IMAGES
of America

NEEDLES

ON THE COVER: Lt. Amiel Weeks Whipple, while conducting a government survey in 1854, saw the "needlelike" mountains in the distance and gave the name "Needles" to the small town on the Colorado River. The picturesque scene shows the winding Colorado River in the forefront. (Courtesy of Dona Schulz Wyzlic.)

IMAGES
of America

NEEDLES

Linda Fitzpatrick and
James M. Conkle

ARCADIA
PUBLISHING

ISBN 978-0-7385-8064-7

Published by Arcadia Publishing
Charleston, South Carolina

Printed in the United States of America

Library of Congress Control Number: 2009942100

For all general information contact Arcadia Publishing at:
Telephone 843-853-2070
Fax 843-853-0044
E-mail sales@arcadiapublishing.com
For customer service and orders:
Toll-Free 1-888-313-2665

Visit us on the Internet at www.arcadiapublishing.com

To everyone who enjoys the history of small towns. To those who knew Needles when she enjoyed the travelers coming and going from east to west and have the vision to see her flourish again. For those who join with us in promoting Needles, a piece of American history on the highway called Route 66.

Contents

ACKNOWLEDGMENTS

Needles is a wonderful town and may have had its rightful place and recognition in California's history overshadowed by the interstate system that made Route 66 obsolete for daily travelers, but it is becoming a much sought after tourist attraction. We feel this is the beginning to a new "Needles Era," and waking up the spirit of this great community and getting others involved has made this entire project worth all the time and effort we have put into it.

It would be impossible to list everyone, but we would like to thank all those that have assisted us by sharing their photographs and stories and opening their homes and memories to us. We would also like to thank our acquisitions editor, Debbie Seracini, whose encouragement and deadlines helped us to complete this book. Tina McGee-Scott with the Needles Library and the Needles Chamber of Commerce spent time pointing us in the right direction. World War II historian Alain S. Batens from Belgium provided information for our World War II chapter. Pam McCorkle Klemm, Rosemary Weart, Marilyn Kirchner, and Nita Claypool also contributed to the pictorial history. A huge thanks to Georgia Breault for all her help. Old high school friends dug through their albums and shared many of the pictures: thanks go out to Dona Schulz Wyzlic for providing the cover image, and many others, including Linda Daniel Andrews, Jimbo and Cathy McConnell, Larry Ford, Jim and Sue Shephard, Trisha Roark Borden, Janis George, Judy Orzel Browder, Carolyn Brown Holman and Linda Kernaghan Wade, the Needles Downtown Business Alliance, and the Needles Chamber of Commerce. A special thanks to Colorado River Museum, Mojave Valley River Museum, Needles Regional Library, the U.S. Bureau of Land Management, Needles Regional Museum, San Bernardino Public Library, Victorville Route 66 Museum, and the Mohave Museum of History and Art.

INTRODUCTION

Needles became known as an oasis along the journey from Chicago to Santa Monica on U.S. Route 66; a welcome reprieve from the long drive. The daily temperature in Needles often made national news, all the more reason to enjoy the cool Colorado River that embraces the town.

Needles was named after the needle-like mountains in the southwest, at the Arizona-California border, by Lt. Amiel Weeks Whipple. Lieutenant Whipple was conducting a government survey for the railroad in 1854 when he came upon the distinct mountain peaks. The community of Needles was first located on the Arizona side of the river and later moved to its current location on the California side. The town was founded in 1883, and the city charter was adopted in 1913.

The area's early inhabitants were a variety of Native American tribes; the most enduring was the Mohave tribe or Pipa Aha Macava ("People by the River"), known today as the Fort Mohave tribe. Archaeological records show the tribe was in the area thousands of years ago, as evidenced by petroglyphs and pictographs and the Mystic Maze, a series of windrows carefully placed in a geometric pattern, a place where warriors paused for purification as they returned from battle. Many of the modern-day residents in Needles are descendants of the Fort Mohave tribe. The city celebrates the tribe with an annual parade, Fort Mohave Indian Days, and appearances throughout the year by the Fort Mohave Band.

Most people do not think about paddle wheelers in relationship to Needles, but in fact, the early history shows that Needles was an important part of the steamboat trade routes, carrying gold, silver, and ore along the Colorado River. The *St. Vallier* was built in Needles in 1899 by the Santa Ana Mining Company, but litigation kept it tied up until 1900 when Capt. John Babson took command of it. Another steamboat, the *Mohave Searchlight,* was built in Needles in 1902 by F. L. Hawley. Regular service began in 1903. Crossing the river initially was done by ferry and later three bridges were built including a draw bridge built in 1884, each washed away until the final bridge was completed in 1890.

The Atlantic and Pacific Railroad, later known as the Santa Fe Railroad, began laying tracks in 1883. Some of the workers (known as the "Big Hat Brigade" for their large sombreros) came to Needles from Mexico. Additional crews were made up of Chinese workers (some of whom opened a Chinese washhouse along Front Street) and members of the Fort Mohave tribe. For some of these men, working on the railroad meant shoveling coal into the steam engines in temperatures above 100 degrees.

The railroad brought a new hotel. Located inside the train depot was the Harvey House, a part of the Fred Harvey chain of hotels. It was named El Garces in honor of Fr. Francisco Garces, the missionary who first made contact with the Mohave Indians in 1776. The original wooden Harvey House burned down and was rebuilt from 1906 to 1908. It was known for its elegant dining and hotel accommodations. Women known as "Harvey Girls" served the visitors and lived in the hotel. These women had to promise not to marry for the first year of their contract, or forfeit half of their base pay of $17.50 a month. Many famous people stayed at the El Graces, including Wyatt

Earp, Gen. Douglas MacArthur, Gen. George S. Patton, and Judy Garland. The hotel closed in 1949. Much of the building was then used for offices by the Santa Fe Railroad until 1988, when it closed completely. The El Garces is currently under restoration, soon to return to its place as the crown jewel of the Harvey Houses. When reopened, it will again provide fine dining and lodging and will feature a historical museum.

Needles played a part in World War II, with an army field hospital and a prisoner of war camp both nearby. The largest combat-training facilities in the country, known as the Desert Training Center, consisted of 18,000 square miles that stretched from Pomona to Phoenix, south to the Mexican border, and north to Boulder City, Nevada. Ten division camps (or "auxiliary camps") were located within the center. The auxiliary Camp Ibis was located 21 miles northwest of Needles.

Route 66 was completed through Needles in 1926. Travelers coming and going from all points east and west drove through Needles on the two-lane road. As a result, the town began to grow with the construction of motels, restaurants, gas stations, a drugstore, and a new and larger Claypool's, which sold everything from spaghetti to Skilsaws.

Nearby communities looked to Needles for their entertainment and weekly shopping. The Needles Theatre opened in March 1930 and was a favorite spot for visitors and locals as well. It boasted of the most modern "talkies" and was equipped with a pipe organ. Its water-based heating and cooling system was the height of modern technology.

One of the early moviegoers was future cartoonist Charles Schulz, who arrived in Needles in 1929 and attended the second grade at the D Street School. His father opened a barbershop on Front Street. Though young Charles only spent a short time in Needles, his famous cartoon *Peanuts* often mentioned Needles and Charles's dog, Spike. Several streets in town, Spike and Schulz Roads, recall the little second grader who became one of the world's most famous cartoonists.

In 1939, the film crew for John Ford's *The Grapes of Wrath* came through Needles and filmed in several locations. They stayed at Carty Camp in Needles, which is still standing—though in need of repair. Other movies filmed in the area over the years have included *Route 66*, *Two-Lane Blacktop* (starring singer James Taylor and Dennis Wilson of the Beach Boys), *Convoy*, *The Amazing Race*, and *Domino*.

Known for its annual Marathon Boat Races, the town prepared each year for an influx of competitors with their racing boats. Several thousand tourists came from all over the country and shared in the festivities, including the deep-pit barbecues and Marathon Parade. The excitement of the racing boats going up and down the river was something that the Needles residents looked forward to every year.

Woodrow Wilson stopped in Needles during his presidency. As Needles grew and prospered, the main street, Route 66, was lit up with neon signs up and down the street. Most of its gas stations, motels, and restaurants stayed open all night to serve travelers. The 1950s brought with it the famous 1957 Chevy, the old Sweet Shoppe, snake dances from Claypool's to the high school, summer dances at the recreation center above the police department, and visits by Eleanor Roosevelt, Ann Landers, and Vincent Price.

As the freeway system progressed with the development of I-40 and Highway 95, fewer travelers were soon coming through town, and like many Route 66 communities, Needles began to decline. Today efforts are underway to restore the historic downtown.

With the images in these pages, the authors seek to celebrate old-time Needles so that the reader can relive the story of a small town located at the spot where travelers once traversed the Colorado River, traveled the railroad, and drove the two-lane road that wove its way through Needles called Route 66.

One

Early Inhabitants
Aboriginal Tribes

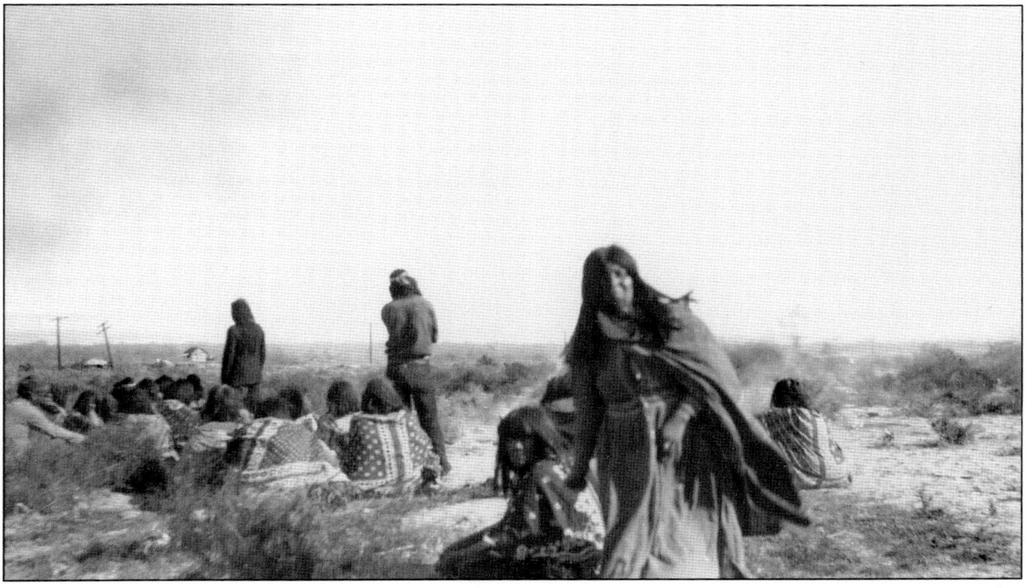

Native American Tribes. There were primarily three groups of Native Americans in the 16th-century American Southwest: the Matha Laythum, the Kavi Laytham, and the Hutto-pah. The Native Americans known as Pipa Aha Macava ("People by the River") were the first inhabitants along the Colorado River near Needles. They trace their origin to Spirit Mountain, located northwest of the current reservation. Their beliefs taught that at death, they would follow the Warrior Master Spirit up Avi Kwa Ame on their way to heaven, which is why they named it Spirit Mountain. In 1865, the Colorado River Indian Reservation was established. It was renamed Fort Mohave on April 5, 1890. Native Americans living in and around the fort became known as the Fort Mohave Indians. Many of the Needles residents can trace their ancestry to the early inhabitants. The people of the Fort Mohave tribe are part of the Needles community and add valuable history to the community with their yearly Fort Mohave Indian Days, which celebrates their heritage with a parade, cultural workshops, and bird singing. (Courtesy of the Needles Regional Museum.)

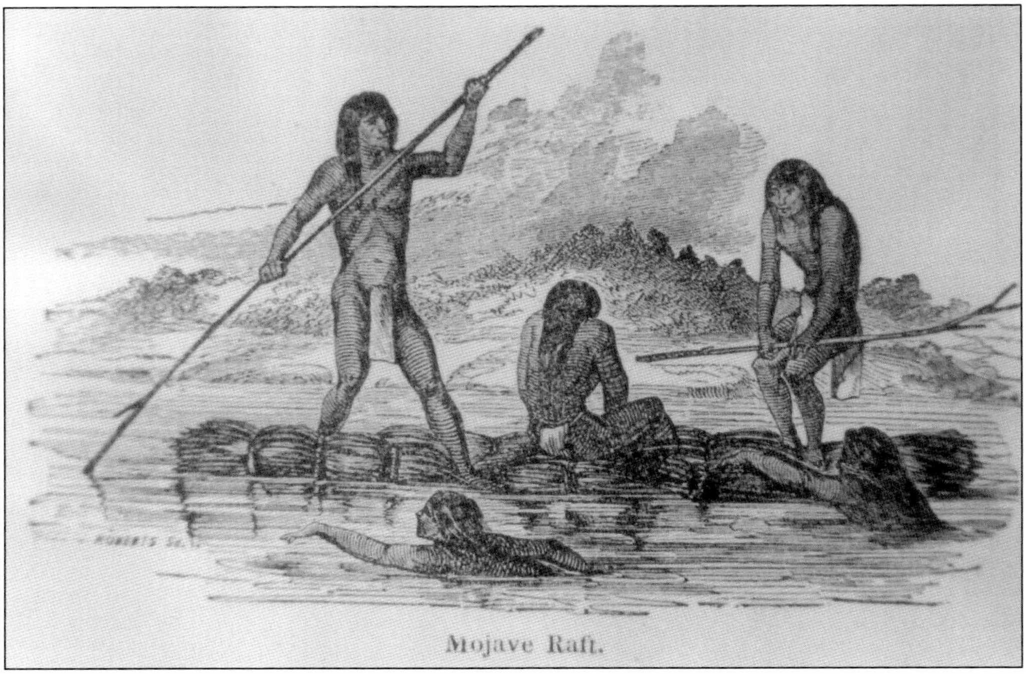

CROSSING OVER. The artist shows early Mohave Indians along the Colorado River. Because the river was very shallow in certain parts, they were able to use poles to direct their rafts. The swift current transported them downriver, but the use of poles allowed them to maneuver to the opposite shore. Below, a survey party, along with Lieutenant Ives, crosses the river after a failed attempt to cross the canyon upstream. (Courtesy of the Mojave River Valley Museum.)

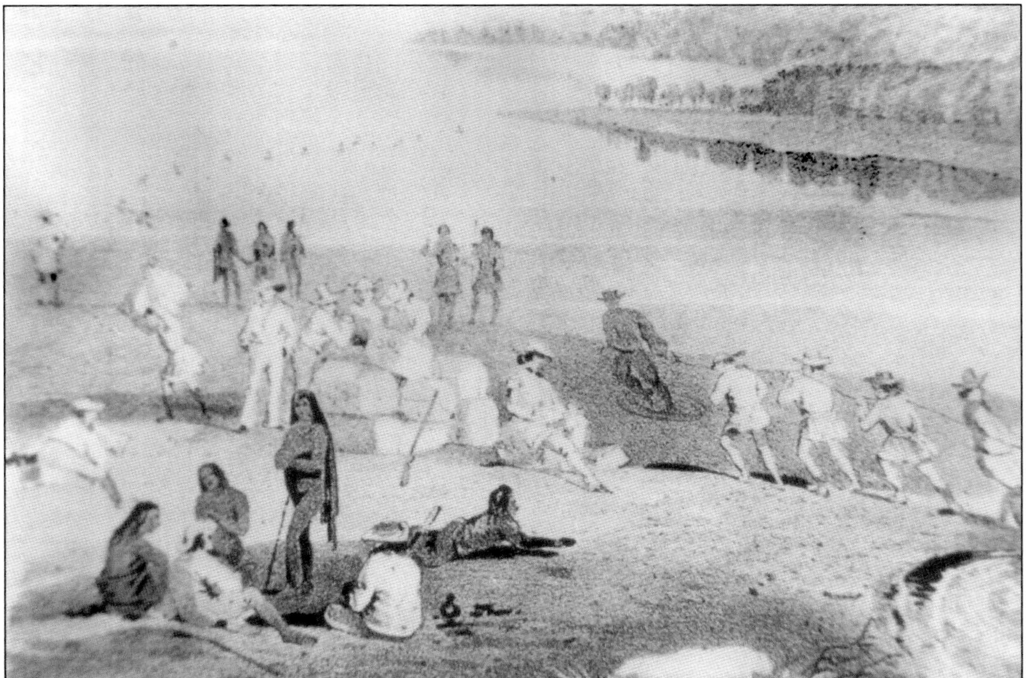

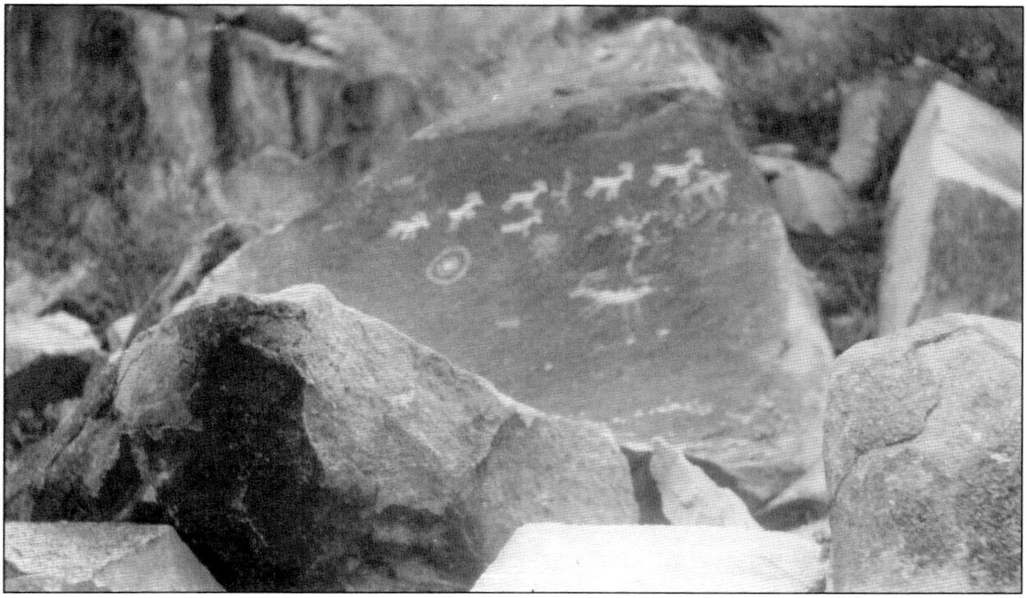

PETROGLYPHS. The Mohave Indians had two different ways of writing: petroglyphs (symbols carved into stone) and pictographs (images painted onto a stone). The petroglyphs are more common. The origin is thought to be religious in nature, the work of shamans' supernatural helpers. The carvings were a means of communicating or telling a story. (Courtesy of Judy Orzel Browder.)

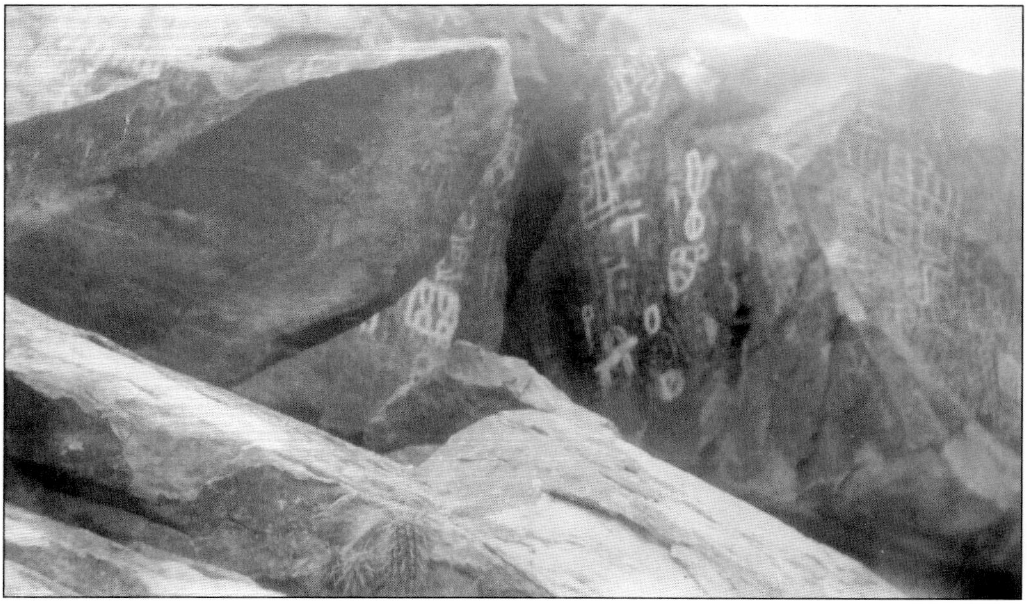

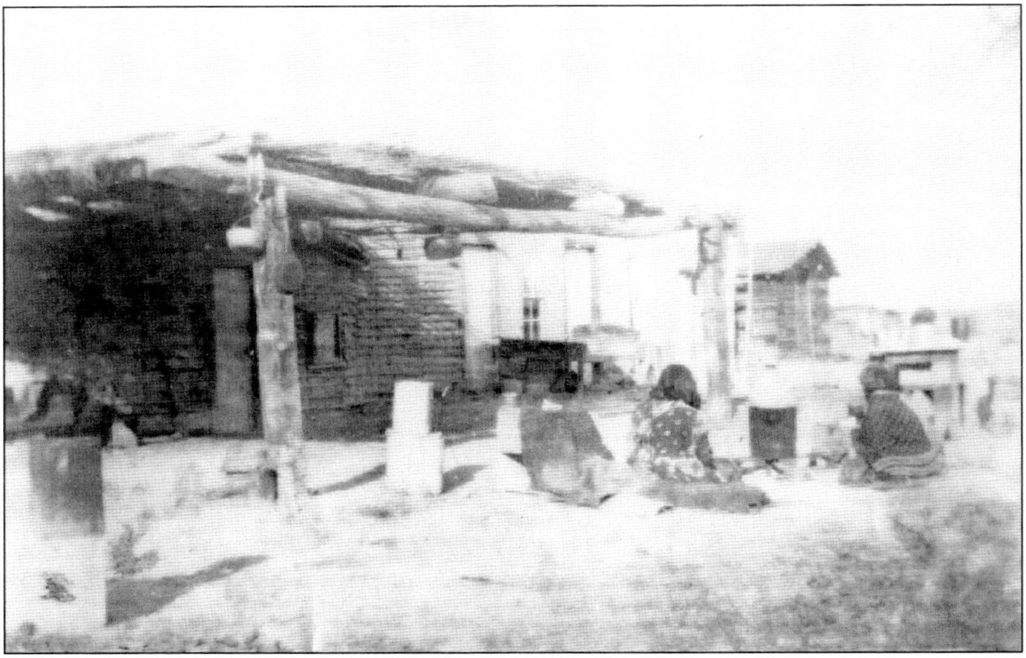

Native American Women. The Fort Mohave women were also pottery makers, forming their wares from clay and crushed sandstone and seashells. They often traded their pottery for the seashells and beads, which they turned into jewelry and decorative items. Harvey Houses throughout the Southwest displayed large amounts of the Mohave Indians' handiwork. Below are a series of thatched-roof houses used by early Native Americans. (Courtesy of Pam McCorkle Klemm.)

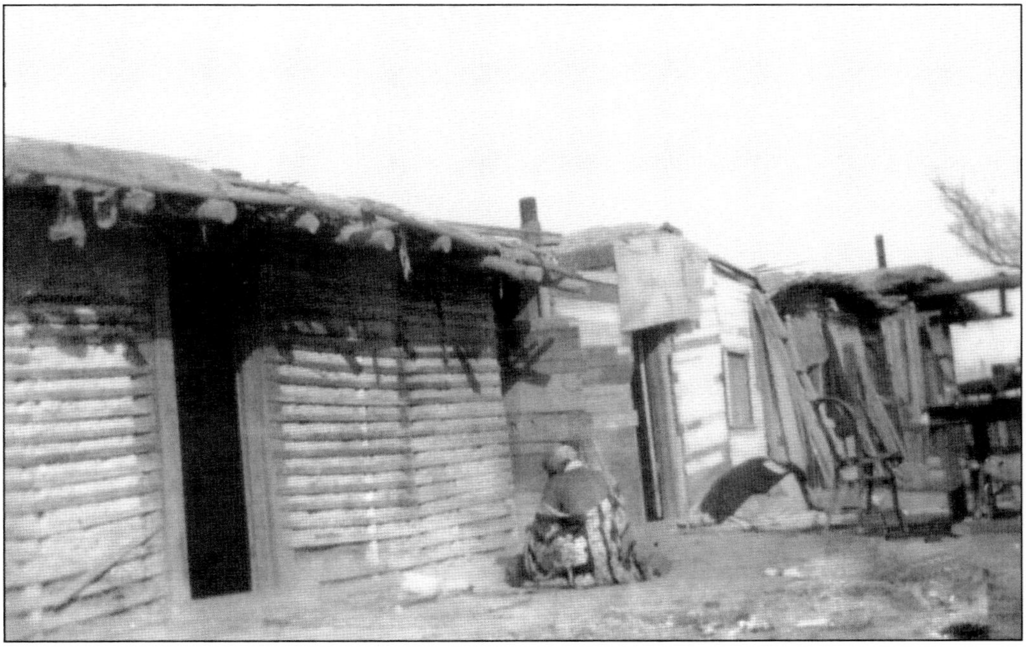

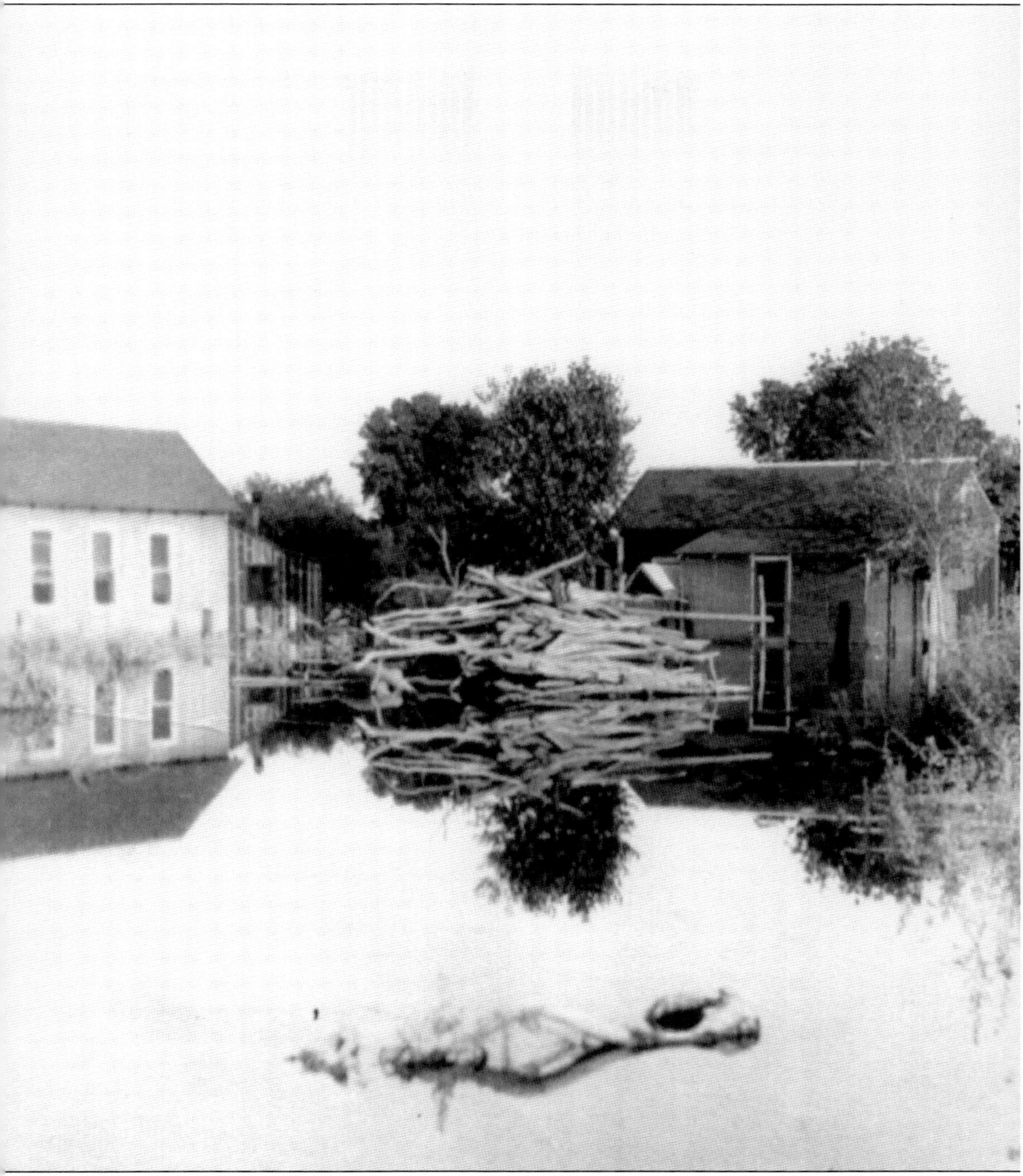

Flooded Native American Village. The early inhabitants along the Colorado River near Needles relied upon the annual overflow of the river to irrigate their crops of corn, beans, melons, and pumpkins. In addition to the overflow of the river, there were flash floods created by heavy rainfall in the mountains. While the overflow of the river was helpful for agriculture, the floods created difficulty for the entire community. Since Needles is located in a bowl, floods were frequent. (Courtesy of Mojave River Valley Museum.)

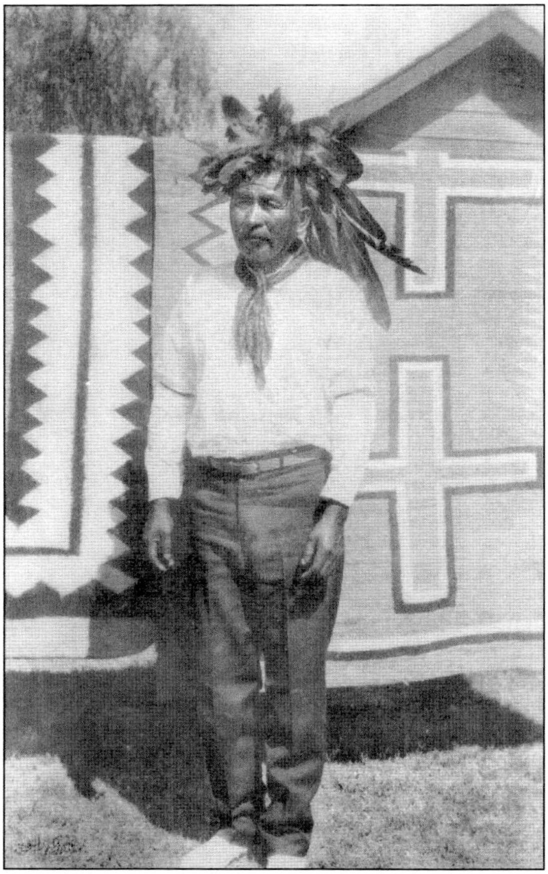

Chief Sherman Ross. This Fort Mohave Indian chief was highly regarded and referred to as Avi Chavar ("next to the highest mountain"). Chief Ross fought hard for water and land rights that the tribe has today. He died in the late 1920s. (Courtesy of the Needles Regional Library.)

Gathering. This gathering of Fort Mohave Indians appears to have been taken in the early 1900s as the women are wearing store-bought dresses with hand-woven shawls. The men are also in store-bought clothes and hats. (Courtesy of the Mojave Valley River Museum.)

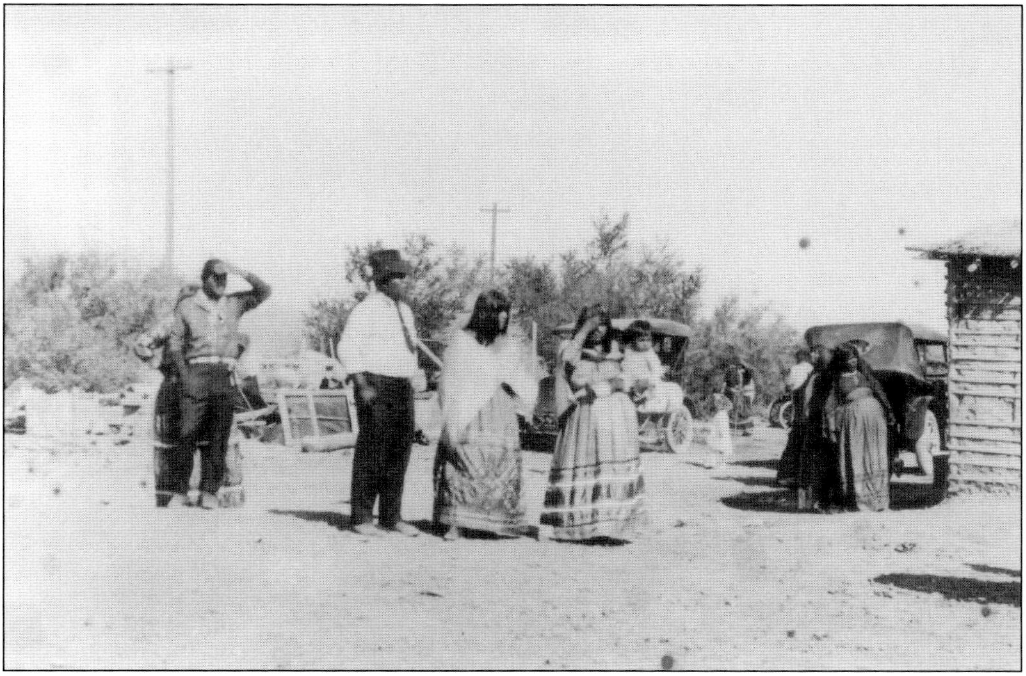

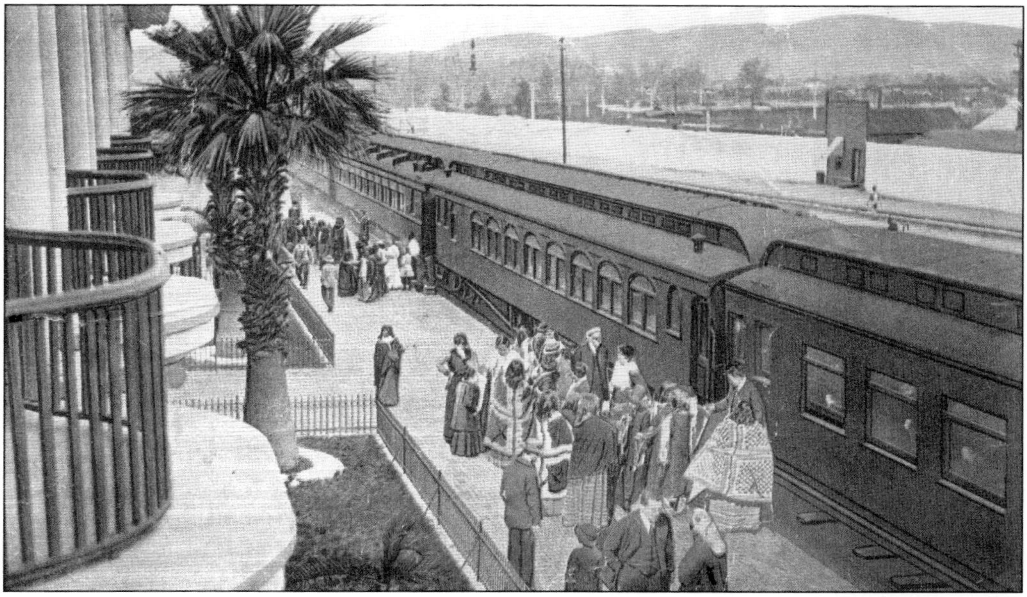

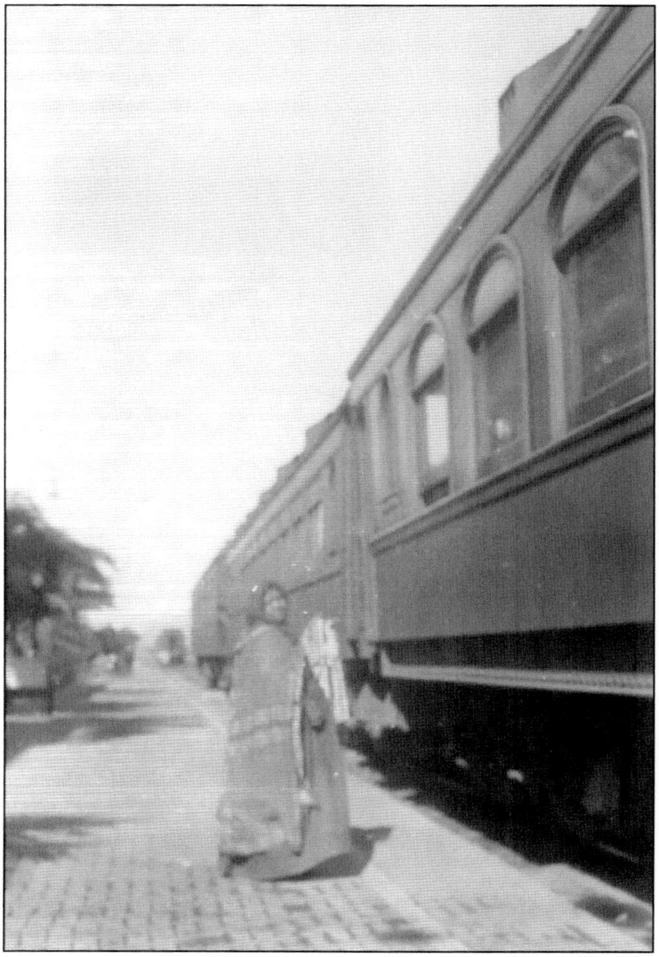

SELLING JEWELRY. Fort Mohave women wait for the train to come into the Needles train depot. They sold their handcrafted jewelry and beaded handbags to Santa Fe passengers as they left the train to dine at the El Garces Harvey House. Passengers traveling to the West for the first time were intrigued by the materials and designs and bought the handmade items as souvenir treasures. (Courtesy of the Needles Regional Museum; Dona Schulz Wyzlic.)

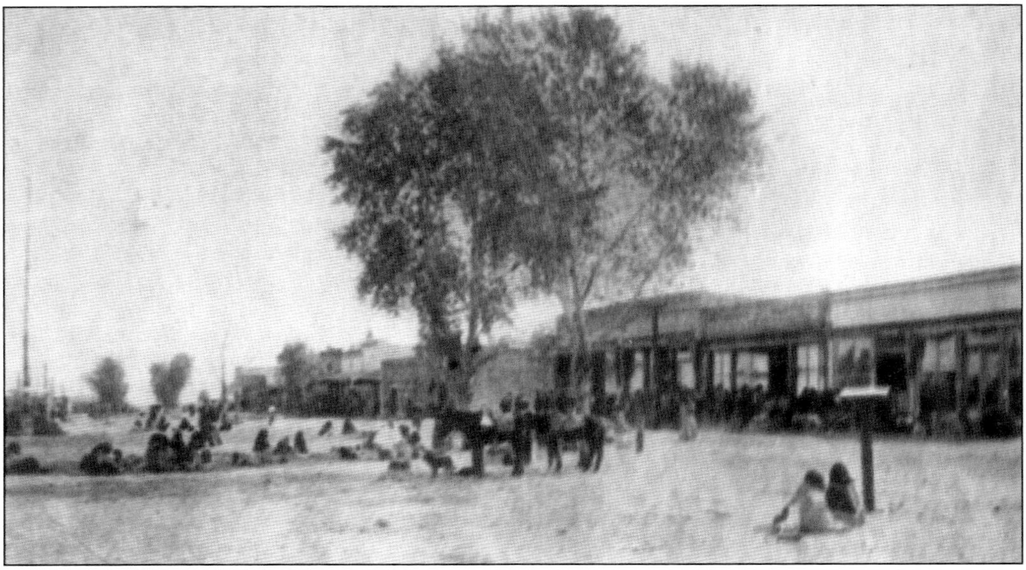

Front Street, 1890. Fort Mohave Indians gather across the street from Murphy and Monaghan's (the first grocery store in Needles) to be paid for work. The store paid them in silver dollars—that was the only form of payment they would accept. To the left is a speaker's stand and a flagpole. This area was used for community events. (Courtesy of Jim and Sue Shephard.)

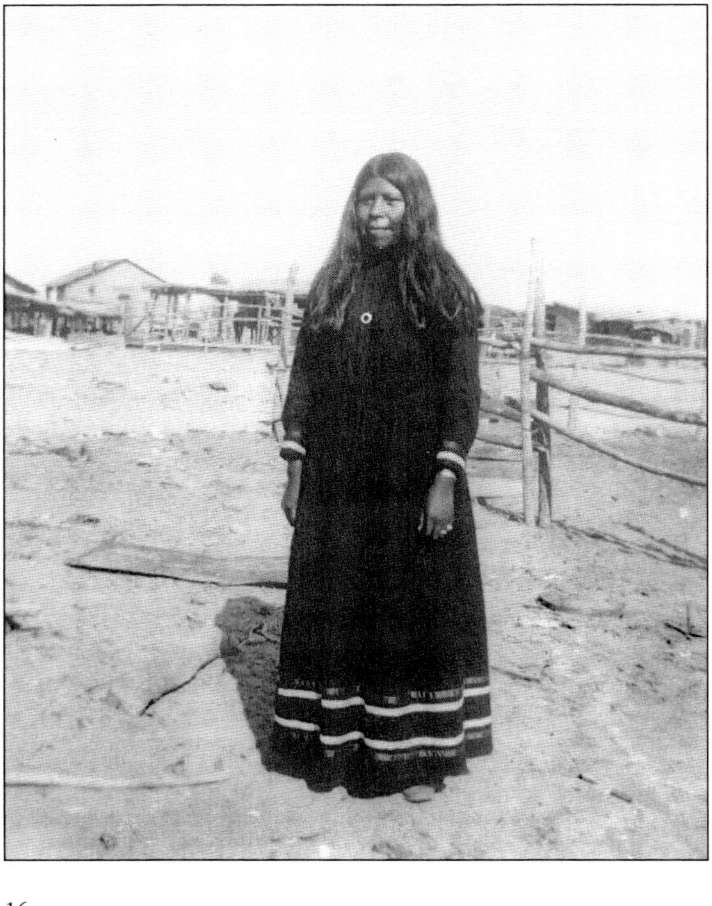

Native American Woman. This woman is wearing her handmade dress with ribbons along the bottom and on the sleeves. Some of the ceremonial dancers wore similar dresses when doing their dances. In the background is a Native American village. (Courtesy of the Needles Regional Museum.)

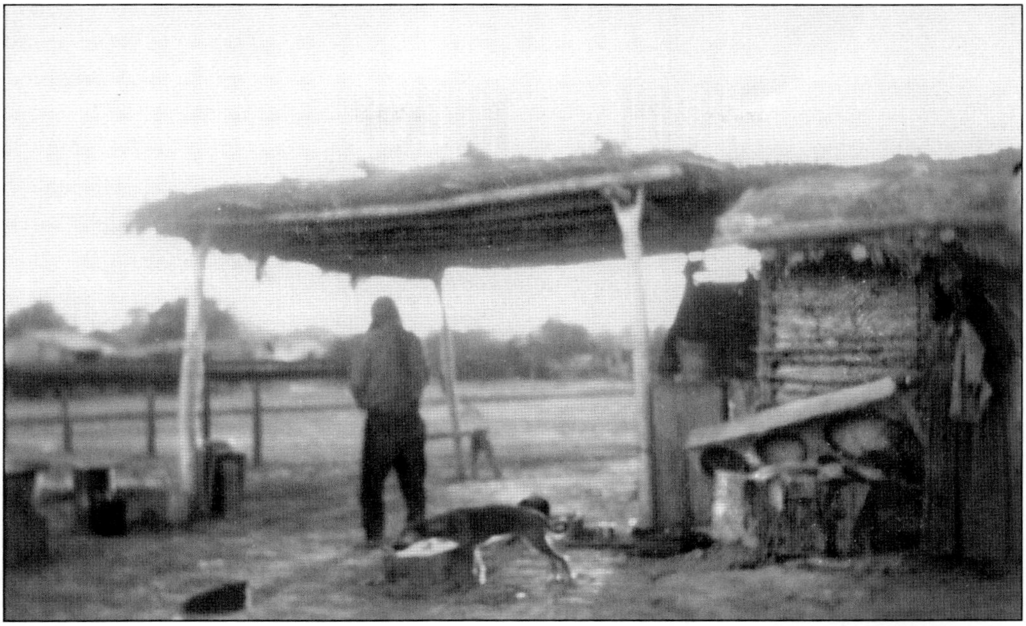

Mohave Indian Home. The Fort Mohave Indians living along the Colorado River around Needles built their homes on stilts with a thatched roof made of bundles of reeds and grass. The stilts were necessary, as the river would overflow from time to time. Mohave homes located further inland were made with four posts planted in the ground to support the thatched roof and timber, as seen in this photograph. (Courtesy of Dona Schulz Wyzlic.)

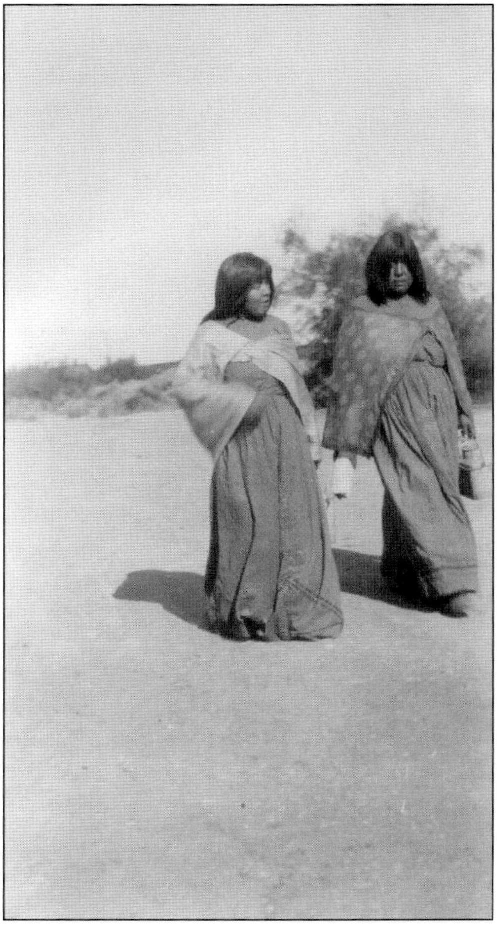

Two Women. This picture captures two Fort Mohave Indian women wearing typical everyday clothing. It appears that these women are dressed in store-bought dresses, which was common after 1909. Prior to that, dresses were made of trader's calico. The shawls were woven by hand. (Courtesy of Rosemary Weart

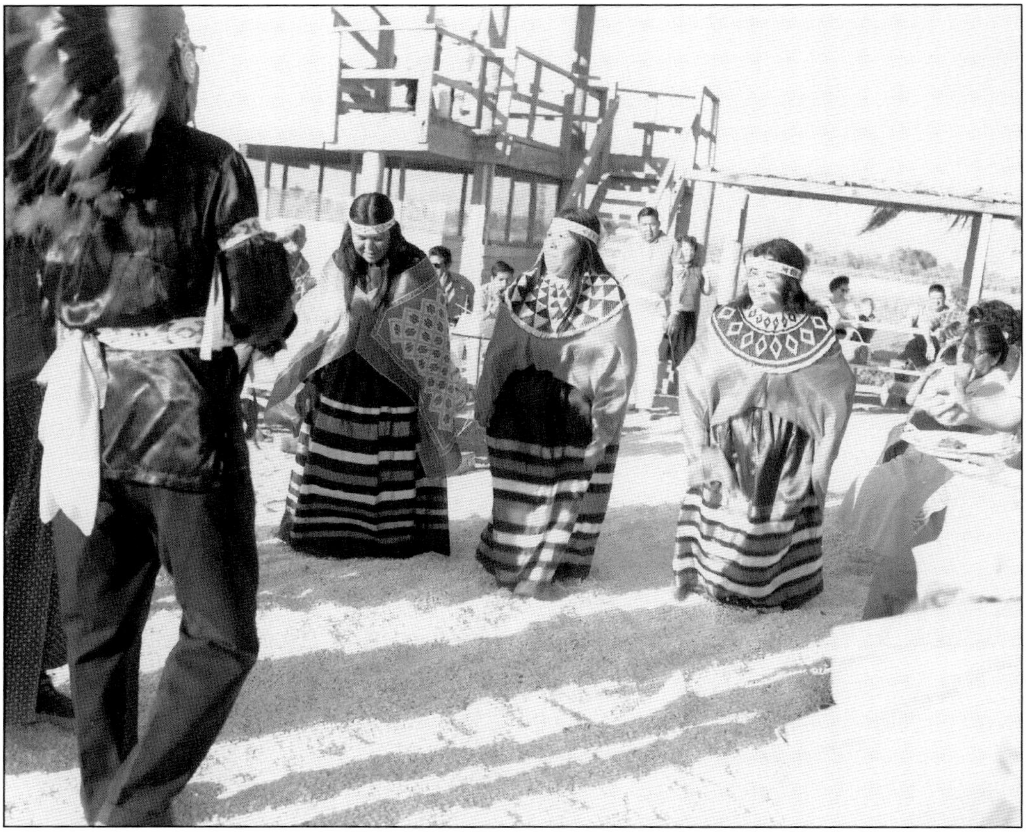

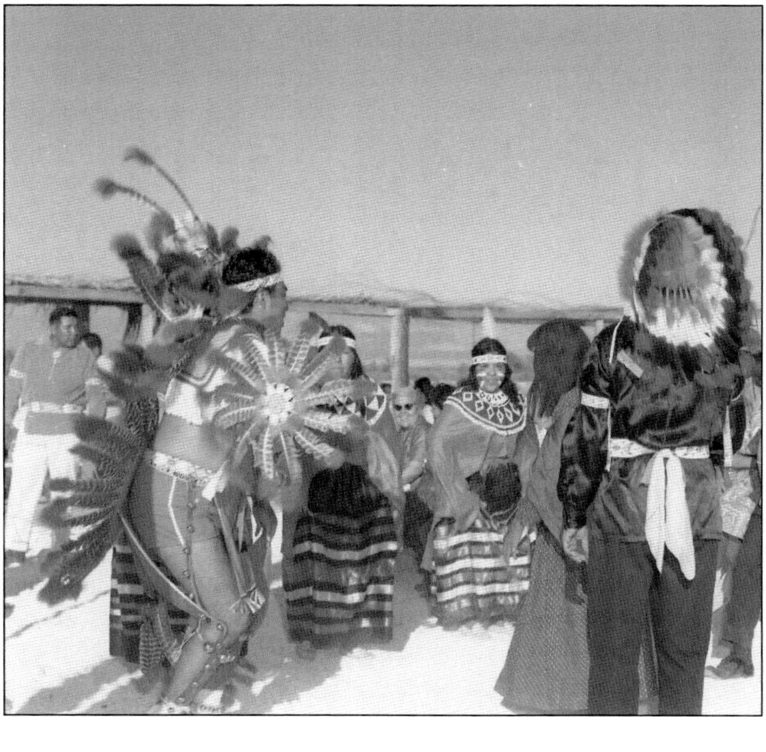

Ceremonial Dance. The Fort Mohave Indians are rich in their spiritual beliefs, their etiquette, and their community events. The group above is performing the Bird Dance during the Marathon celebration. The Fort Mohave dancers at left wear their ceremonial dress with beautiful beaded shawls. The men are also dressed in ceremonial clothes. (Courtesy of Judy Orzel Browder.)

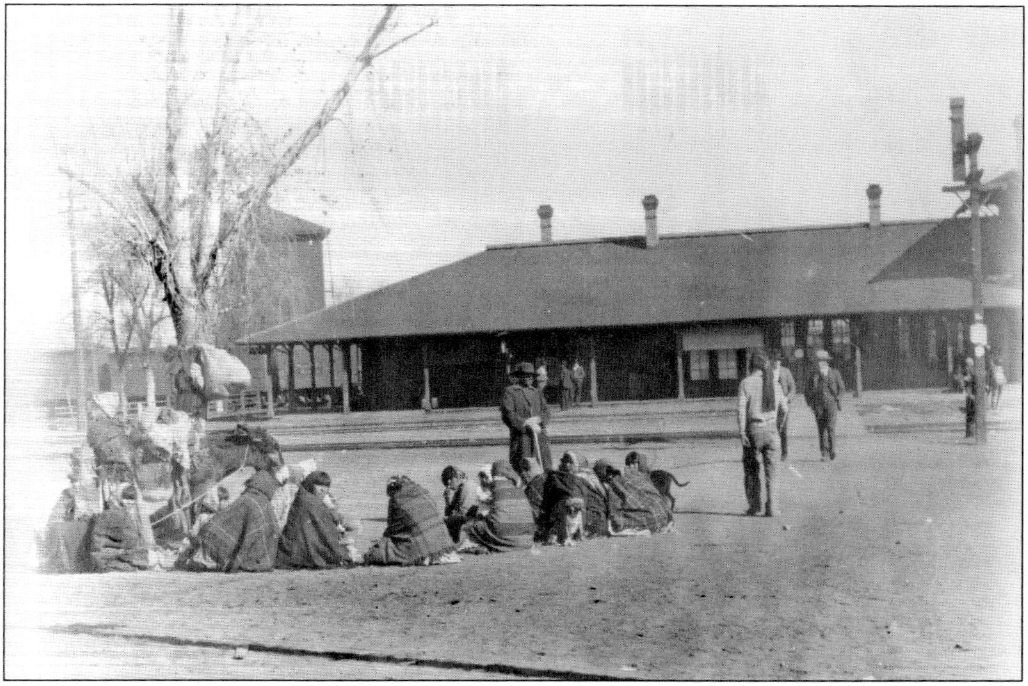

PARK. Fort Mohave Indians gather in front of the first El Garces Harvey House, in an area that later became Santa Fe Park on F and Front Streets. The park was landscaped in 1908 after the Harvey House was rebuilt. (Courtesy of the Needles Regional Library.)

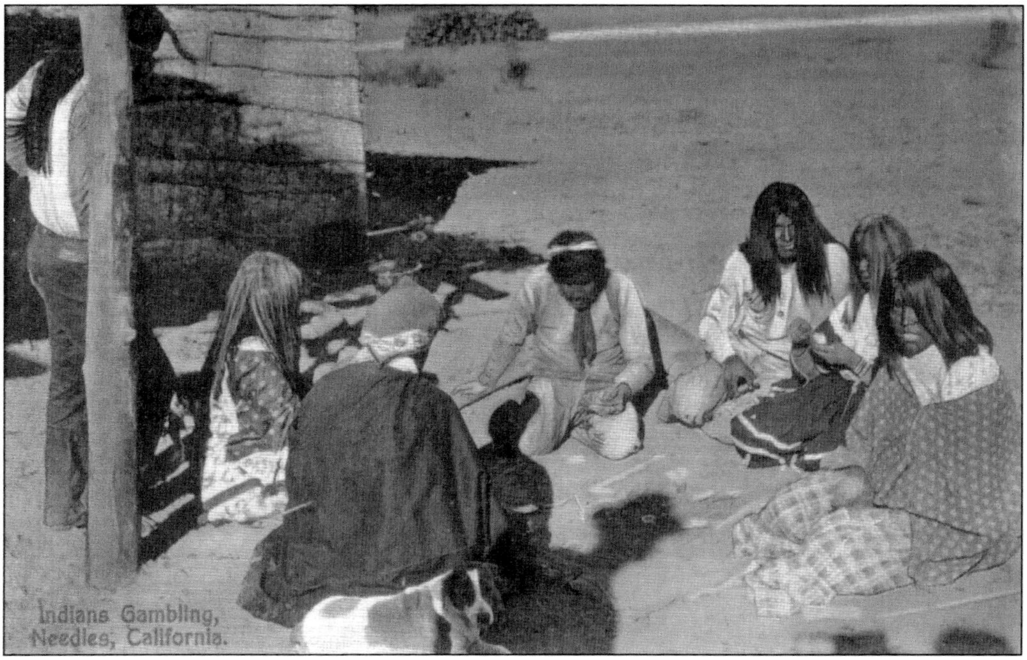

MOHAVE INDIAN GAMES. While Mohaves did not have cards, they played a number of games that closely resembled popular American card games. In one game, players divided straws into piles; whoever ended up with the odd number of straws won. They would often bet on the games, normally wagering stones or beads. (Courtesy of the Needles Regional Museum.)

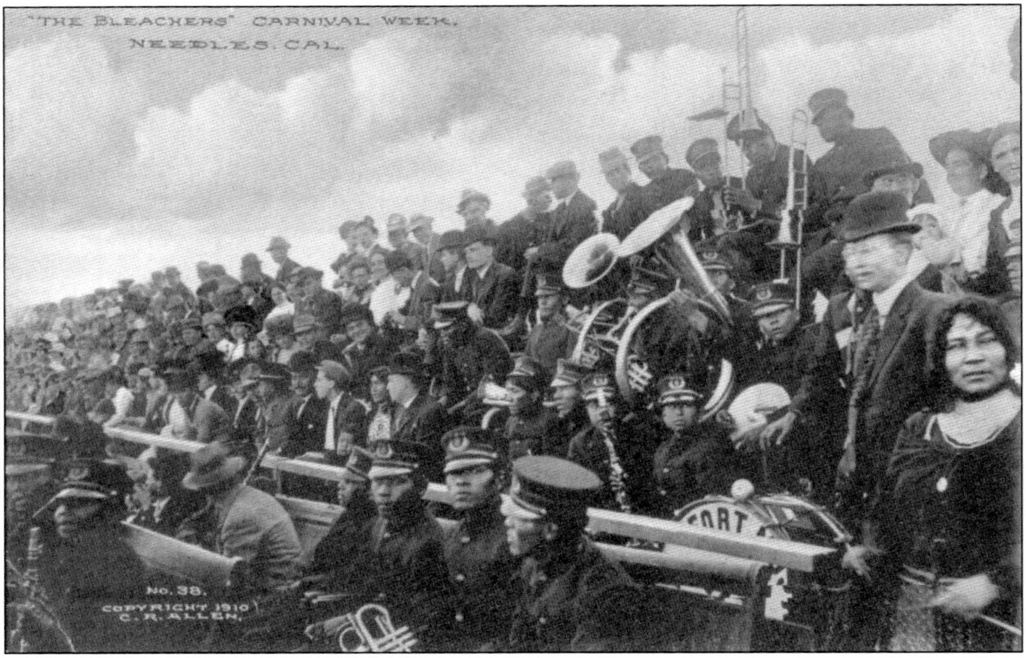

FORT MOHAVE BAND. Albert J. Eller taught music to the children at the Fort Mohave Indian boarding school. Eller had played with the John Philip Souza band. In 1906, the school band played at the first Orange show in San Bernardino and won first place under the direction of Fort Mohave's Ned White. Here the Fort Mohave Band waits to perform during the Carnival Week celebration. (Courtesy of the Needles Regional Library.)

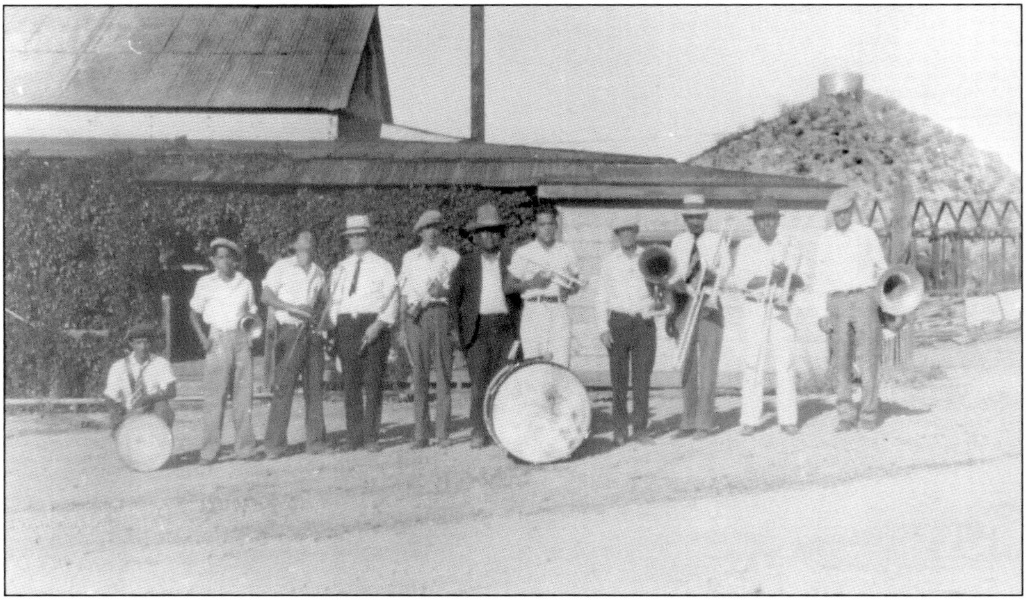

BAND. Needles enjoys the participation of different bands at many local events. Wearing a hat in the center of this early-1900s photograph of local musicians is Jack Jones, who taught music to many of Needles's young people. (Courtesy of the Mojave River Valley Museum.)

Two
Steamboats on the Colorado
Trade Routes

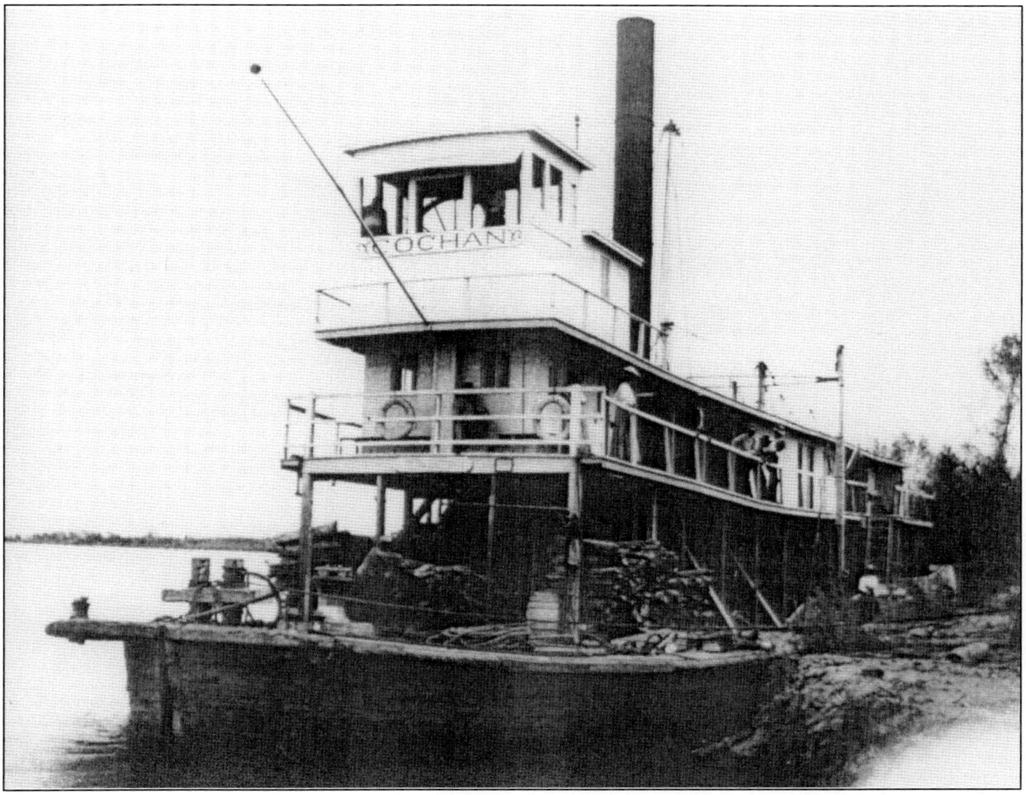

The *Gila* to the *Cochran*. A number of steamboats operated along the Colorado River from 1849 until the early 1900s, carrying gold, silver, and ore. One of the first steamboats along the river was the *Gila*. It was renamed the *Cochran* in 1899 and brought upriver to Needles. After completion of the railroad at Needles, however, river trade fell off. In addition, declining silver prices closed several mines, which further reduced the need for the steamers. (Courtesy of the Mohave Museum of History and Art.)

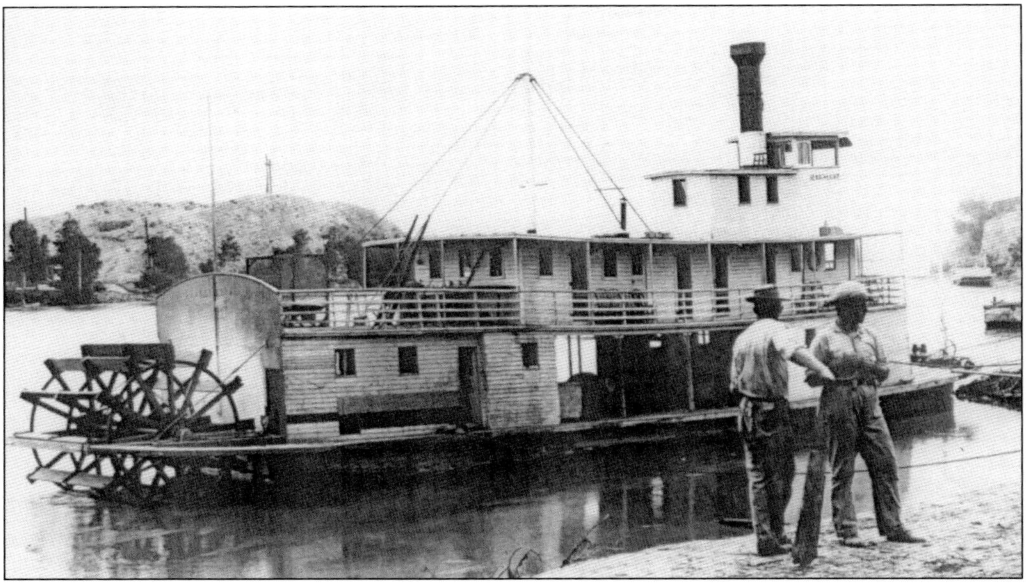

THE *SEARCHLIGHT*. F. L. Hawley of Needles and F. L. Forrester organized the Colorado River Transportation Company and, along with a crew of carpenters, built the *Searchlight* in 1902. It began service in 1903, making its way to the mining camp at the Quartette Landing. This sternwheeled steamer carried 60 tons. (Courtesy of the Colorado River Museum.)

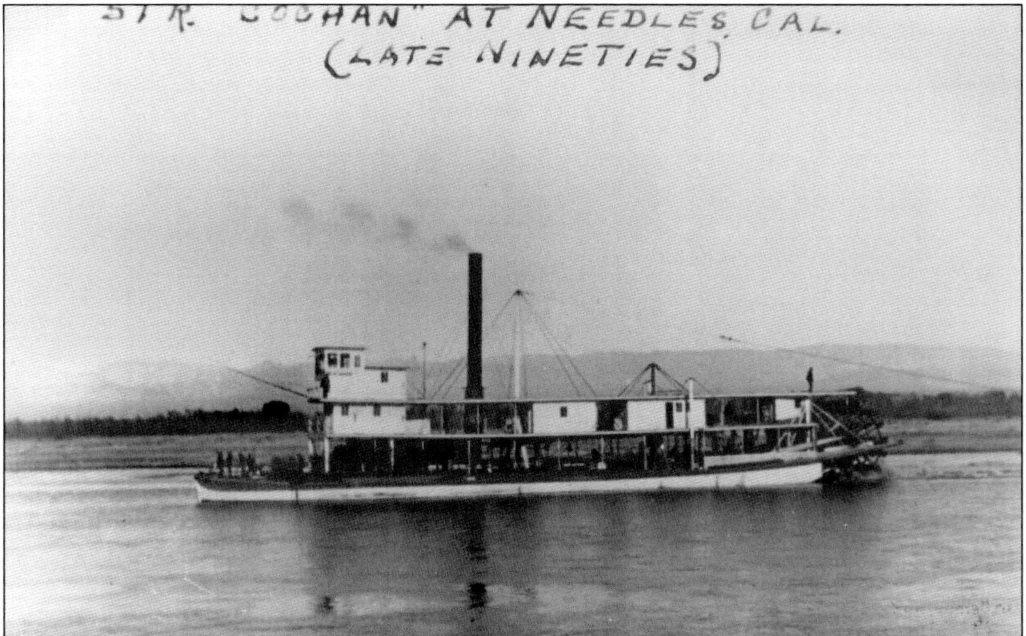

THE *COCHRAN*. After the drawbridge was built in 1884, the *Cochran* stayed mainly below the bridge to accommodate the trade on the lower Colorado River. The boat was piloted by a former barge captain named Pelham. It made a trip upriver only once every six weeks or so. (Courtesy of the Colorado River Museum.)

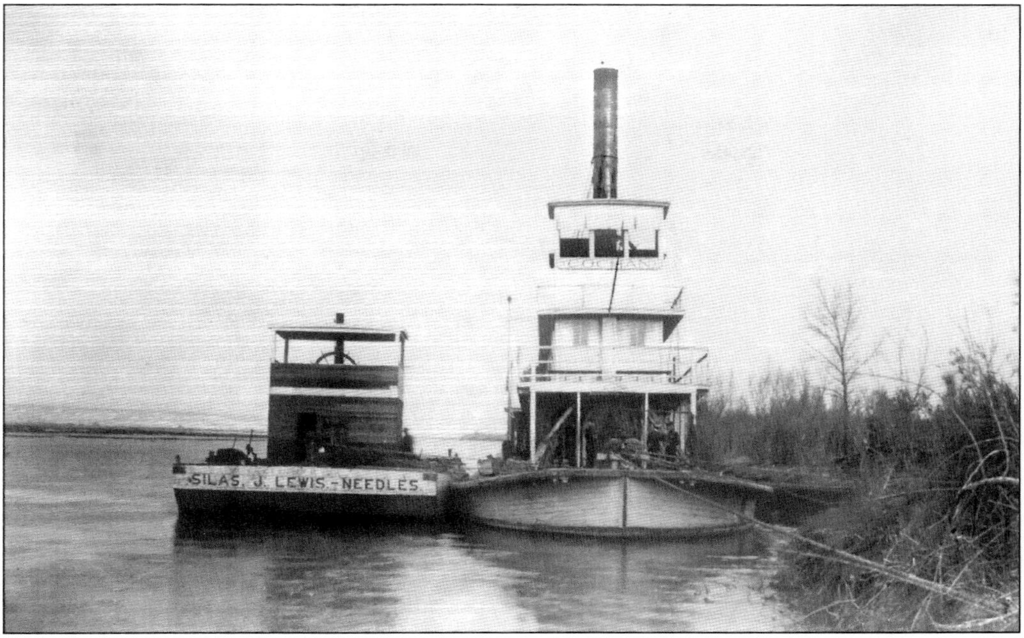

ST. VALLIER. This picture captures the steamboat *St. Vallier* sitting along the Colorado River waiting for supplies. This 74-by-17-foot steamboat was built by the Santa Ana Mining Company in 1899. It was, however, tied up in litigation until 1900. Alfonso Smith and his backers purchased the *St. Vallier* and added four cabins and an upper deck. (Courtesy of the Mohave Museum of History and Art.)

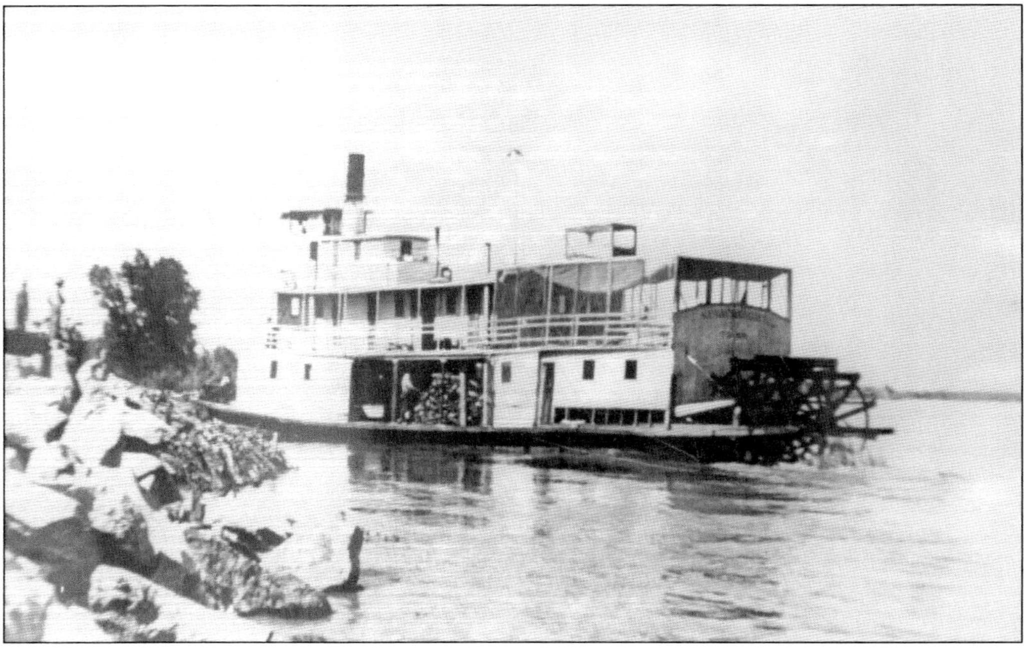

THE *SEARCHLIGHT*. This steamer was the last steamboat that operated below the Grand Canyon. The *Searchlight* was 91 feet long with an 18-foot beam. Passengers enjoyed six staterooms, a smoking room, and a galley. The Quartette Mining Companies short-line railroad then took passengers and supplies to the mining camp. (Courtesy of the Mohave Museum of History and Art.)

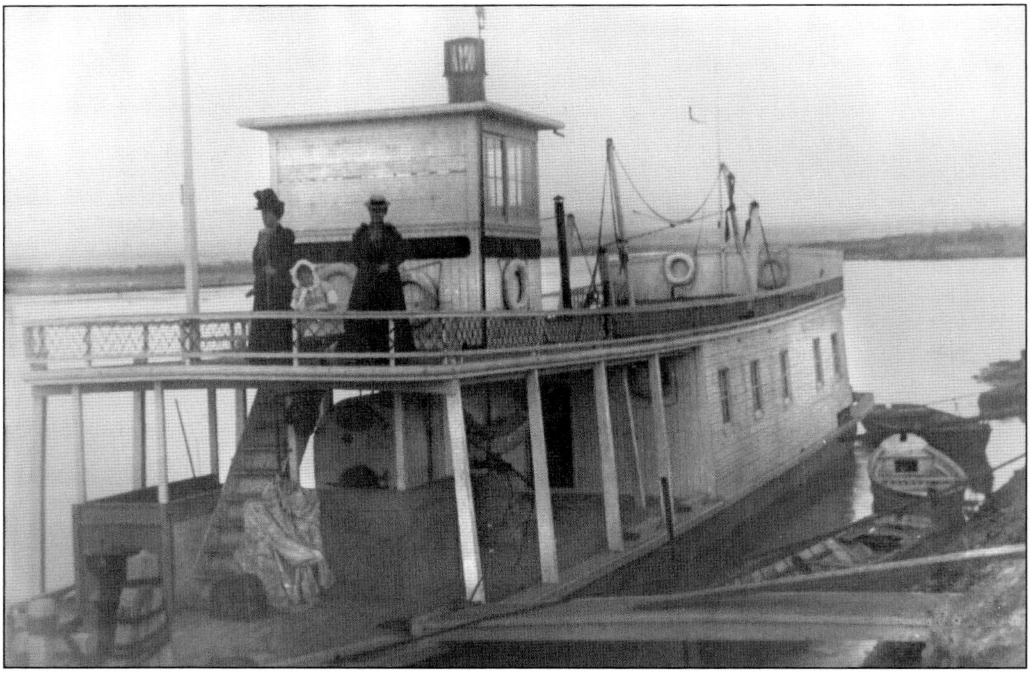

Women Traveling to the Quartette Mining Company. At Needles, passengers connected with the Quarttett Mining Company short railroad that took them up the river to mining camps. (Courtesy of Marilyn Kirchner.)

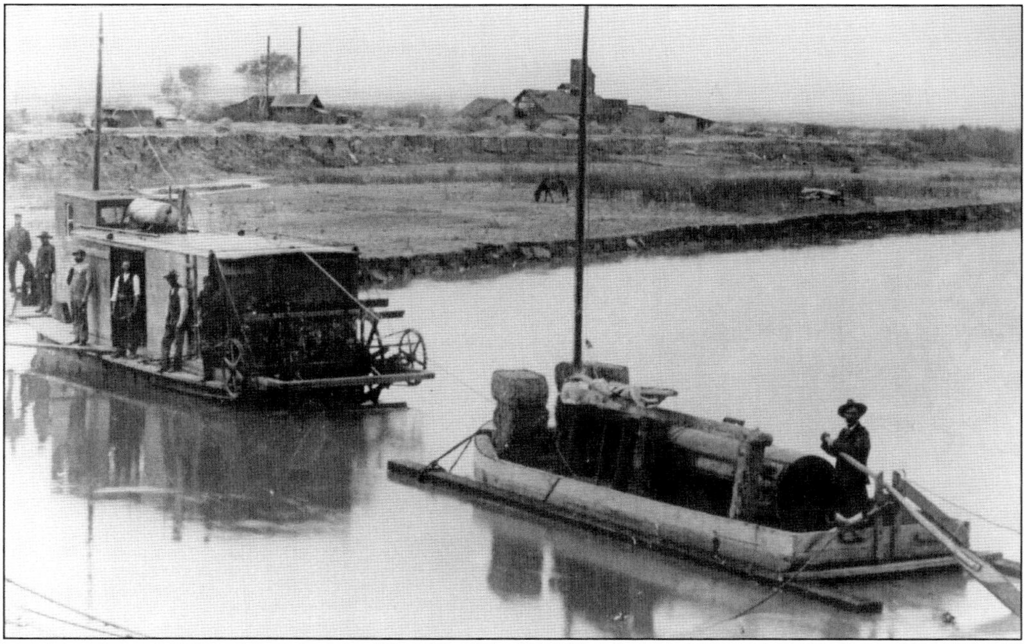

Paddleboat and Barge. Another means of getting across the river was the use of smaller paddleboats and ferries. In this photograph, large trunks are being transported behind the paddleboat as passengers get ready to leave the boat for dry land. This location is above Needles on the banks of the Colorado River. (Courtesy of Dona Schulz Wyzlic.)

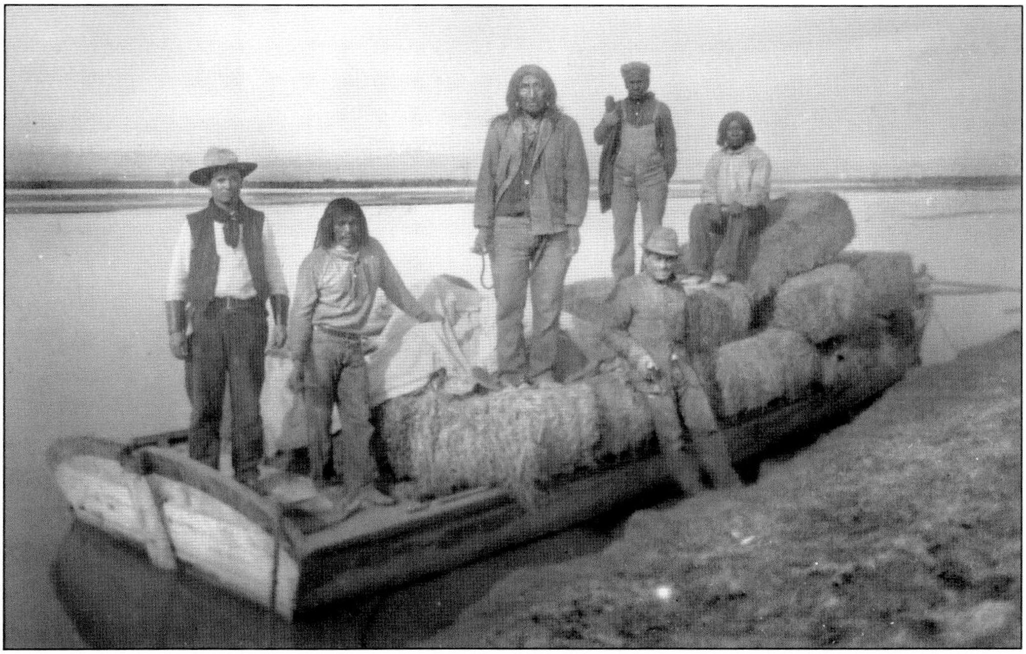

BOAT ON THE COLORADO RIVER. This is a view of Native Americans and others traveling on the Colorado River. These small boats were used up and down the river to pick up supplies for personal use and deposit workers and other passengers at Needles and other points along the river. Several bridges were built across the Colorado River at Needles. The swift current washed them away until a more formidable bridge was completed in May 1890. In the interim, ferryboats transported travelers and automobiles across the river to the other shore, where they resumed their travel. (Courtesy of the Mohave Museum of History and Art.)

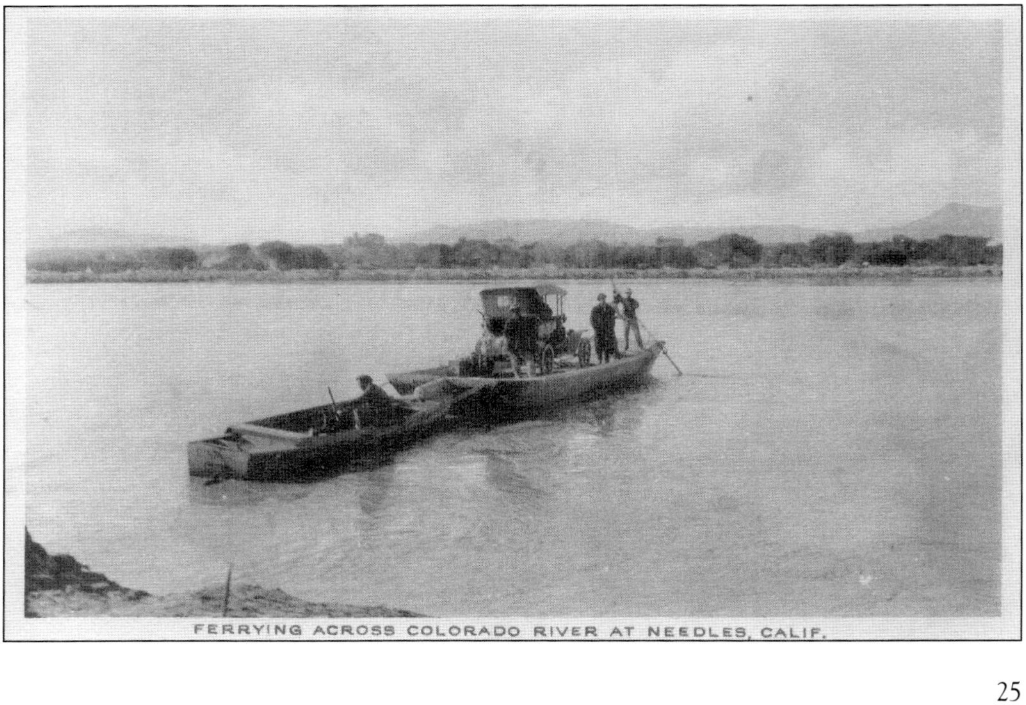

FERRYING ACROSS COLORADO RIVER AT NEEDLES, CALIF.

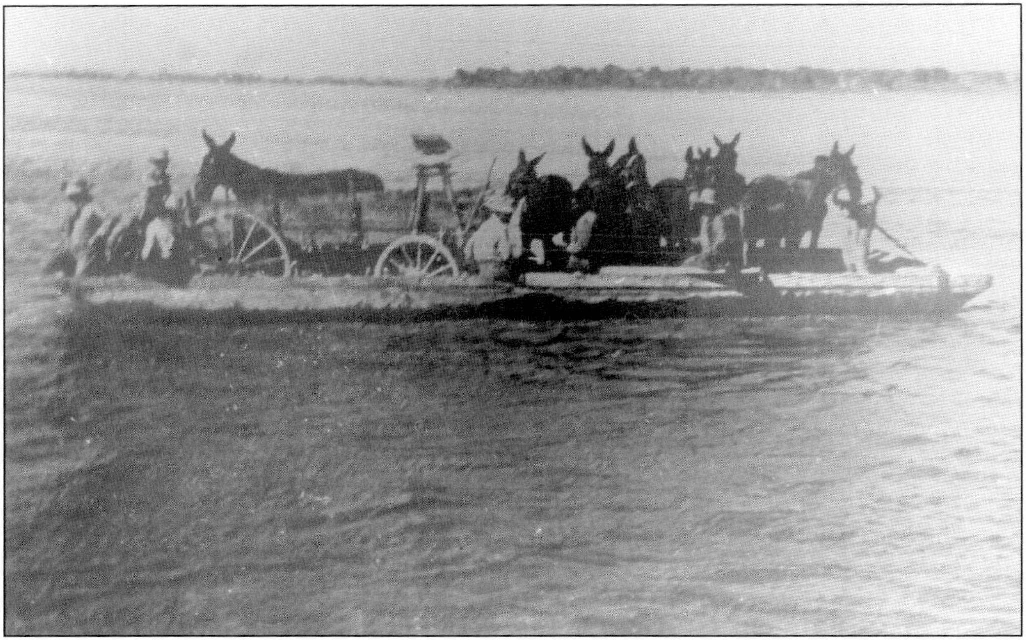

DONKEYS TRAVEL THE RIVER. The Colorado River, with its swift current, was also very shallow in certain spots. This allowed ferryboats to use poles to guide their boats. Here are men with their wagon and most precious cargo, the donkeys, traveling down the river. The Colorado River at Needles was as much as a mile wide in certain spots. (Courtesy of the Mojave Valley River Museum.)

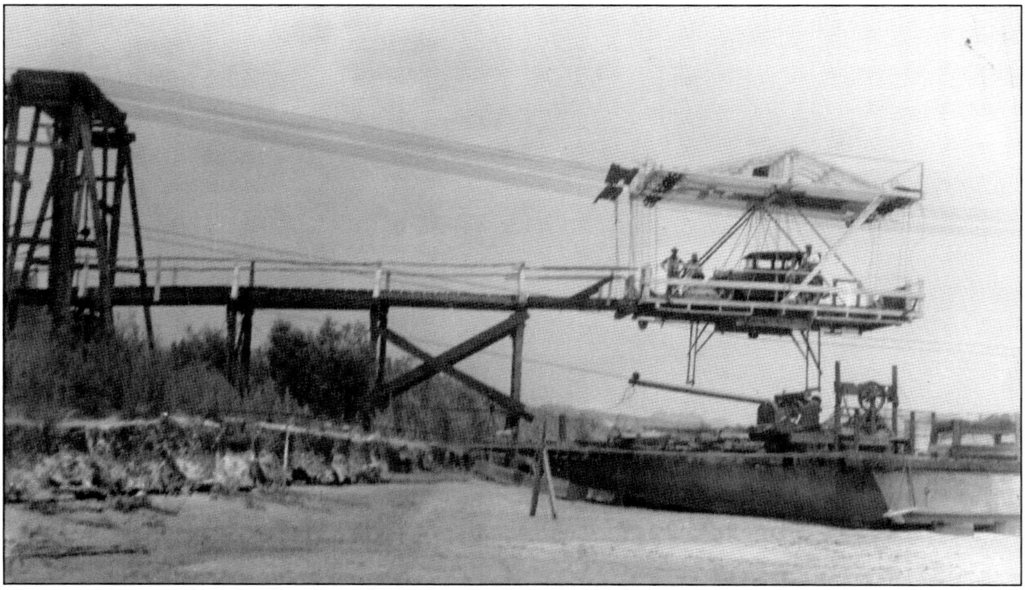

NEEDLES FERRY. The Needles Ferry brought travelers across the river from Leonard's Landing—also known as Glenwood—to the California side of the river. It was located just above Booth Avenue. The ferry also brought automobiles across the river. Built in 1901, it operated until a 1914 flood destroyed it. In order to get cars on land, ferrymen laid wooden planks on the bank so that the cars could be driven over the planks to dry land. (Courtesy of the Mohave Museum of History and Art.)

Three

Railroad Era
El Garces Hotel and Depot

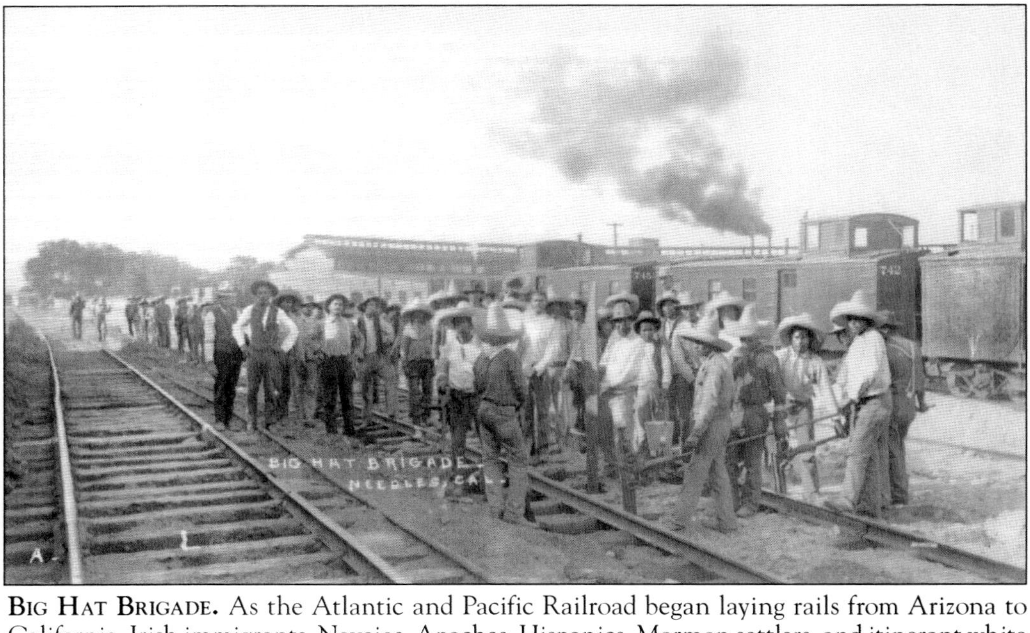

Big Hat Brigade. As the Atlantic and Pacific Railroad began laying rails from Arizona to California, Irish immigrants, Navajos, Apaches, Hispanics, Mormon settlers, and itinerant white laborers worked to complete the rails. The Hispanic workers pictured here were nicknamed the "Big Hat Brigade" since they wore sombreros for protection from the 100-degree-plus temperatures. The rails at Needles were completed in 1883. (Courtesy of the Needles Regional Library.)

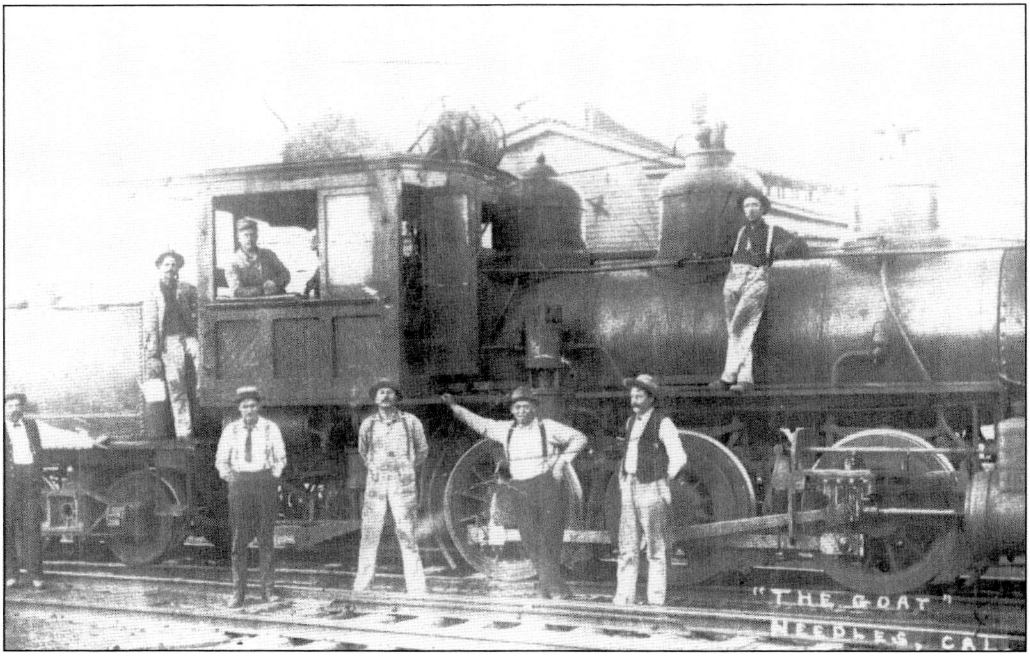

SWITCH ENGINE. This yard switch engine was a larger version of the "goat," and it was used to move boxcars into the yard and deliver goods to a number of warehouses. In addition, the switch engine put the caboose on trains and moved freight cars east of the Needles roundhouse for repair. (Courtesy of the Needles Regional Museum.)

The Needles Engineers

To those engineers of Needles, of nigh fifty years ago,
We will pay our little tribute, speak a kindly word or so,
For we rode behind them often in those dim and distant years,
And our mem'ry fondly lingers o'er those Needles engineers.

George Hastings, Emmet Hodgdon, John Coons and "Blackie" White,
Hilarious "Windy" Colcord, full of frolic day and night;
Staid, methodic Jesse Thompson—oh, as recollection clears
We shall call a fuller roster of those Needles engineers.

Bob Brockie ran to eastward, Johnny Husher did the same,
Division point was then Peach Springs, a most deceptive name.
Still, in lieu of springs and peaches there were whiskies, wines and beers,
"Missouri" Moore, Bill Skinner, and the jovial Dad Goodell,
They rolled 'em 'cross the desert, yes, they gave 'em merry hell.
The pay-car eased all burdens, although sometimes in arrears,
Ah! "them was happy days," indeed, for Needles engineers.

When Nellie Bly* raced homeward in the year of eighty-eight,
Completing her world journey 'gainst the wiles of time and fate,
Bill Skinner pulled her swiftly, and amid our ringing cheers
He delivered her in safety to his brother engineers.

So we gladly doff our headgear as we sing this modest lay,
To those runners of the Eighties—pioneers of Santa Fe.
Their intestinal development dispersed all normal fears,
Yes, they sure had guts in plenty, those old Needles engineers.

*Two engines pulled the Bly special out of Needles.

A RAILROADER'S POEM. This poem was written around 1888 as a tribute to the Needles engineers who pulled the "Bly Special" out of Needles. The author is unknown. (Courtesy of the Mojave River Valley Museum.)

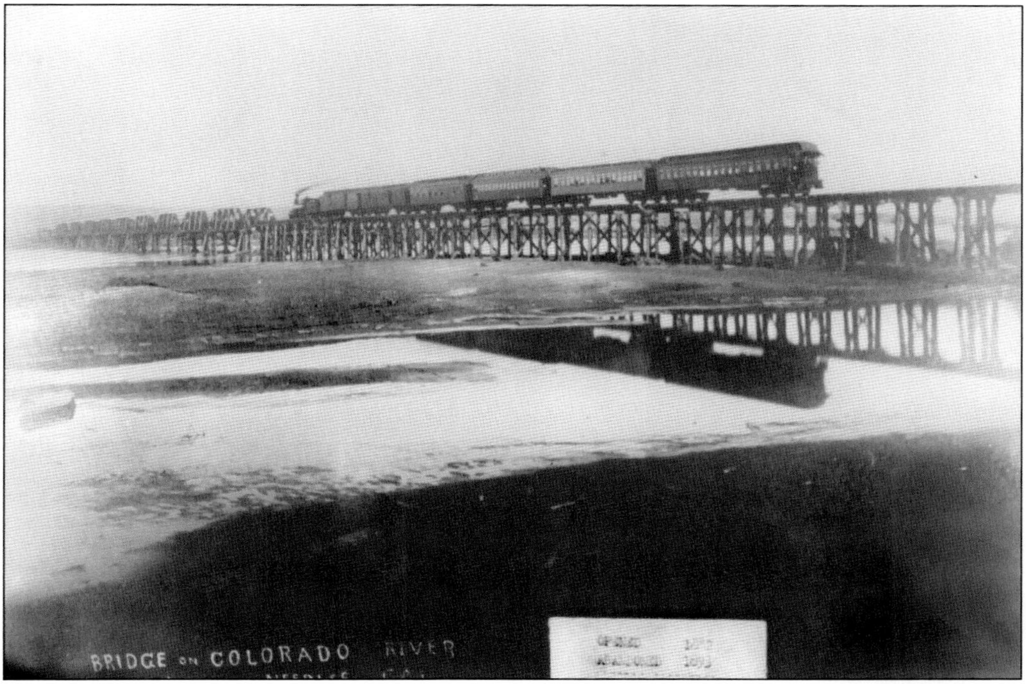

ATLANTIC AND PACIFIC BRIDGE. This was the first bridge built by the Atlantic and Pacific Railroad that spanned the Colorado River. Fast currents washed the bridge away in 1884, 1886, and 1888. Railroad executives realized that they needed a bridge that could withstand the current, and construction of a high-cantilever bridge began and was completed May 1890. This bridge was called the Red Rock Bridge. (Courtesy of the Mohave Museum of History and Art.)

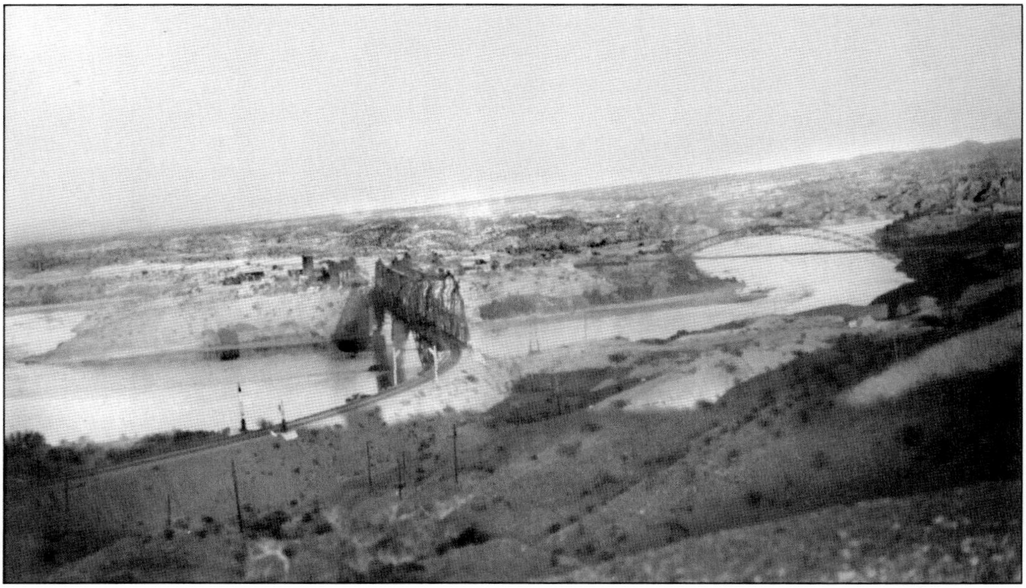

RED ROCK BRIDGE. The Red Rock Bridge was shared by wagons, automobiles, and trains. In 1945, safety concerns led to the removal of the bridge's rails so that reinforcements could be made. The bridge reopened for traffic in 1947. It was finally dismantled in 1976. (Courtesy of Dona Schulz Wyzlic.)

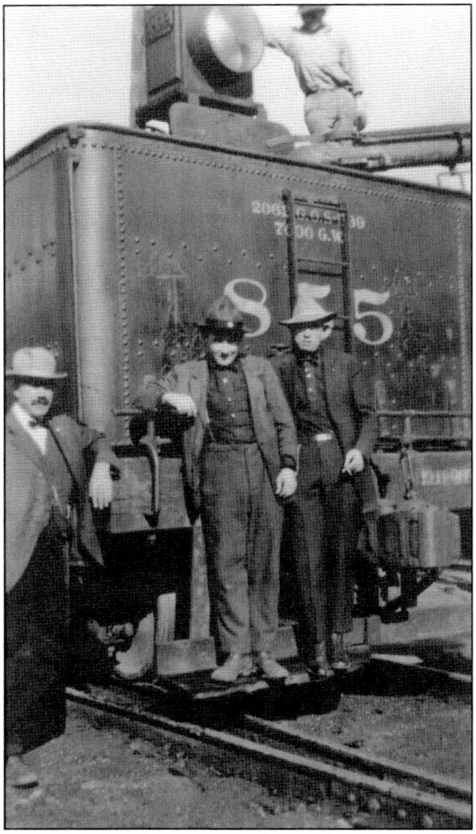

The Goat. This larger steam locomotive was also referred to as the "goat." Standing on the rear wooden platform, the Needles switch engine crew is seen here waiting to move engines into the roundhouse for maintenance or repair. The wooden platform occasionally gave way; after a number of injuries, it was removed. (Courtesy of the Needles Regional Museum.)

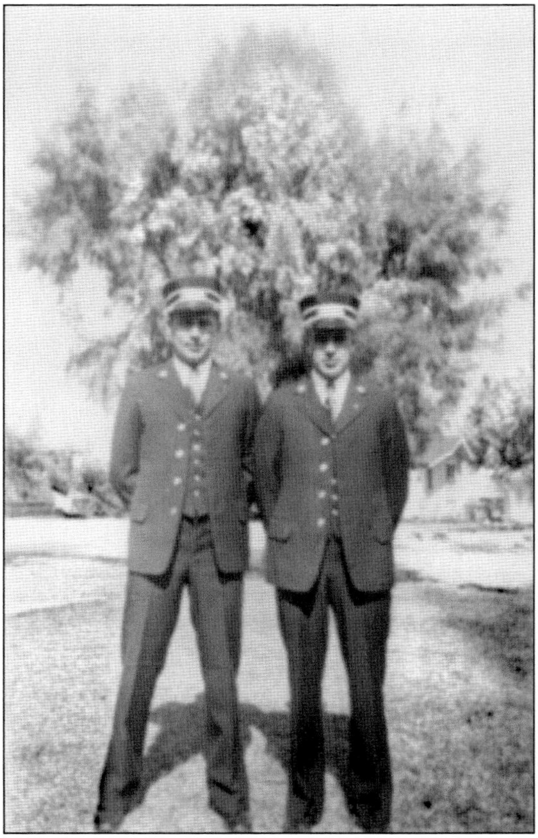

Conductors. Standing on the grounds of the El Graces, conductors Ernie Schulz and Roland Pratt, Needles residents, pose for a picture before boarding the train. The conductors were responsible for the safety of the crew and the passengers. After collecting the passengers' tickets, conductors signaled the engineer that the train was ready to leave the station and conveyed how many passengers would dine at the next Harvey House or train depot. Once the trains arrived at another station, the conductors were responsible for telling officials how many passengers were on board and what the train's departure and arrival times were. (Courtesy of Dona Schulz Wyzlic.)

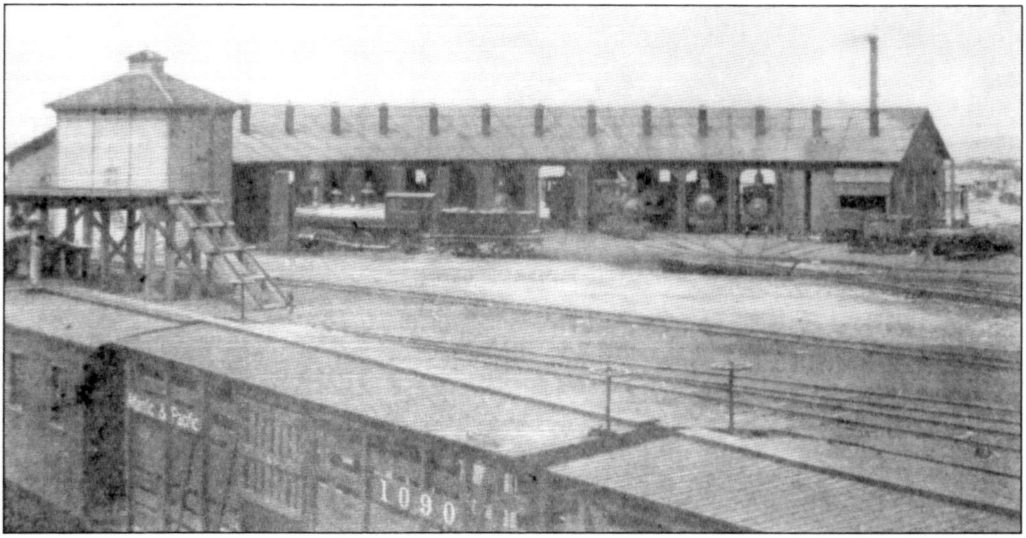

ROUNDHOUSE AND TURNTABLE. Beyond the tracks is the roundhouse. Atlantic and Pacific locomotives backed to the turntable to pull the engine into the stalls where they were maintained and rebuilt. This semicircle was necessary since trains could not back up on the track. The turntable (seen below) was in the center of the roundhouse. Once an engine was on the turntable, it was then delivered to an open stall to be worked on. The square building in these pictures is the water tank, housed according to the Southern Pacific style. The elevated track is the east end of the coal chutes. The roundhouse in Needles was the largest west of Kansas City. (Courtesy of the Mojave River Valley Museum, Robert Flink Collection.)

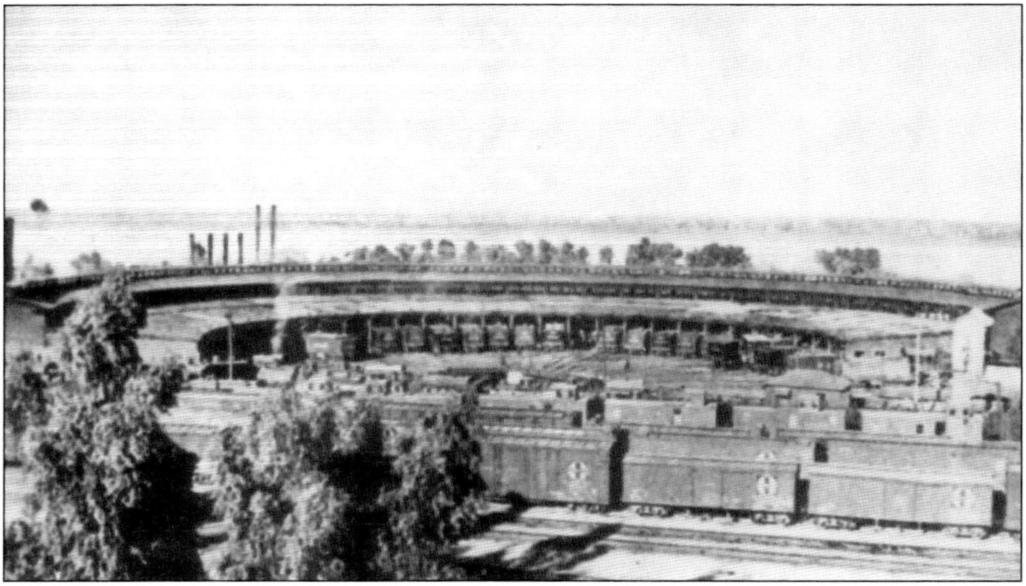

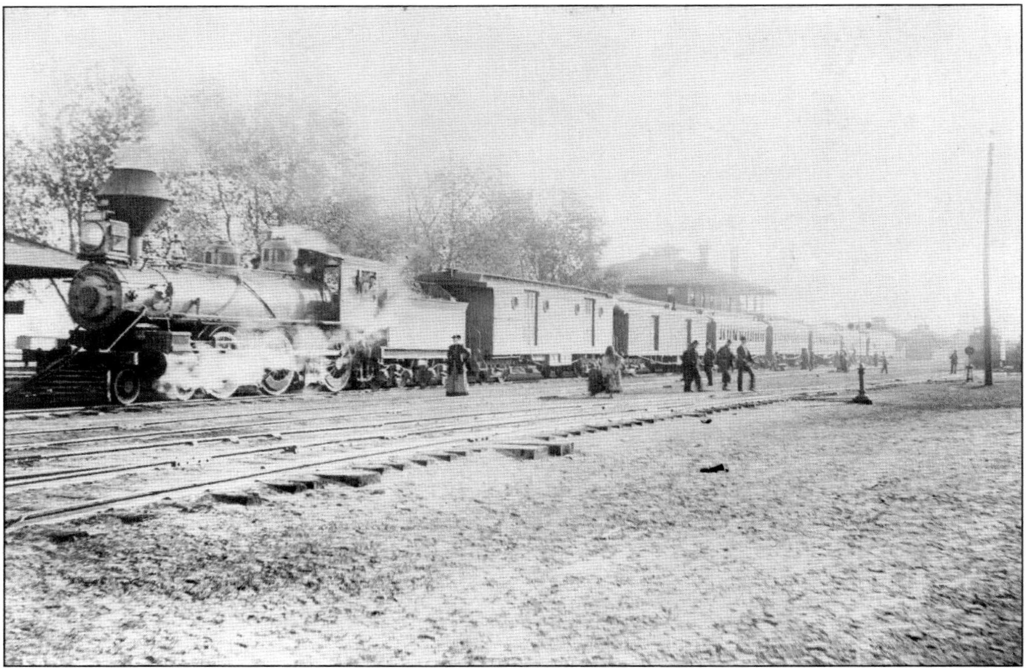

Santa Fe Overland. In 1903, the Santa Fe Overland sits at the Needles train depot as passengers mill around. In the left corner of the picture is the express office with a small park between the express office and depot. A portion of the upstairs of the old wooden Harvey House containing the telegraph office is visible. The first switch stand is an old Atlantic and Pacific with a bar across the top. (Courtesy of Jim and Sue Shephard.)

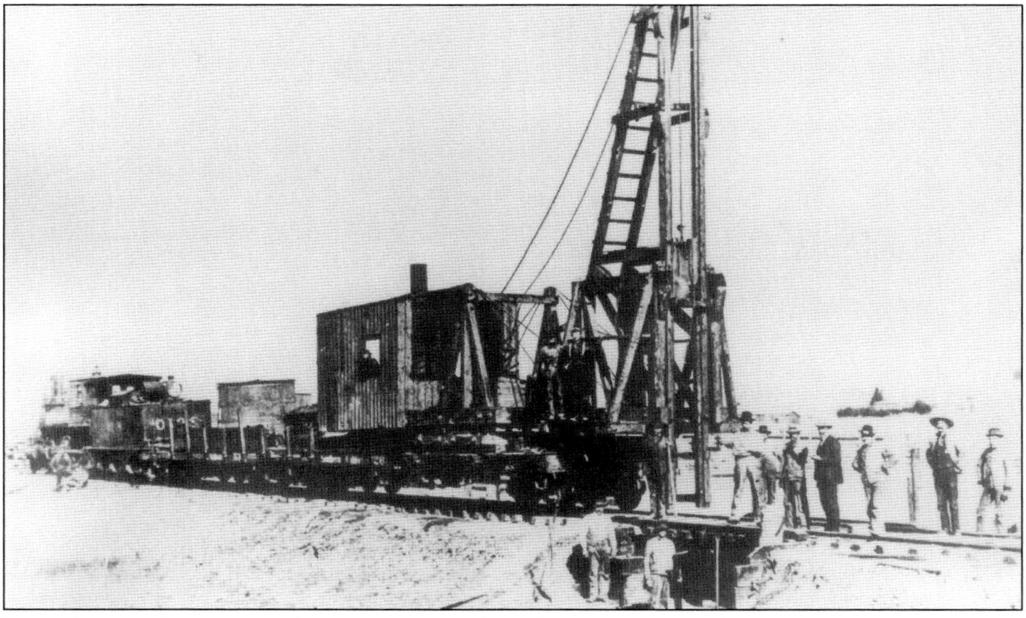

Pile Driver. The piece of equipment on the railroad flatbed is known as a pile driver, also referred to as a bridge derrick. This Needles crew is driving a piling to stabilize the ground around a culvert. The culvert may have been caused by a flash flood. (Courtesy of Mojave River Valley Museum.)

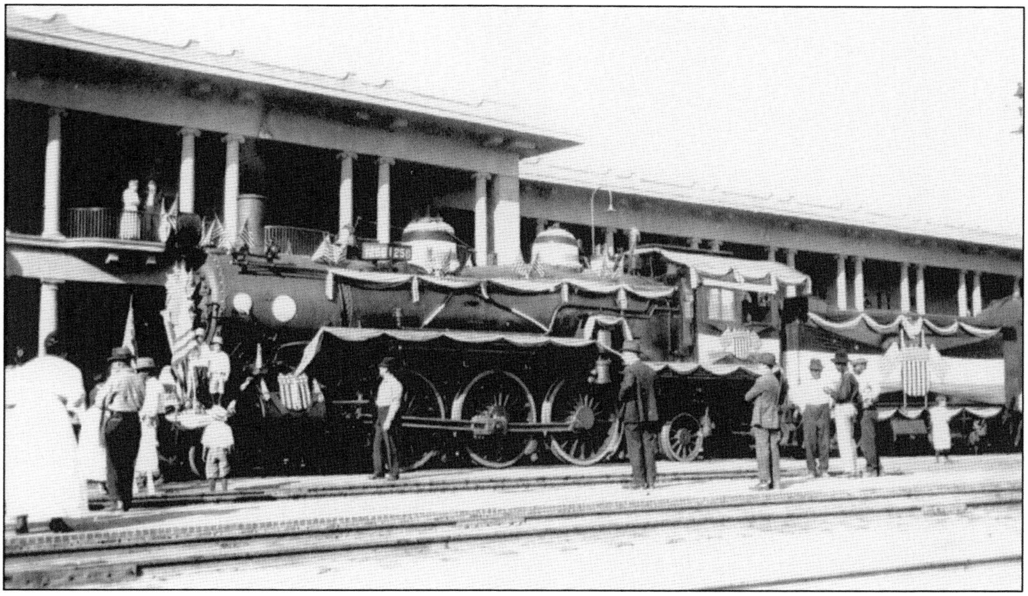

Victory Train. This is the train that Pres. Woodrow Wilson took across the country in July 1919 on a whistle-stop campaign to solicit the support of the American people for entry into the League of Nations, which was intended to promote international peace. In the photograph below, the president's train is at the El Garces train depot, sitting on a turntable to allow other trains to pass while the president and his staff ate at the El Garces Harvey House. At the end of the tour, Wilson suffered a debilitating stroke. (Courtesy of Pam McCorkle Klum.)

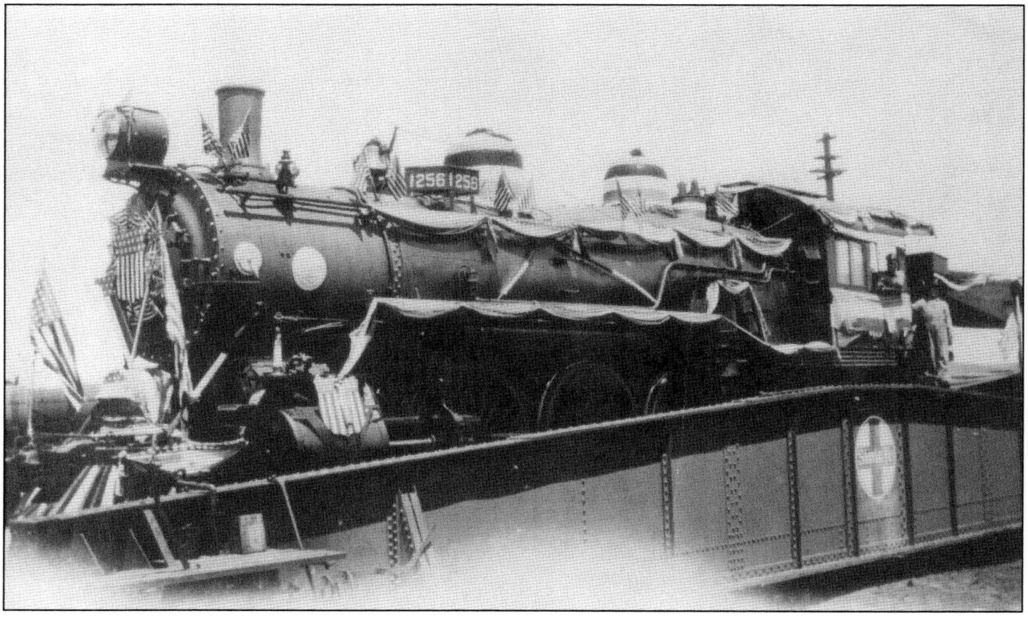

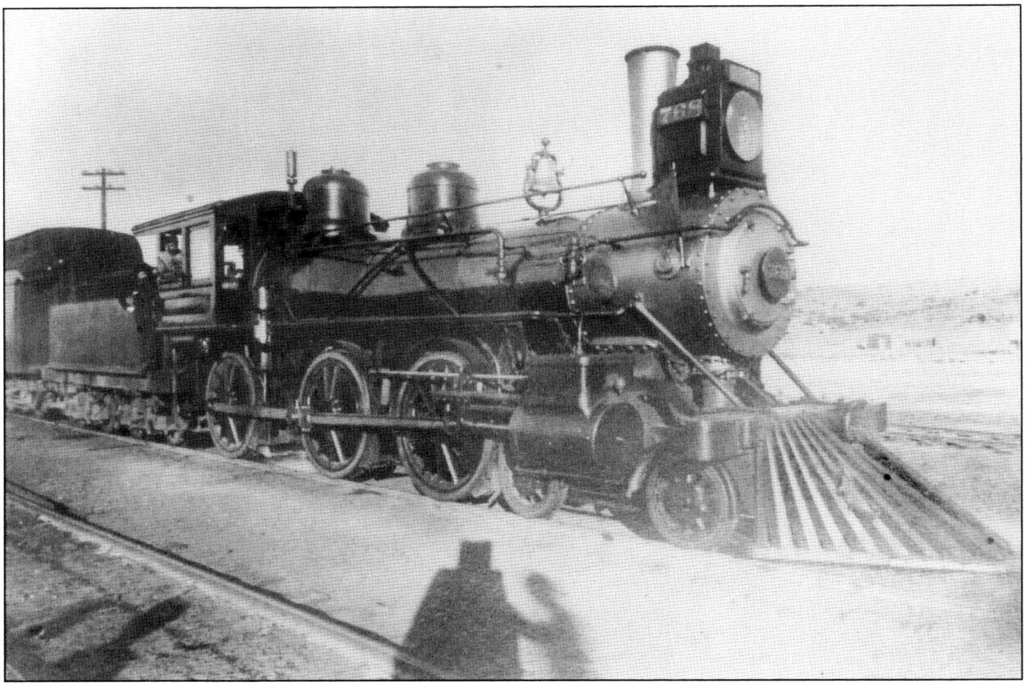

STEAM LOCOMOTIVES. The United States began developing steam locomotives about 1829. The locomotives carried freight and passengers until they began to be phased out starting in the mid-1900s in favor of diesel locomotives. Pictured are early steam locomotives at the El Garces train depot in Needles. (Courtesy of Mohave River Valley Museum, Dona Shulz Wyzlic.)

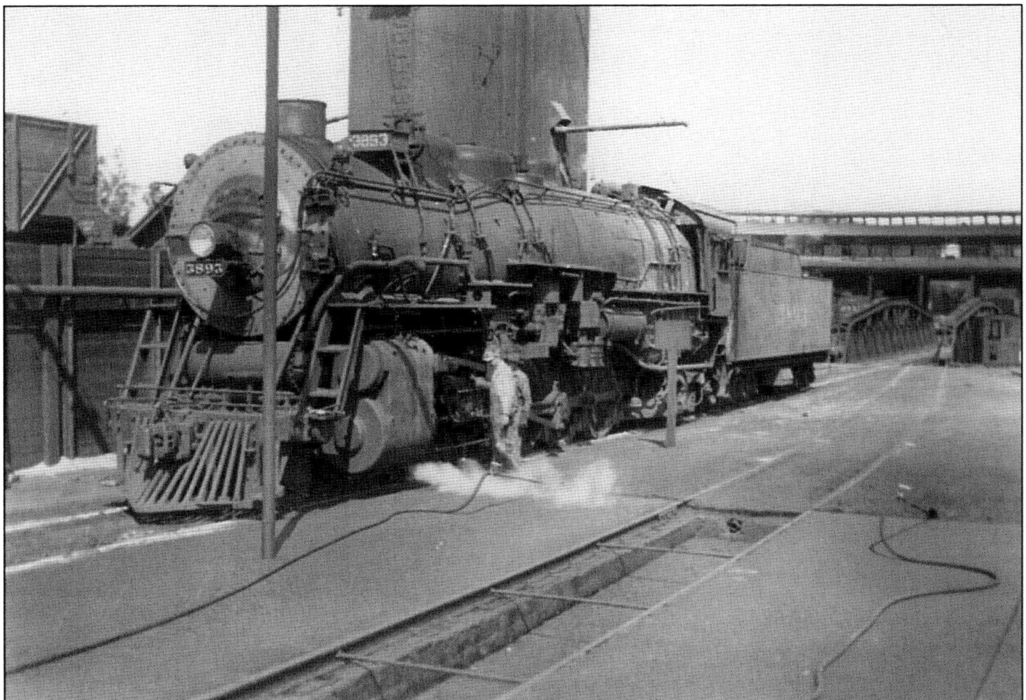

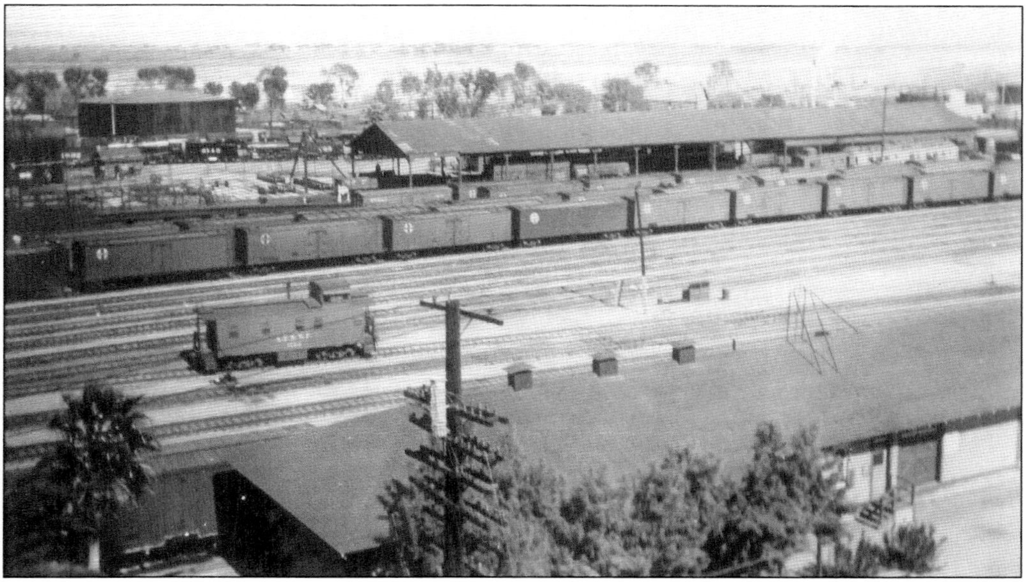

RAIL YARD. The Needles trainsmen get ready to take the caboose to pick up loads and deliver them to warehouses down the tracks. The rail yard has many tracks in parallel to keep cars from interfering with the flow of traffic. Cars are stored while they wait to be loaded or unloaded. (Courtesy of Dona Schulz Wyzlic.)

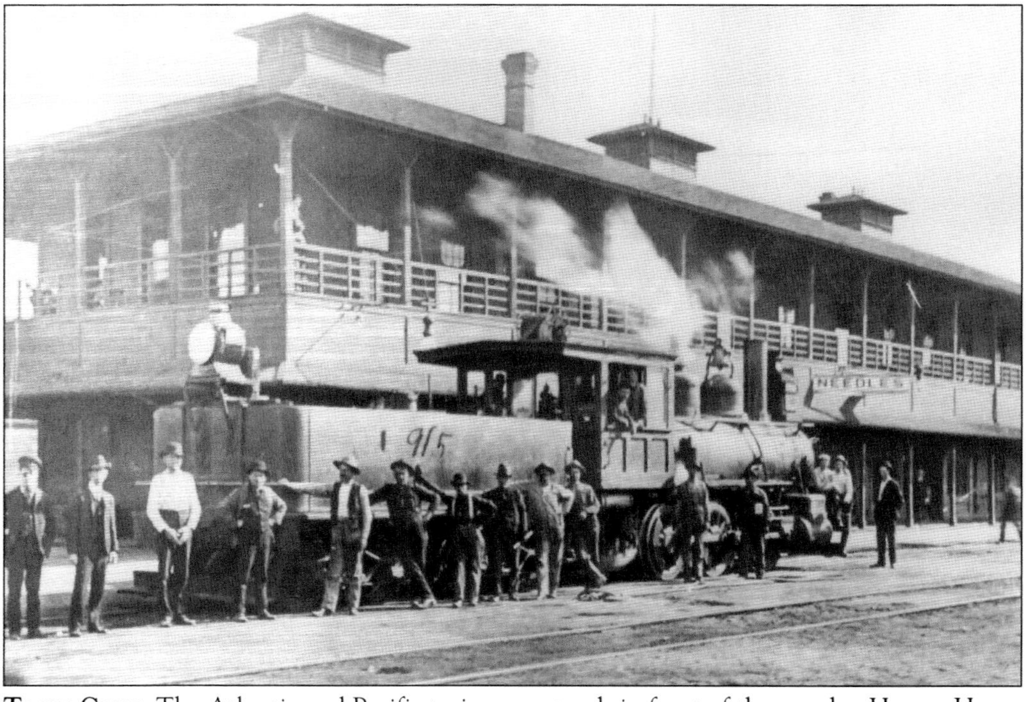

TRAIN CREW. The Atlantic and Pacific train crew stands in front of the wooden Harvey House hotel and train depot in Needles in the early 1900s. The crew did a variety of jobs, including inspecting couplings and handbrakes and working the track switch to reroute cars. They would signal the engineer when to stop and start when coupling or uncoupling. (Courtesy of the Needles Regional Museum.)

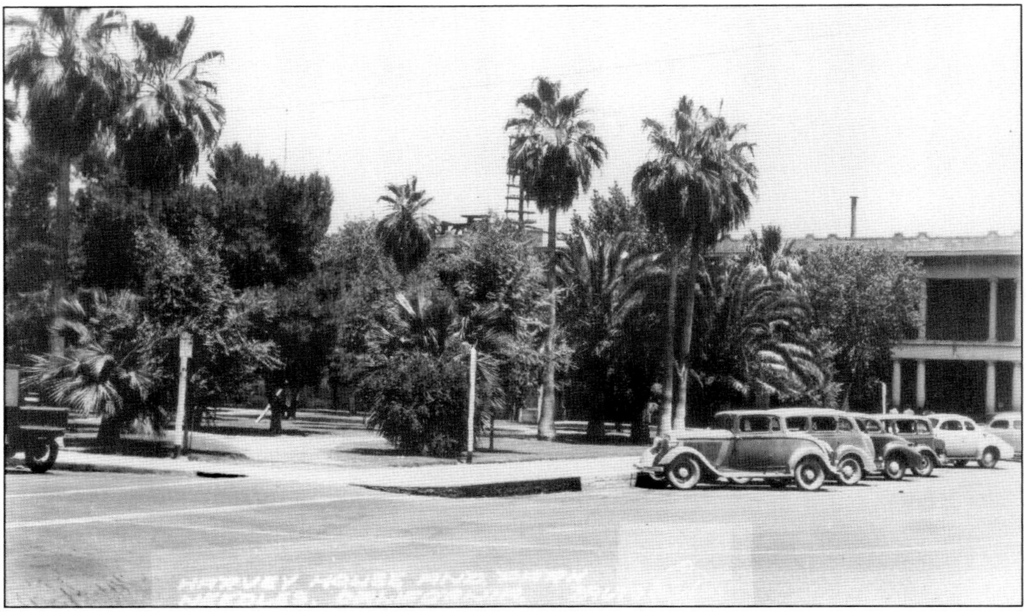

SANTA FE PARK. The Santa Fe Park sits in front of the El Garces Harvey House. It was landscaped in 1908 upon the completion of the new concrete Harvey House. The park is used throughout the year for community events and gatherings. The annual Rodeo Picnic is held the weekend of the Needles Rodeo. (Courtesy of Marilyn Kirchner.)

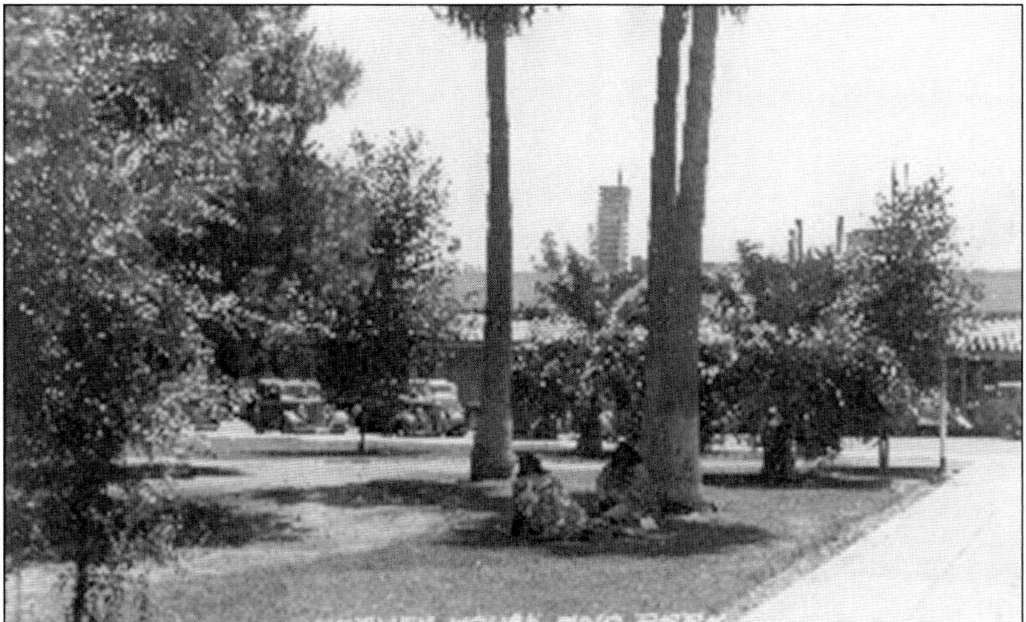

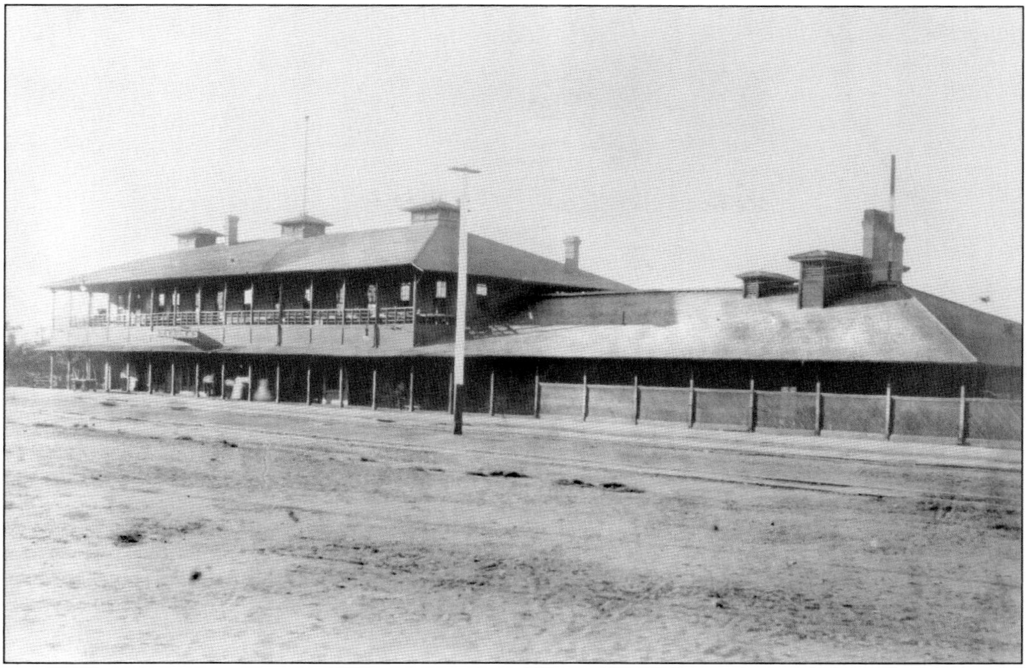

Harvey House. The original wooden Harvey House was destroyed in a fire, and construction on the new building began in 1906 and was completed in 1908. It was named the El Graces in honor of missionary Padre Francisco Garces, who traveled through the area in 1776. The El Garces was part of the Fred Harvey chain of hotels and restaurants that provided Santa Fe Railroad passengers with food and lodging. (Courtesy of the San Bernardino Public Library.)

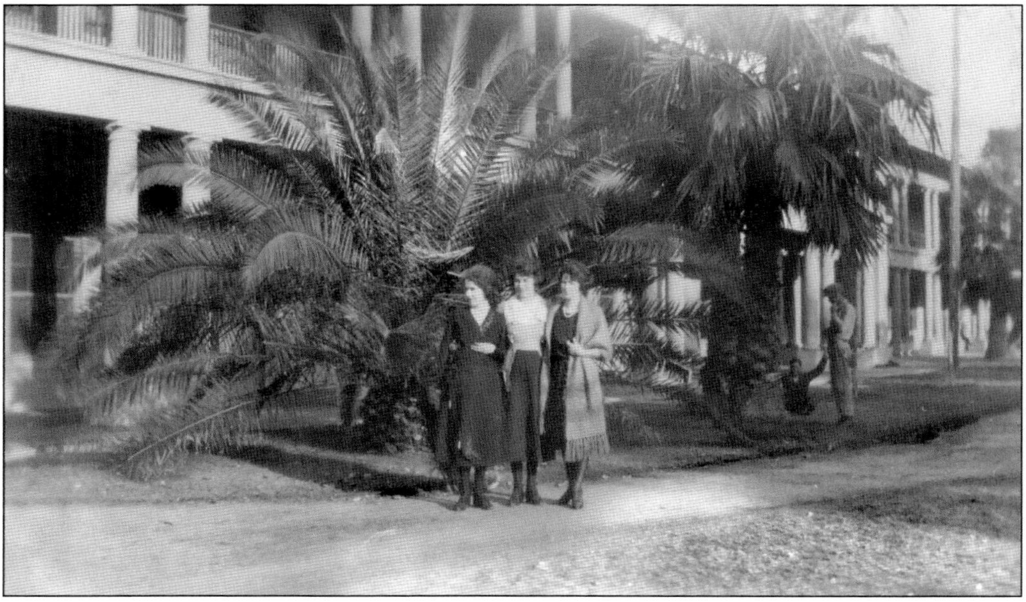

Hotel Visitors. The Harvey House with its mature palm trees was a favorite location for picture taking. These visitors pose as a reminder of their visit to Needles. Whether traveling by car or on the passenger train, a picture of the "crown jewel" of the Harvey Houses was an important reminder of a visitor's trip. (Courtesy of Rosemary Weart.)

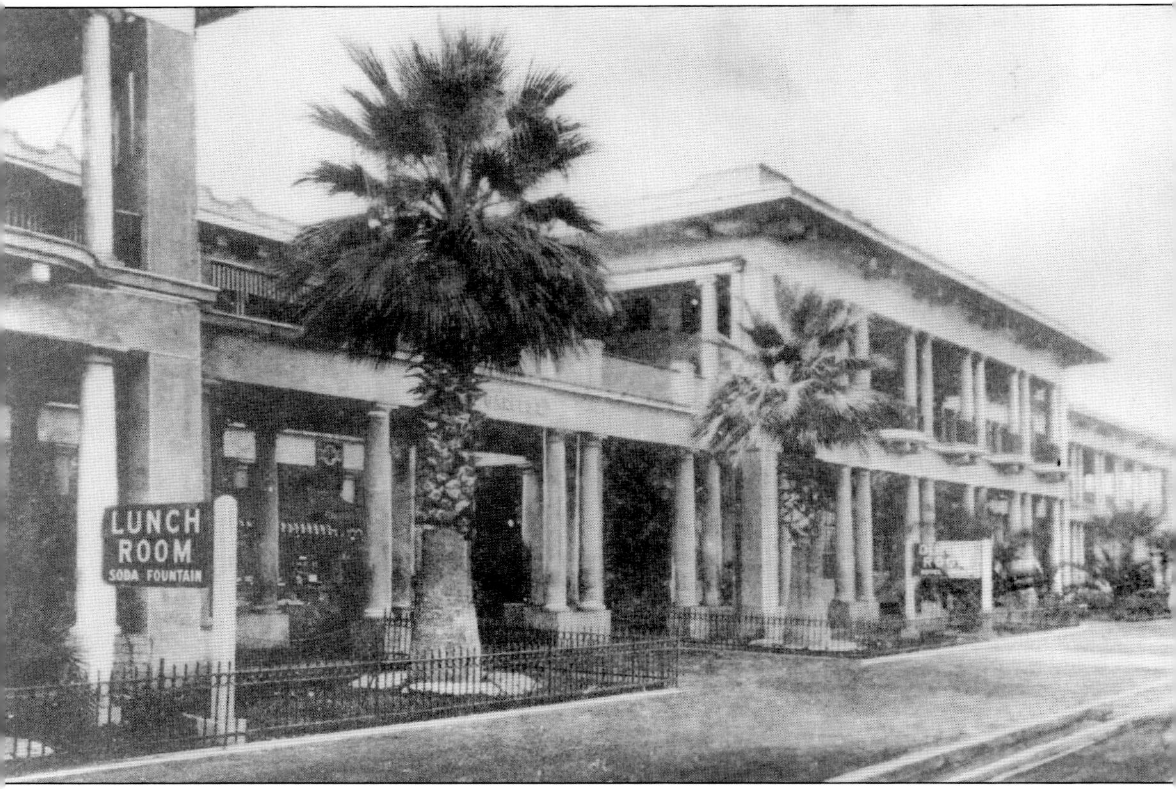

Rebuilt Harvey House. After the fire destroyed the original Harvey House, it was reconstructed using concrete and steel. The rebuilding also included landscaping around the hotel and in the adjacent Santa Fe Park. Some guests preferred the hotel rooms that looked out on the park; train enthusiasts booked rooms overlooking the train station. There was a horseshoe lunchroom and a very elegant dining room displaying the finest china and linen. They imported the finest linen from John S. Brown and Son's of Belfast. The pattern on the napkins matched the pattern on the china. Harvey invented the oversized napkin so that men could tuck them under their chins and in their waistcoats. Some of the Harvey Houses also had a newsstand where drinks and sandwiches were sold. Fred Harvey had the only Coca Cola franchise and bottled the drink in his own plant. These bottles of Coca Cola were sold exclusively at the Harvey Houses. (Courtesy of the Mojave River Valley Museum.)

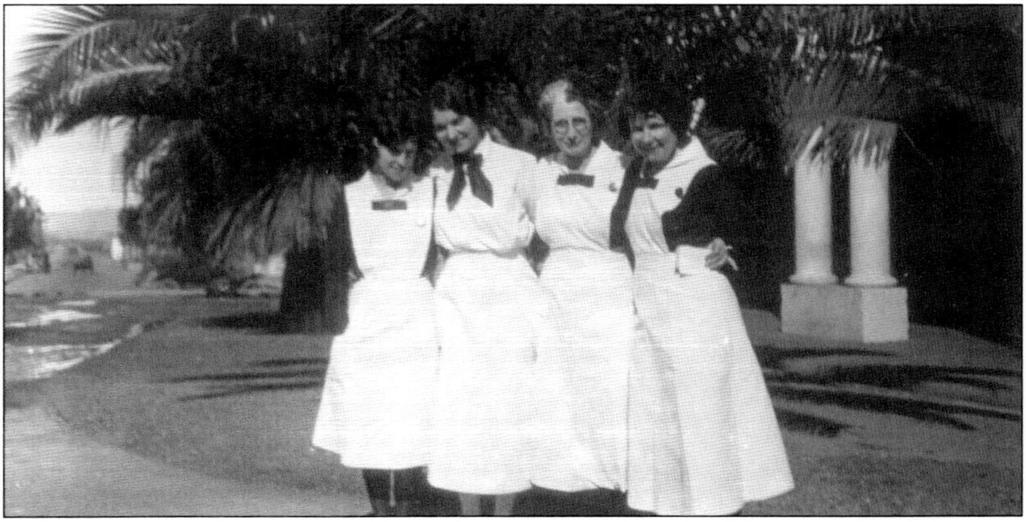

Harvey Girls. Initially the Harvey House's waiters and hosts were all male, but in the 1880s, Fred Harvey, tired of the rowdy male staff, replaced them with young women, known as "Harvey Girls." These unmarried Harvey Girls pose in front of the Needles El Garces Harvey House. They were hired under a contract that prohibited them from marrying for one year. If the contract was broken, they forfeited a portion of their $17.50 monthly base pay. They were not allowed to wear makeup and had a strict curfew. Many women were hired from abroad. It was important that they exhibit the finest manners and provide excellent service. (Courtesy of Rosemary Weart.)

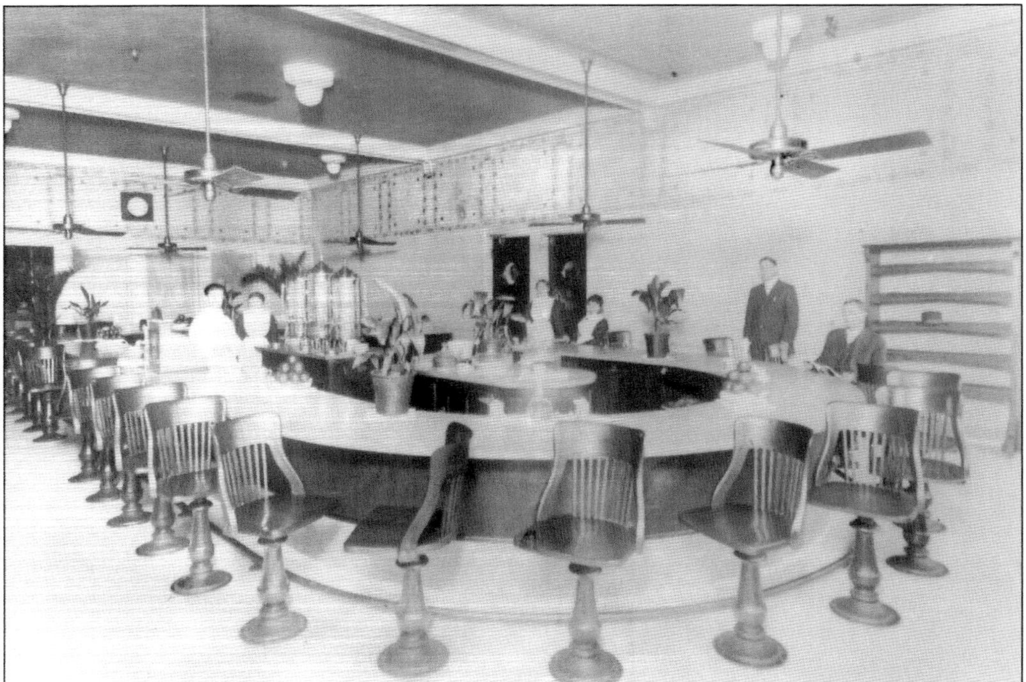

Harvey House Lunchroom. Though each Harvey House exterior was built to uniquely complement the surrounding landscape, the interiors were similar in design. As an example, Harvey Houses all featured horseshoe-shaped lunchroom counters; most had two. Most hotels had a newsstand as well. (Courtesy of Mojave River Valley Museum.)

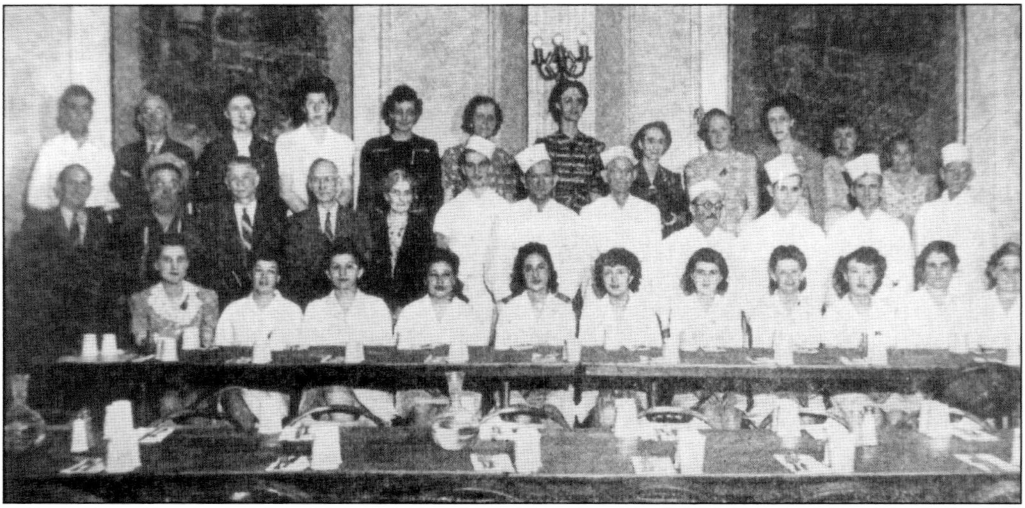

Harvey House Employees. The above image shows 34 employees in the Needles El Garces Harvey House. The restaurant was built to serve railroad passengers, so its daily routine revolved around the train schedules. A spotter waited by the railroad track for the first sign of the train. When he sighted the train, the spotter would bang on a bell to alert the rest of the staff. Employees would position themselves at the door of the dining room and ring a bell to direct travelers to the dining room. This streamlined system allowed the Harvey House restaurant to serve as many as eight trains a day. The picture below shows a typical Harvey House kitchen. (Courtesy of Mojave River Valley Museum.)

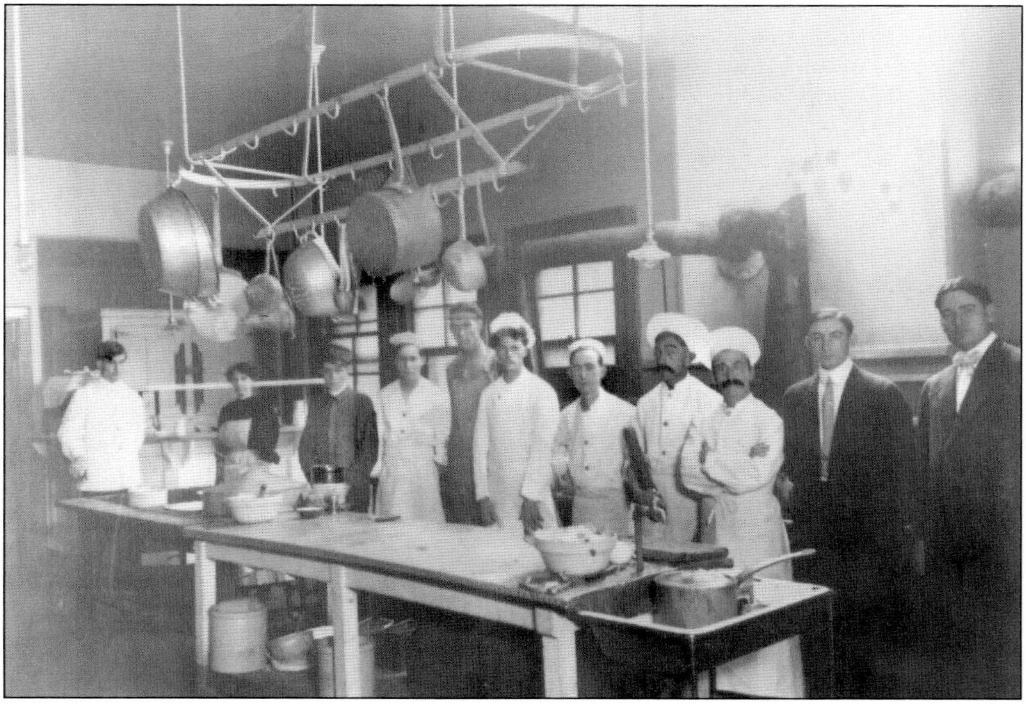

Four

Early Needles
Birth of a Town

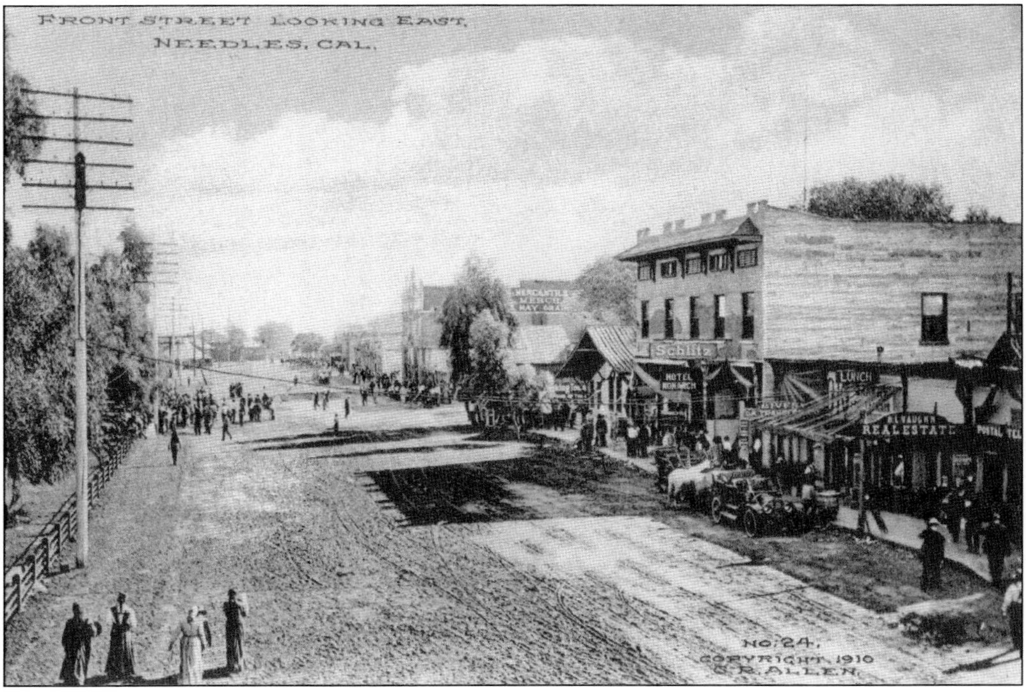

Front Street. This 1910 street scene on Front Street shows the original unpaved street that later became part of Route 66. Located across from the train depot, many early Needles businesses grew to support the travelers who came to town on the railroad. As the main street in Needles, Front Street featured a drugstore, barbershop, saloon, and a hotel, and was the scene of many of the town's events. (Courtesy of Marilyn Kirchner.)

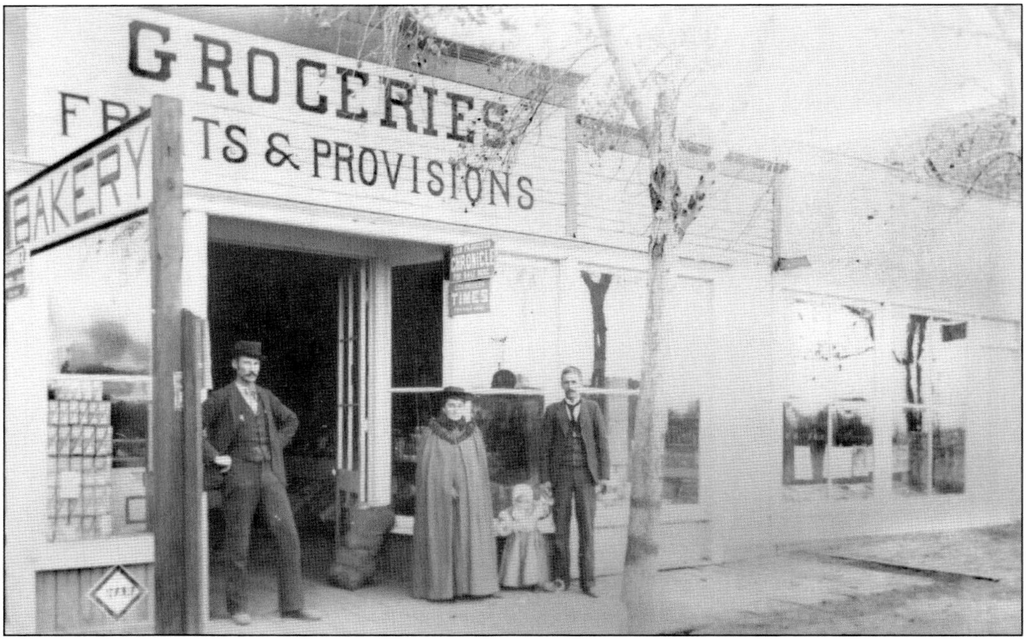

Holcomb Store. Samuel Frost Holcomb Jr. opened one of the town's first bakery and grocery stores, located on Front Street. It was a welcome addition since Needles residents no longer had to make long trips for provisions. Standing in front of the store are Samuel and his wife, Louise, with their daughter, Joy, and an unidentified man on the left. The Holcomb home (seen below in 1884) was located several blocks away from the store on Third Street. Pictured here are Louise Holcomb (holding daughter Lucille) and fellow Needles resident Ina Sperry. (Courtesy of the Needles Regional Library.)

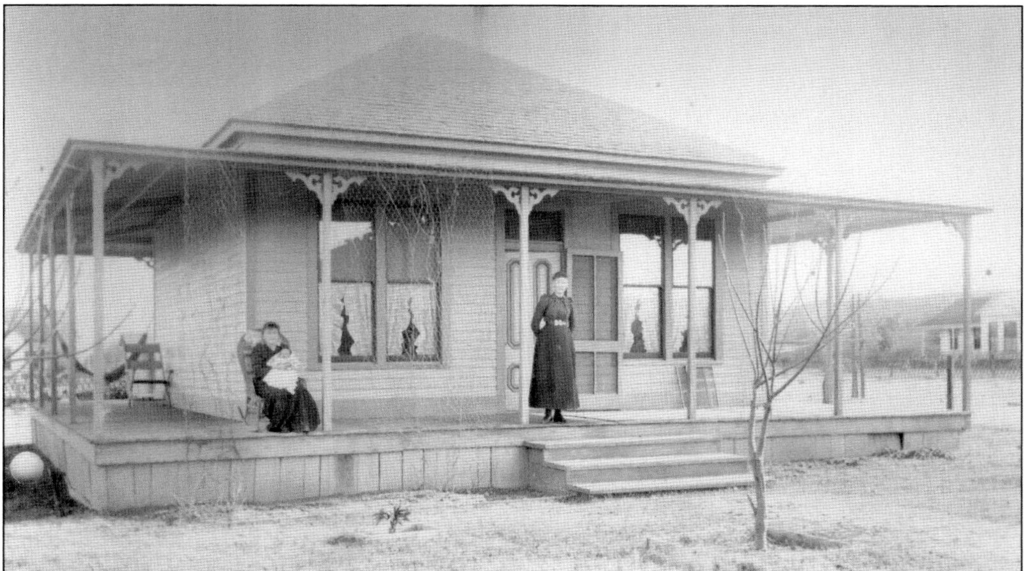

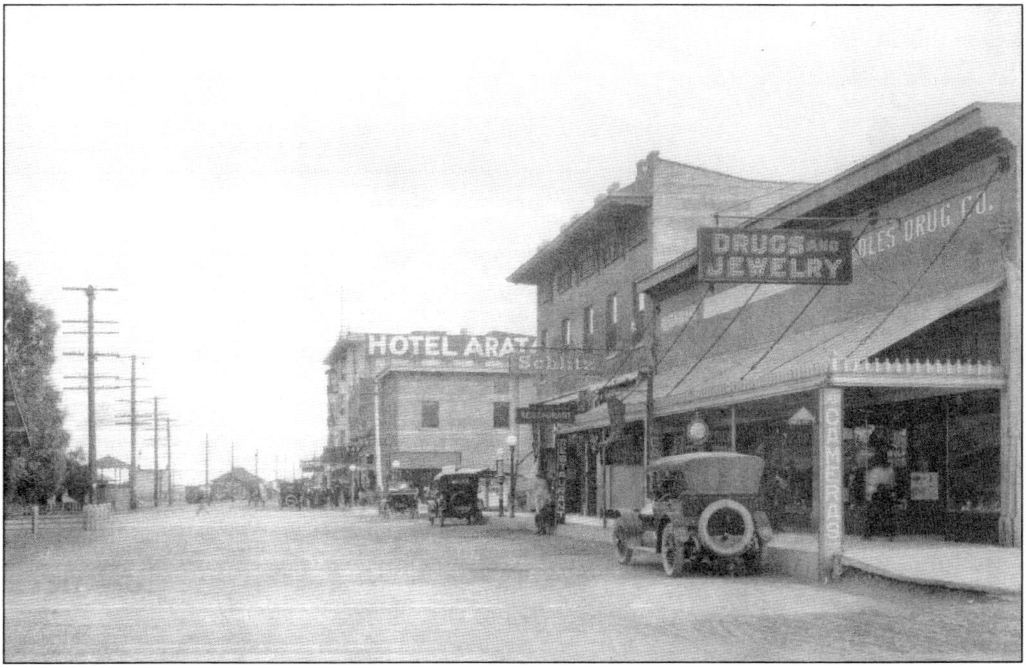

Needles Drugstore. On the corner of Front and F Streets was Needles's first drugstore. Although remodeled several times, the site continued to be the location of the drugstore until the early 1960s, when the shop moved to Broadway Street. In the distance in this photograph is the Hotel Arataba, named for the famous Mohave Indian chief. In the image below is a general merchandise store that served the community in the late 1800s. (Courtesy of the Needles Regional Library.)

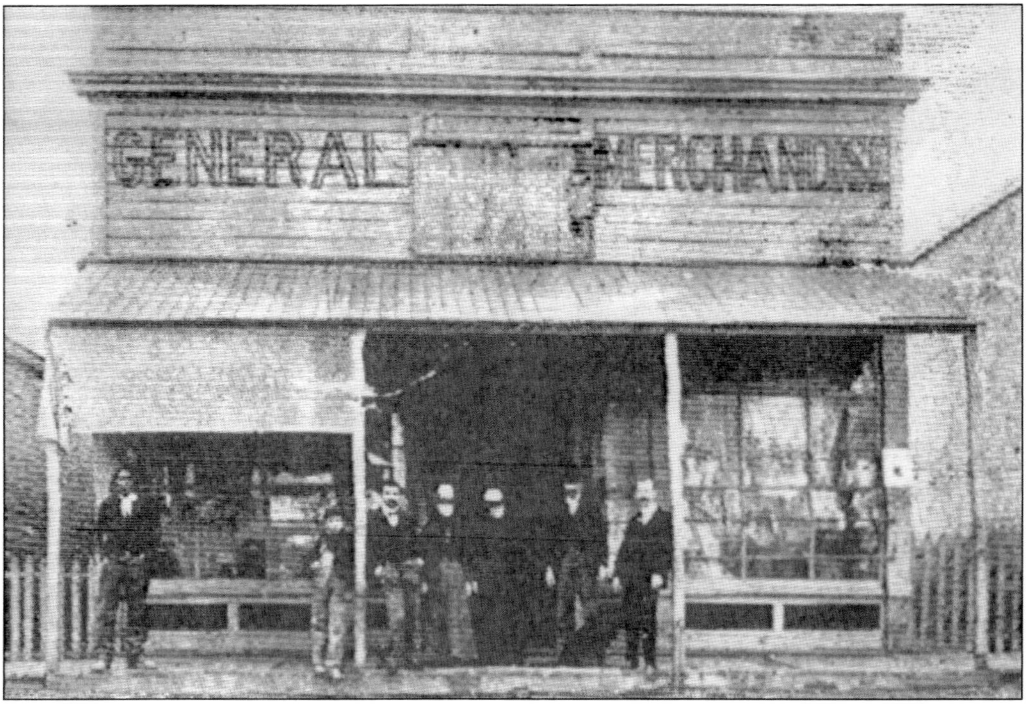

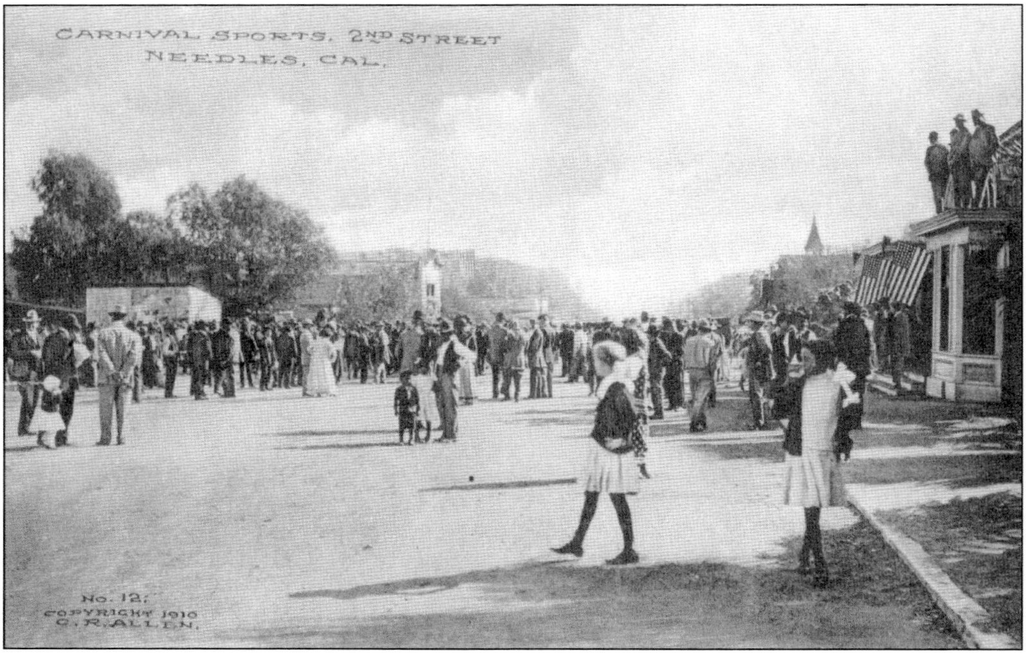

Carnival. The yearly carnival has come to town, and Needles residents are enjoying another weeklong celebration. The carnival was held on Second Street, which is now Broadway, another new alignment of Route 66, and its exhibits drew men, women, and children alike. All sorts of healing remedies were pitched to the onlookers. The image below shows another part of the celebration—a deep-pit barbecue. (Courtesy of the Needles Regional Museum.)

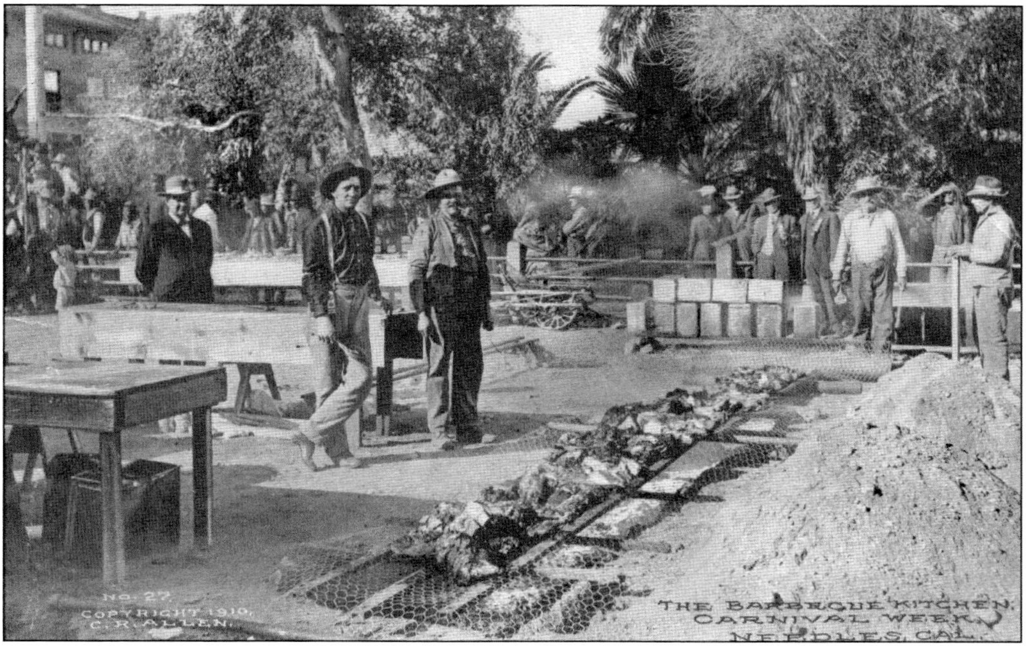

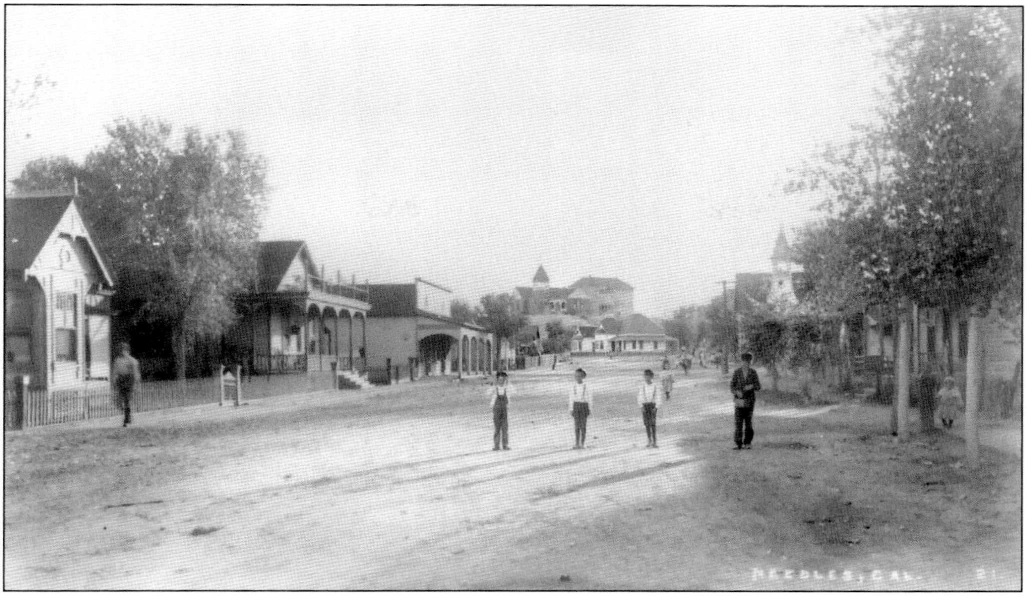

HIGH SCHOOL. School is out for the summer, and the young children here seem to be enjoying that fact. At the end of the street in this *c.* 1911 image stands the first high school built in Needles. (Courtesy of Mojave River Valley Museum.)

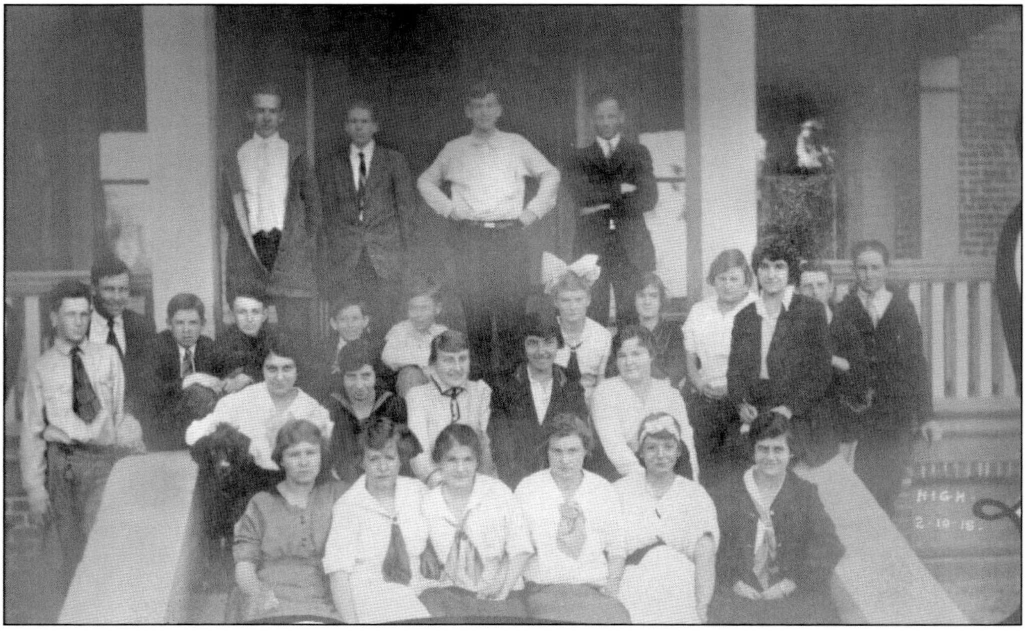

GRADUATION. The class of 1916 poses on the steps of the Needles High School. Some modern-day Needles residents are descendants of the students pictured here. From left to right are (first row) Winnie Greaney, Gertrude Salyman, Zena Wakefield, Myrna Dano, and two unidentified; (second row) Ema Clay, Katy Smith, Sandridge Orr, Edith Jackson, and Jane Crone; (third row) Charles Croneck, Bermond Smith, Ralph Kroeber, Kane "Peewee" Jackson, Emilie Greaney, two unidentified, Monica Hatch, class teacher Michaels, Charles Qurmback, Harry Thompson, and unidentified; (fourth row) Fawn Byers Wakefield, Brett Orr, Harry Rayburn, and Art Qurmback. (Courtesy of the San Bernardino Public Library.)

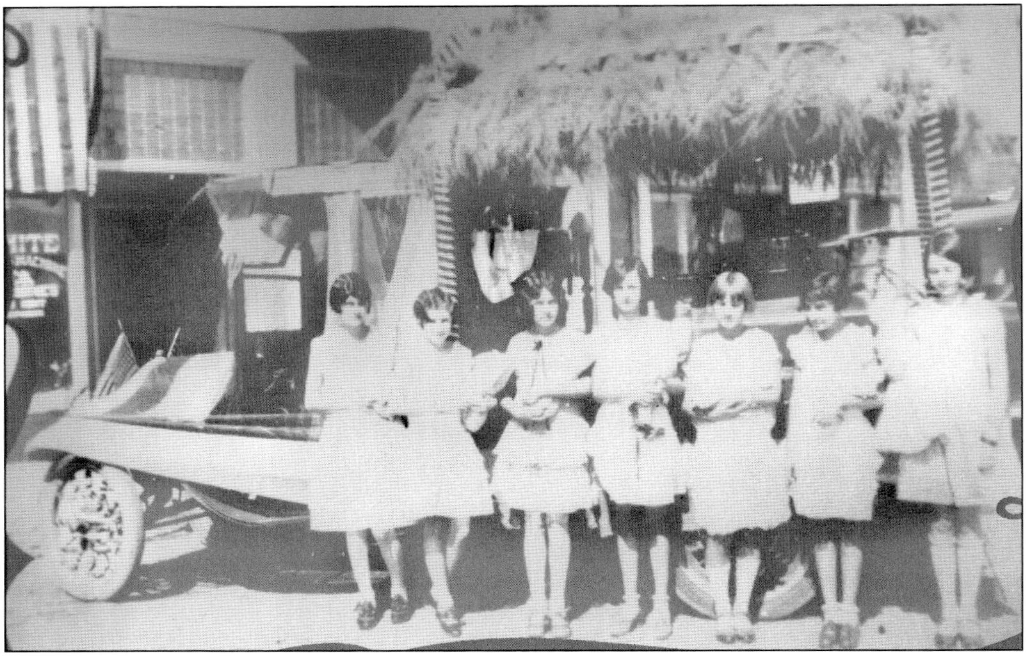

Teens of Yesteryear. Needles has always enjoyed parades, and this photograph records such an occasion. It is apparently a Fourth of July or Armistice Day in the early 1930s. According to Irene Acuna Murry, the truck seen here belonged to Jack Brobrant. He called it Jack's Express and used it to make deliveries to residents. The young women gracing the truck were demonstrating the stitching of doll clothes for the White Sewing Machine Company. (Courtesy of the San Bernardino Public Library.)

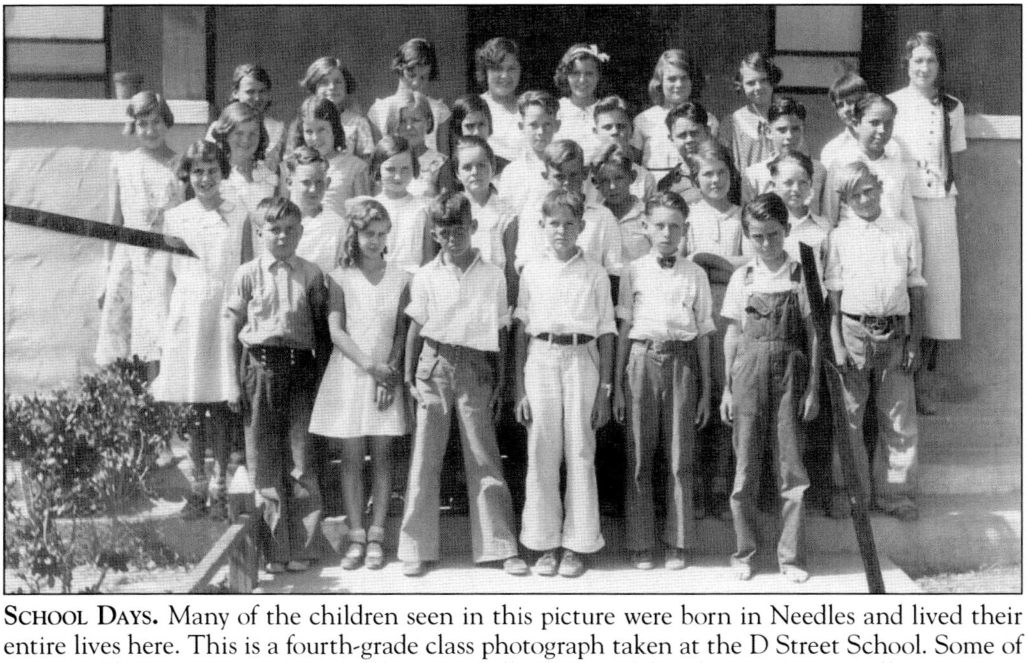

School Days. Many of the children seen in this picture were born in Needles and lived their entire lives here. This is a fourth-grade class photograph taken at the D Street School. Some of these children grew up to raise families in Needles; many of their last names are still common in Needles today. (Courtesy of the McCorkle family.)

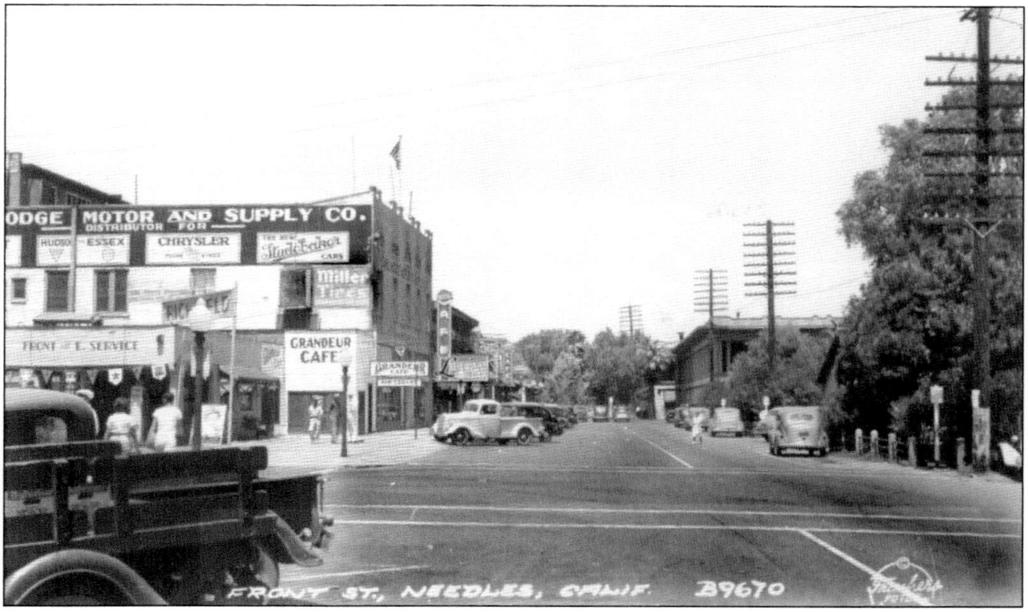

STREET SCENE IN THE 1940S. The picture above looks down Front Street and shows many of the businesses that were part of early Needles. The Grandeur Café holds many memories for those who lived in Needles in the 1940s and 1950s. On the right is Dr. Harward's old office, and at the end of the street on the right is the beginning of the El Garces Harvey House. The image below shows a street scene on Broadway Street (Route 66), which includes the movie theater, the California Hotel, and the Texaco gas station. The streets were lined with palms and a variety of trees. (Courtesy of Hugh Brown.)

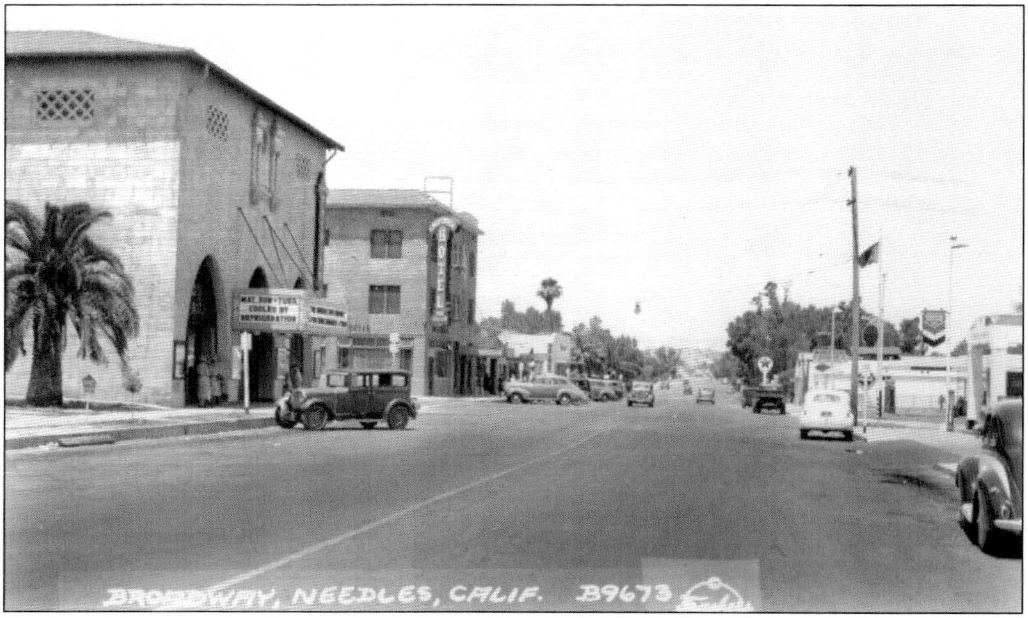

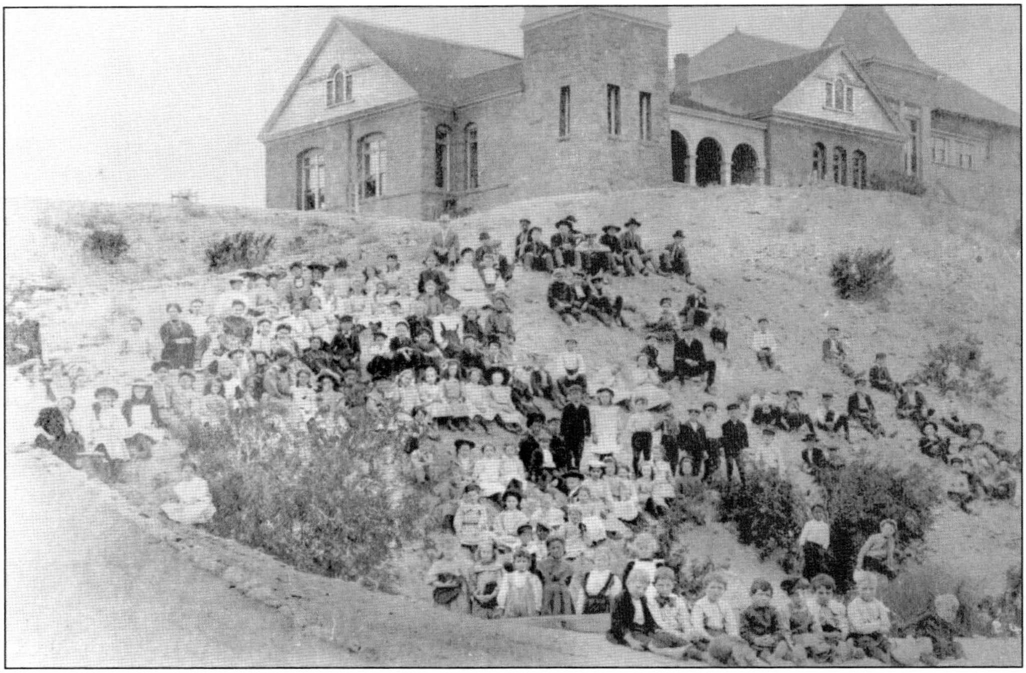

D Street School. Known as the "Castle on the Hill" and built in 1893, this elementary school was torn down in the late 1920s and a more modern structure was built in its place. In 1929, a young boy named Charles Schulz entered second grade at the new D Street School. Below are a group of children who appear to be playing baseball. Standing behind are perhaps parents, family members, and teachers. (Courtesy of Pam McCorkle, Klemm.)

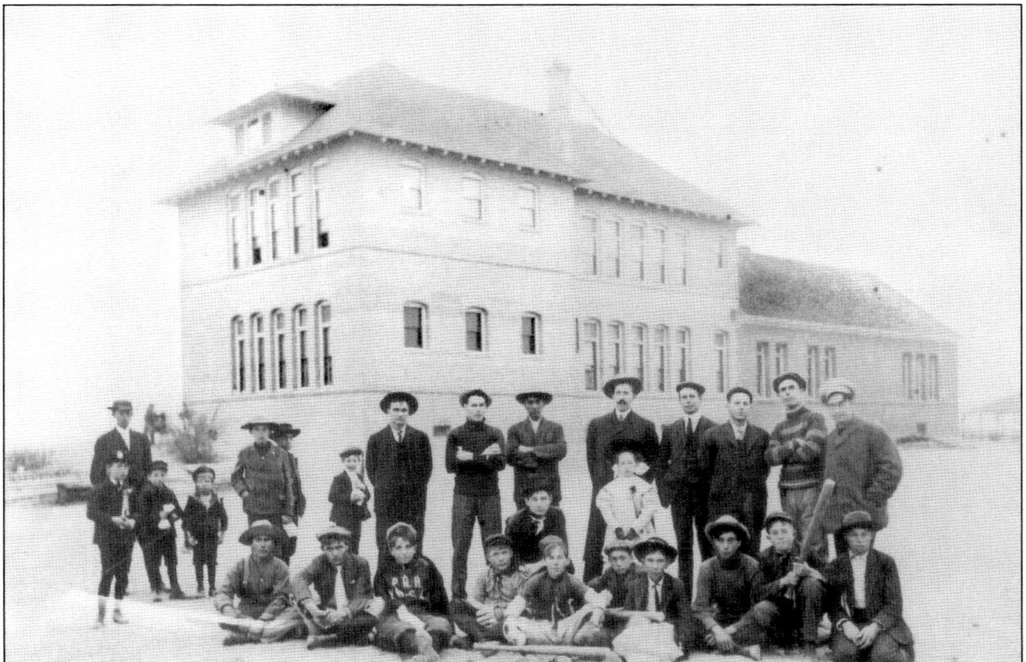

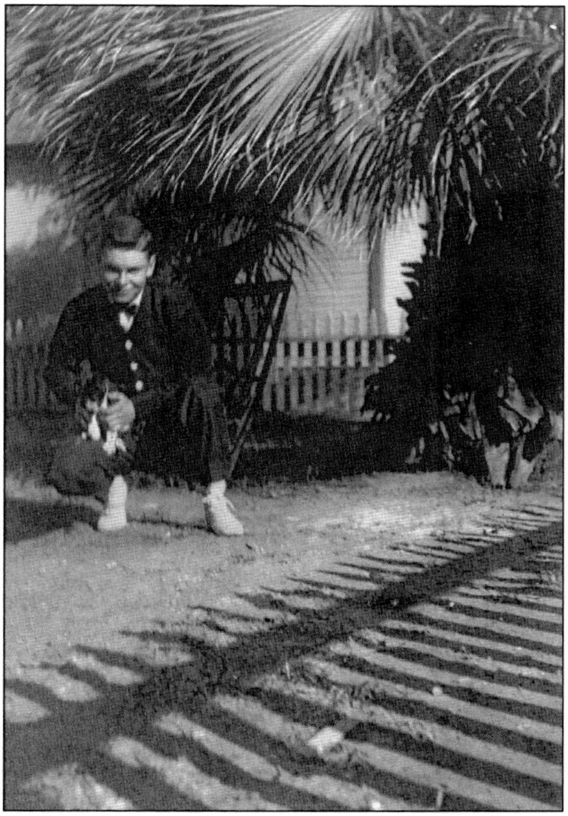

Young Bill Claypool. This image captures young William "Bill" Claypool Jr., all dressed up along the railroad track at the Needles train depot. (Courtesy of the Claypool family.)

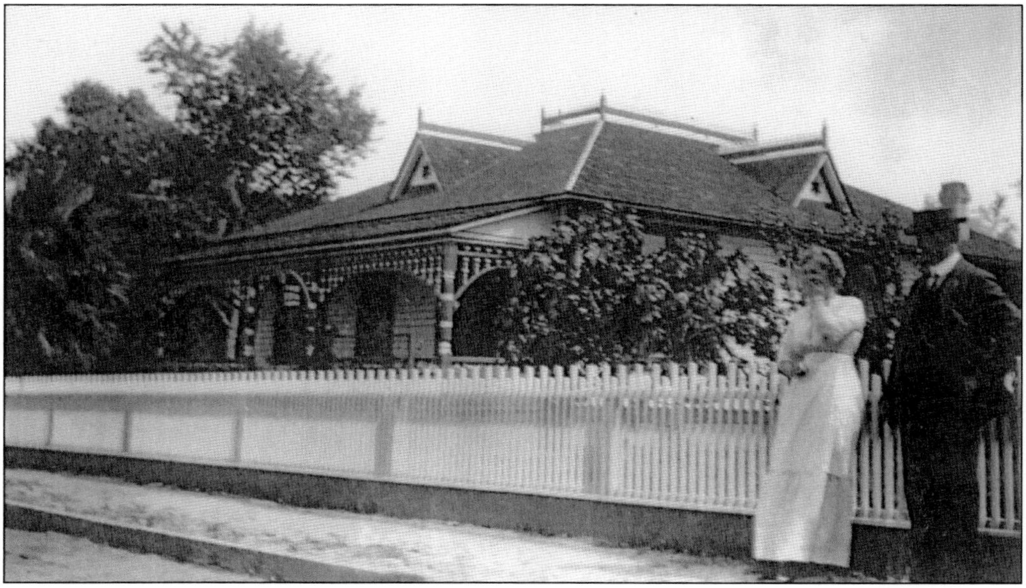

Father and Daughter. William Claypool Sr. stands with his daughter Francis in front of the Claypool home on Broadway Street. Today a vacant lot is in its place. The Claypool family lived in their home until 1924 when William Sr. and his wife, Francis, moved to San Bernardino where they had a feed mill. They remained there until their deaths in the 1940s. (Courtesy of the Claypool family.)

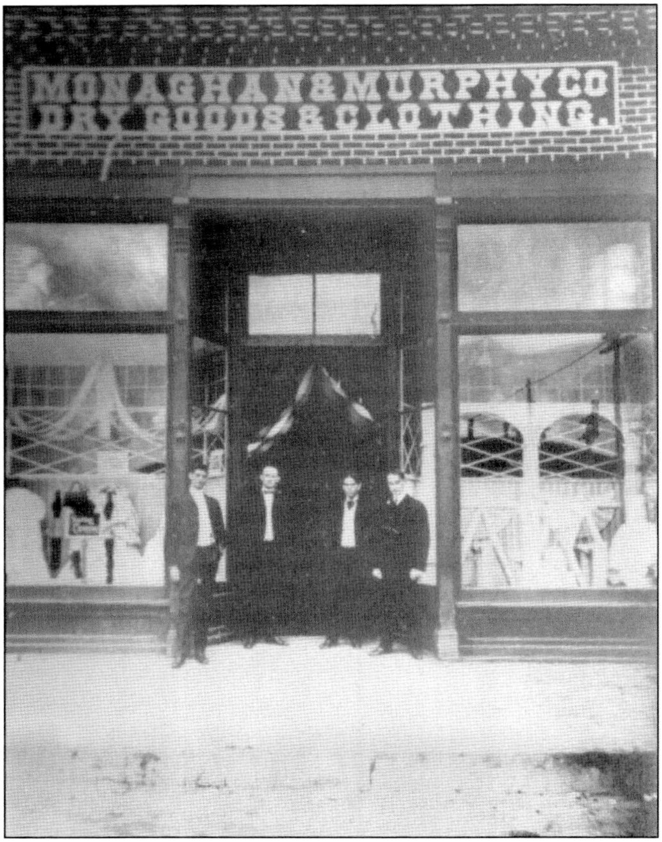

MURPHY AND MONAGHAN. Two merchants, Mr. Murphy and Mr. Monaghan, arrived in Needles, formed a partnership, and opened their clothing and dry goods store about the time that the first steam locomotive came up the Colorado River in 1883. In 1911, they sold the store to the Claypools. (Courtesy of the San Bernardino Public Library.)

NEW STORE. William Claypool purchased the Murphy and Monaghan store, and it became the first Claypool General Store, located on Front Street across from the railroad tracks. At the time the store was purchased, Bill II had just graduated from Berkeley High School. (Courtesy of Needles Regional Museum.)

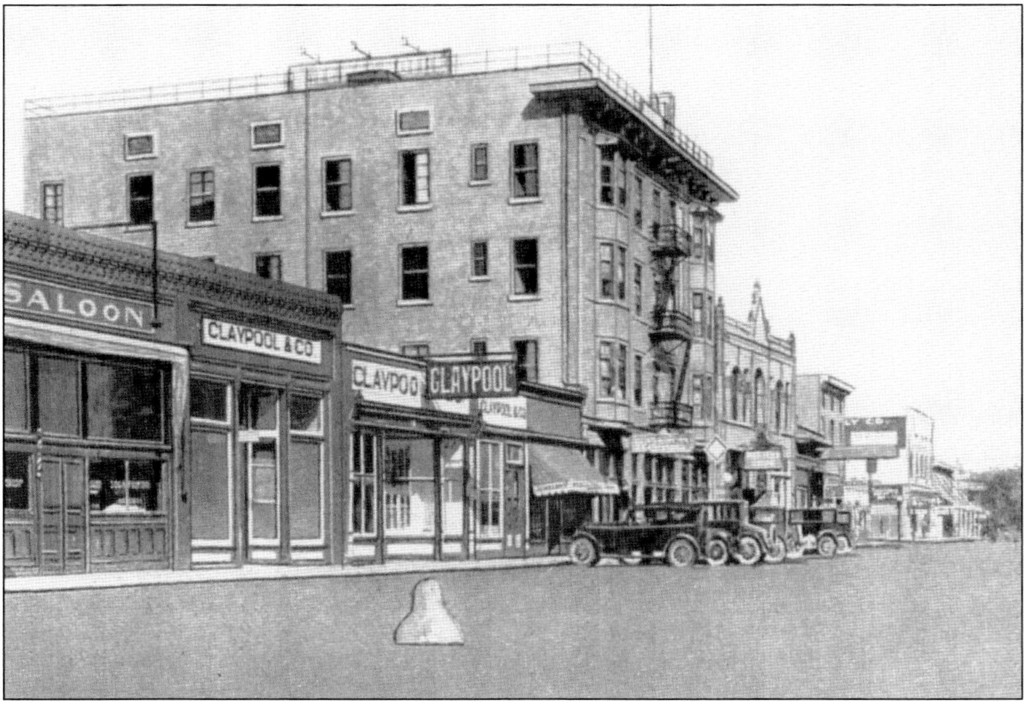

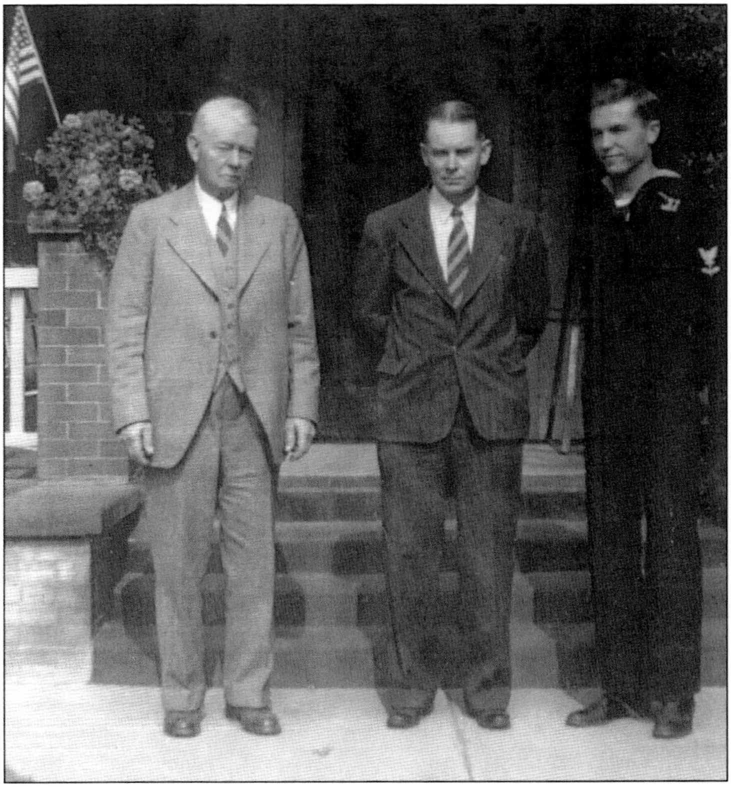

THE CLAYPOOLS. The Claypool family was a very important part of Needles. Pictured here are William Claypool Sr., William Claypool II, and William Claypool III (Bill). The latter was very active in local politics and service clubs and later took over the Claypool store. William III (Bill) remained in Needles until his death in 2008. (Courtesy of the Claypool family.)

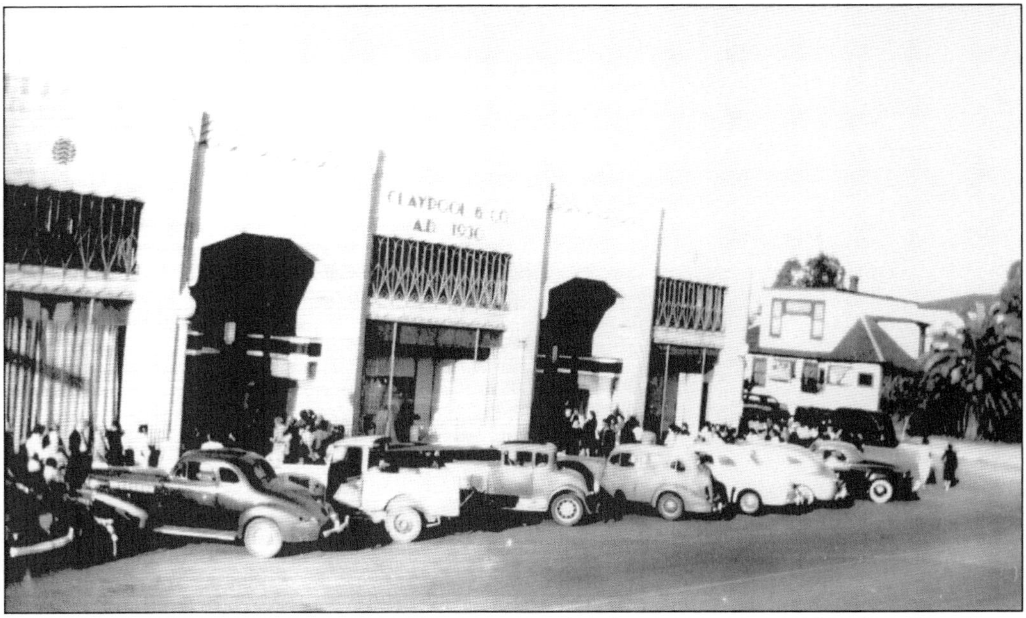

CLAYPOOL'S, 1930. This very large building was completed in 1930. In it could be found hardware items, shoes, groceries, lumber, clothing, and baked goods. It was Needles "One Stop Shopping." The surrounding communities came to town to gather groceries and supplies. After Route 66 was completed through Needles in 1926, the store served people as they traveled the famous highway. (Courtesy of the Claypool family.)

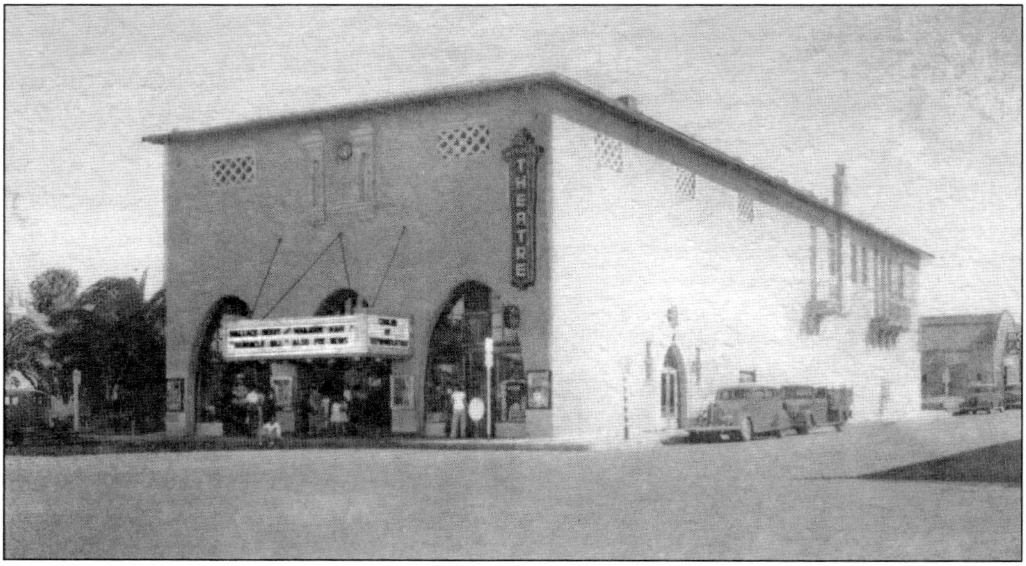

Needles Theatre. The Masons constructed the two-story building in 1929. On March 1, 1930, with the fanfare of the Fort Mohave Band, it opened its doors to some of the first "talkies." The theater seated 700 and had a full-sized stage with an orchestra pit. The water-based heating and cooling system was a new concept. On one side of the theater was a sweet shop; on the other was a real estate office. The Masonic Hall was on the second floor. An electrical fire in the late 1990s caused the theater to close. In the image below, the theater's projectionist is loading the movie projector for the next movie. (Courtesy of the Needles Regional Museum; Larry Ford.)

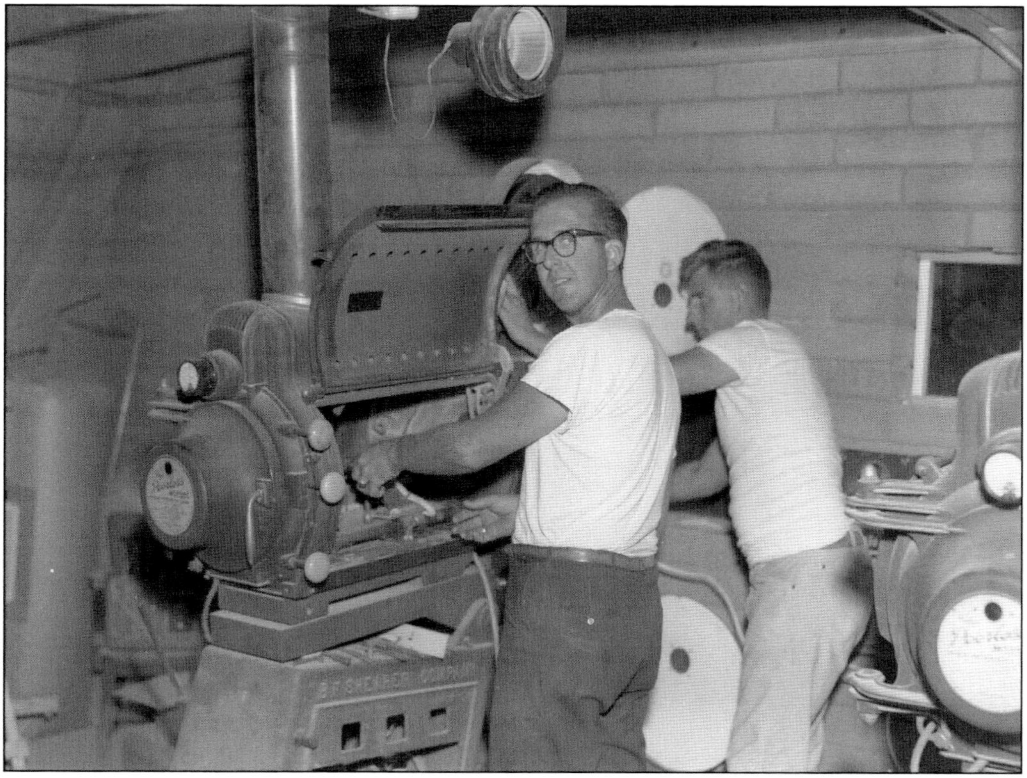

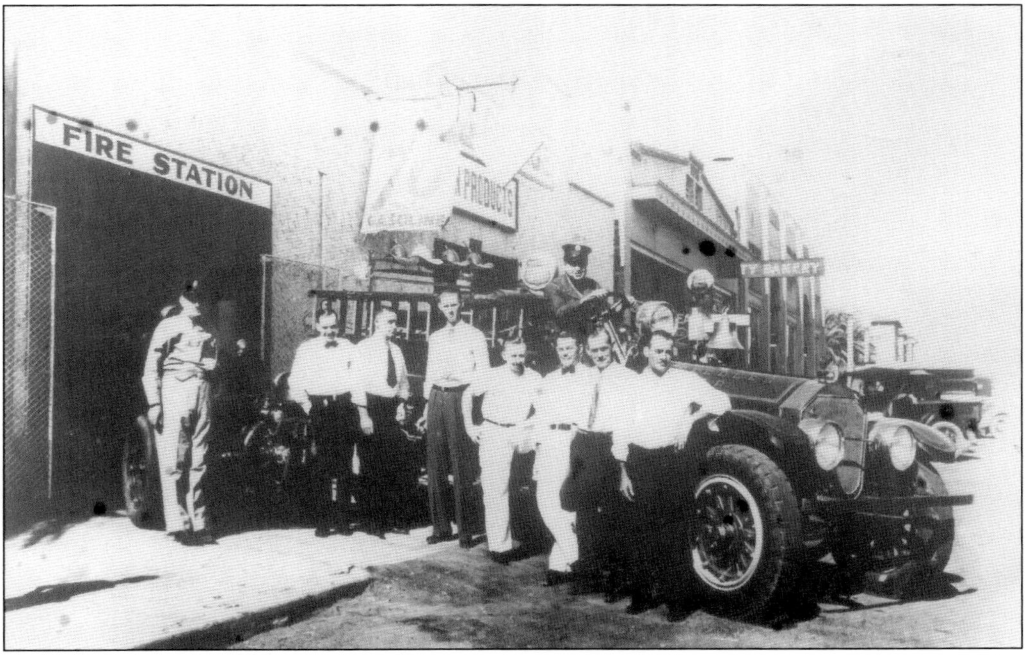

FIRE STATION. All polished and ready to go, this early-1900s fire engine was pulled out of the firehouse for a photograph with the crew and dignitaries on hand. The fire station was located on Front Street across from the train station as it is today. (Courtesy of the Mojave River Valley Museum.)

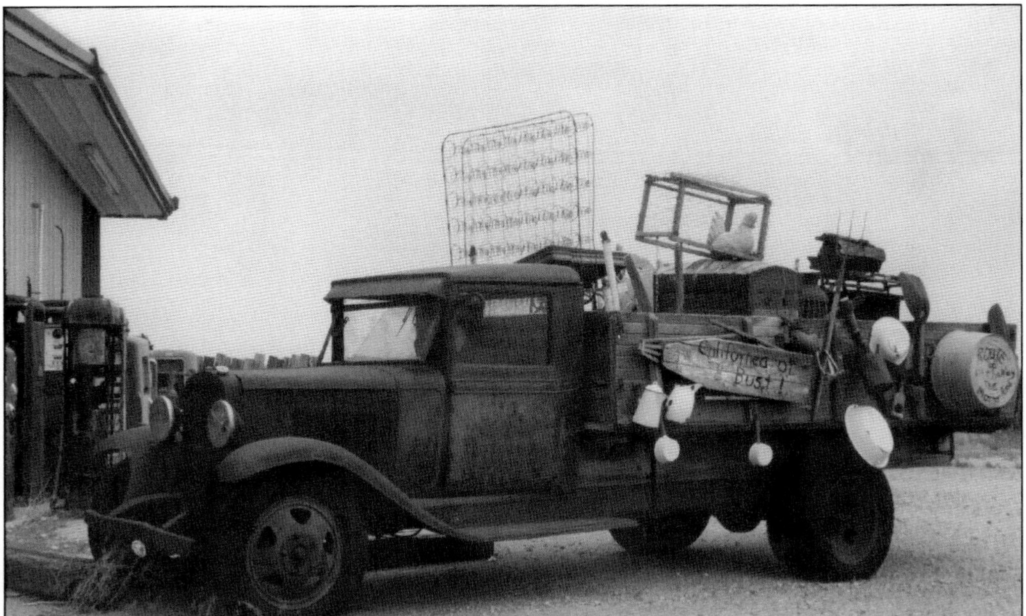

ON THE ROAD. This picture shows a car reminiscent of one from *The Grapes of Wrath*. Presumably the truck holds all of this family's worldly goods, and they are taking it on a trip out West to find their fortune. A coffee pot dangling on the side of the truck and a chicken perched atop says it all. (Courtesy of the Mojave River Valley Museum.)

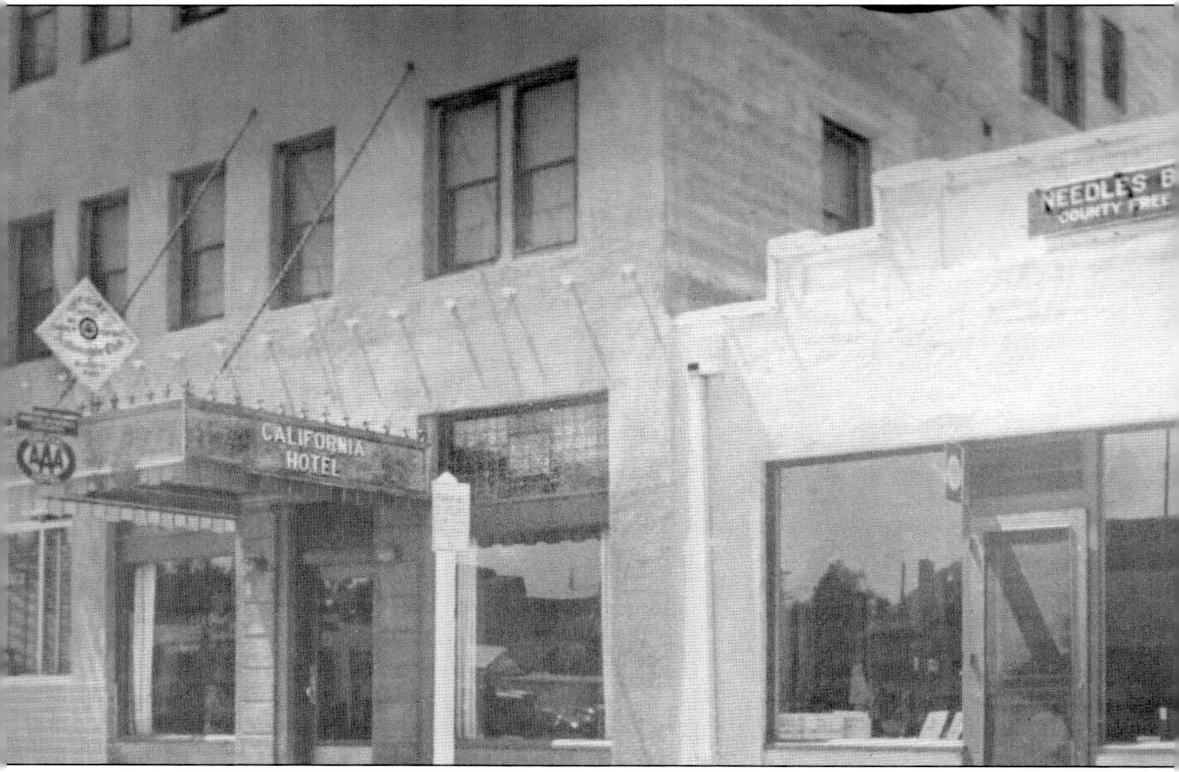

California Hotel and Library. Remember when the San Bernardino County Free Library, Needles Branch was next door to the California Hotel? The last business to occupy the library building before demolition was Bernice Morris's Needles Florist. The library was once located in the old Santa Fe Recreation Building, after the old railroad structure was given to the city for civic use. The California Hotel was a famous stopping point for political leaders. It finally met its death by fire and was demolished by the city. (Courtesy of the Mojave River Valley Museum.)

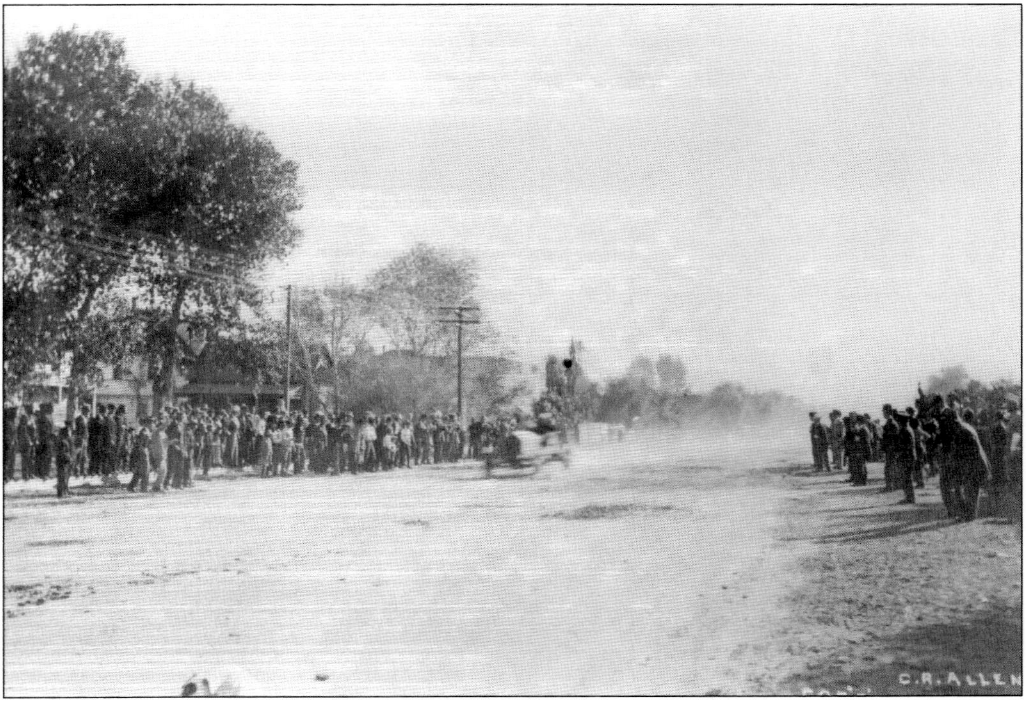

AND THEY'RE OFF! This 1910 photograph taken by C. R. Allen shows crowds of Needles race fans lining the street as dust fills the roadway. In the picture below, men, women, and children bicyclists line up to begin a race along a road that appears to be close to the Colorado River in Needles. (Courtesy of the Mojave River Valley Museum.)

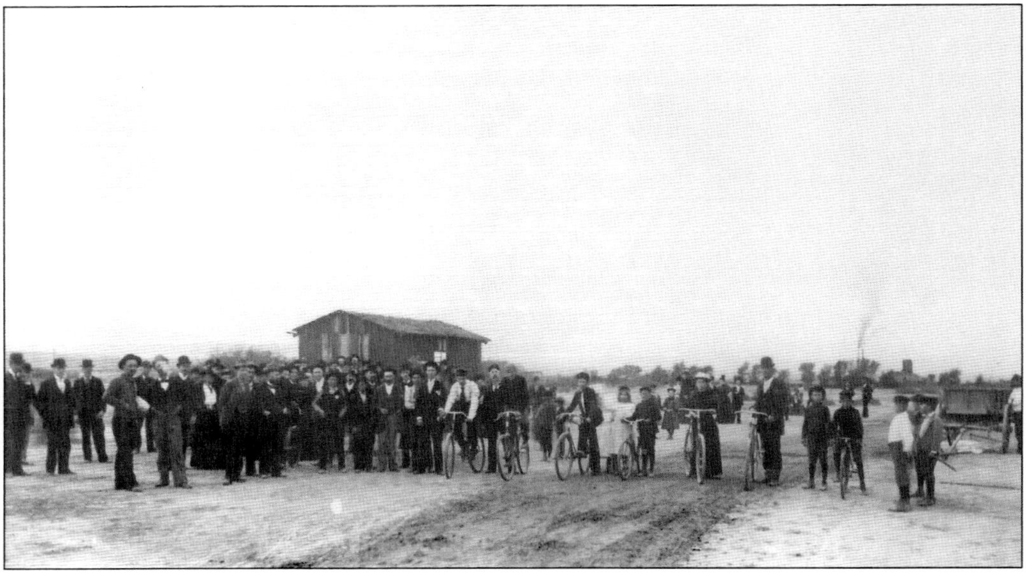

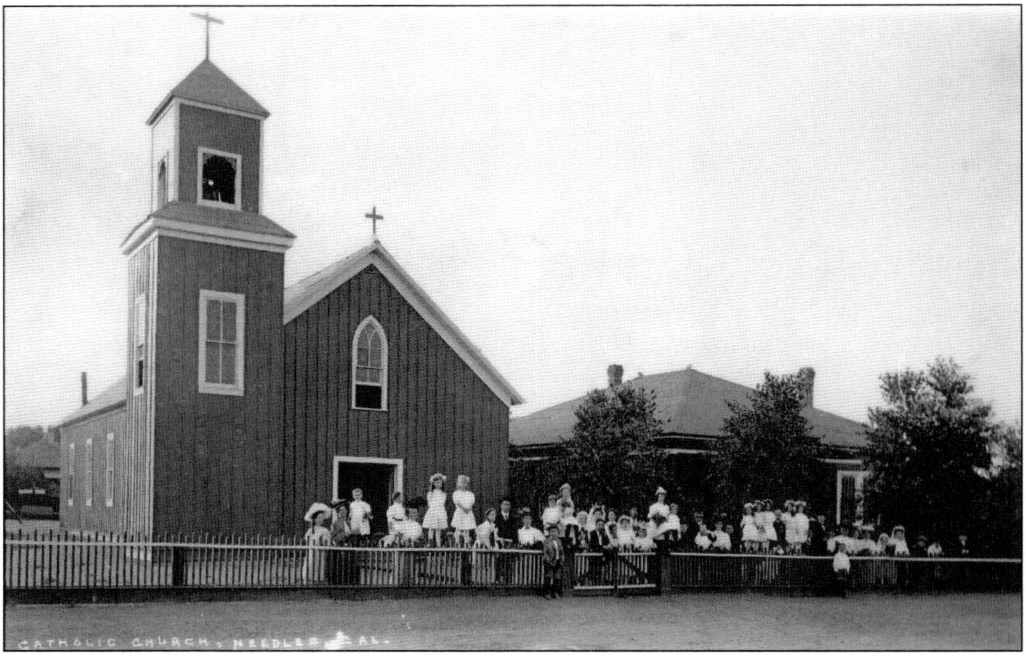

Catholic Church. When Father Garces came through Needles in 1774, he said the first Mass ever held in the area, even though he had no church building in which to say it. The church was built in 1889. A fire destroyed the structure just before Easter in 1920, but it was rebuilt in 1921. The tower bell was salvaged and is in use today. (Courtesy of Pam McCorkle Klemm.)

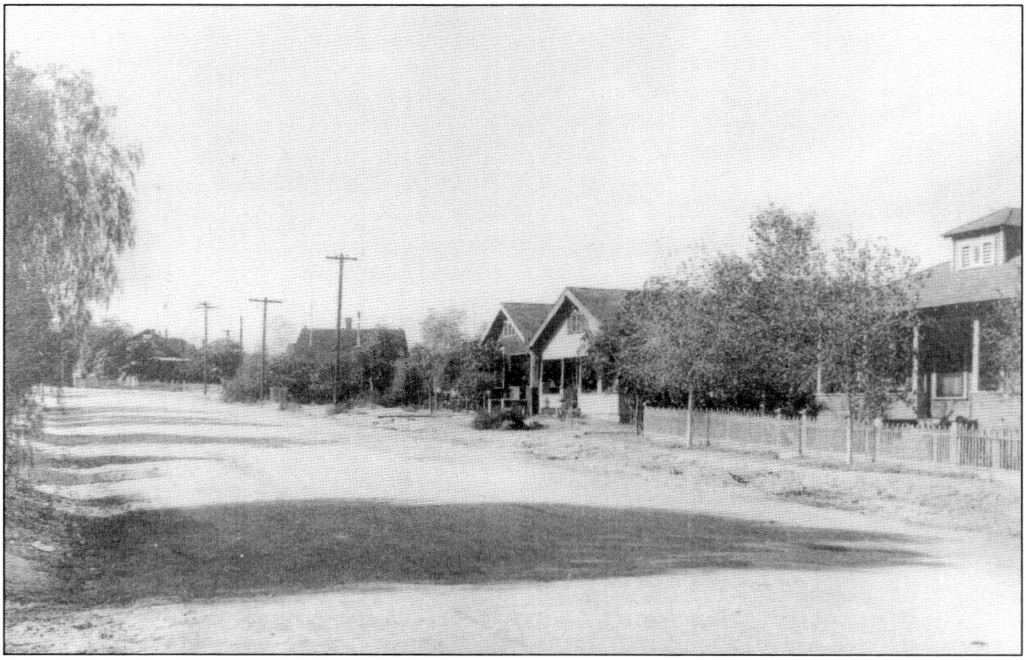

Needles Neighborhood. This is a street scene in Needles in the early 1900s. The streets were still just graded dirt surfaces at that time. Some of the homes in the downtown Needles area can be traced back to 1901. Restoration has begun on several of the homes. (Courtesy of the Mojave River Valley Museum.)

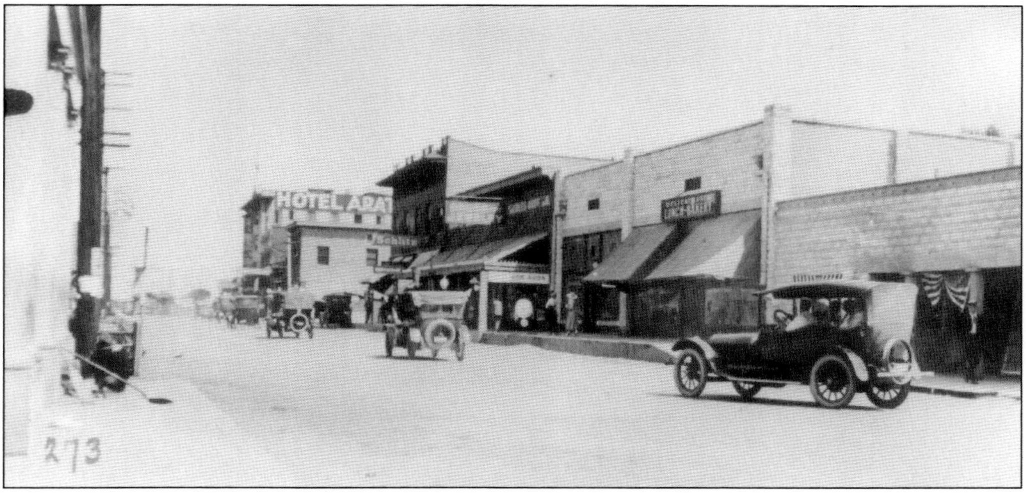

Automobiles of the Day. Here is a familiar street scene along Front Street in Needles, including the cars of the day. Below, on the left, the last letters of the Claypool store sign are visible, dating this image to sometime between 1911 and 1929. (Courtesy of the Mojave River Valley Museum.)

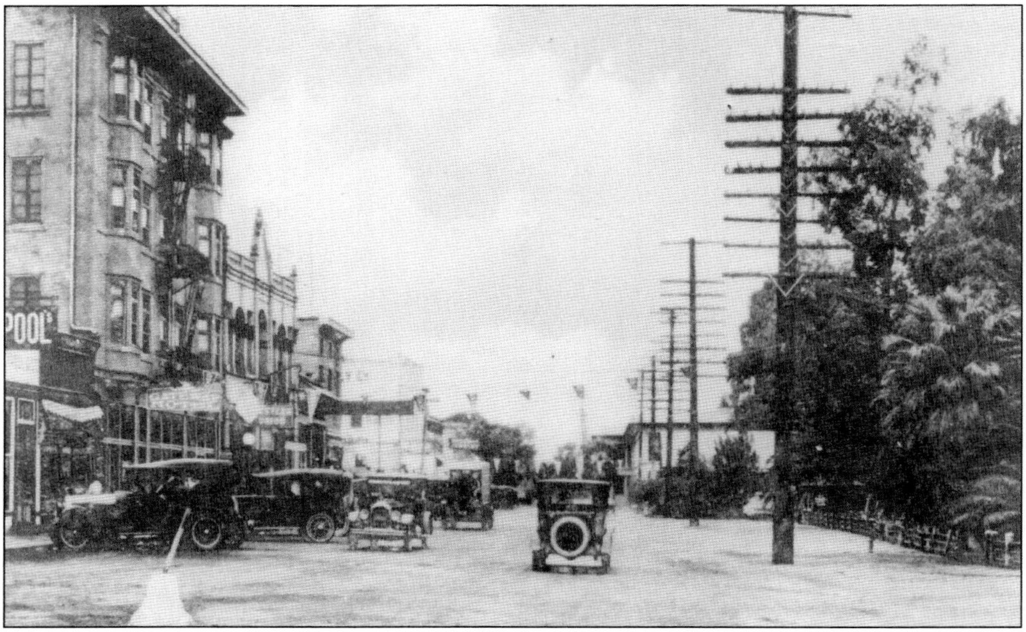

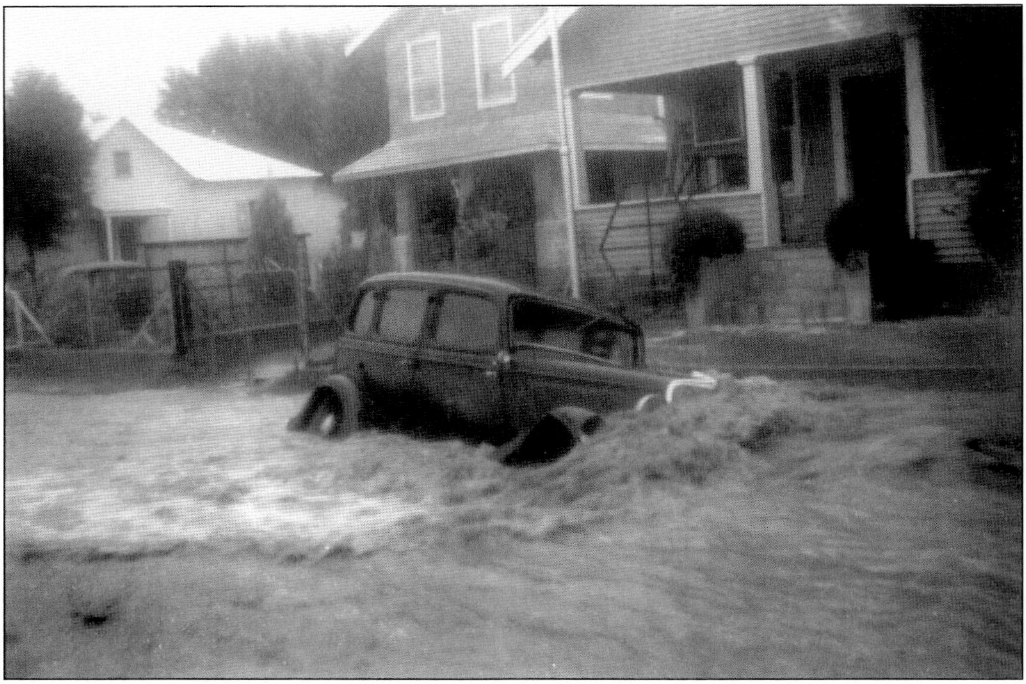

Flood, 1936. The hard-hitting flood of 1936 was particularly devastating. Here water crashes around a car and down a neighborhood street. When the water receded, the town was left with sludge and sand, requiring a difficult cleanup. The image below captures the destruction caused by the rapid water as it surges through the downtown area. The completion of the Davis dam solved Needles's flooding problem. (Courtesy of Needles Regional Library; Pam McCorkle Klemm.)

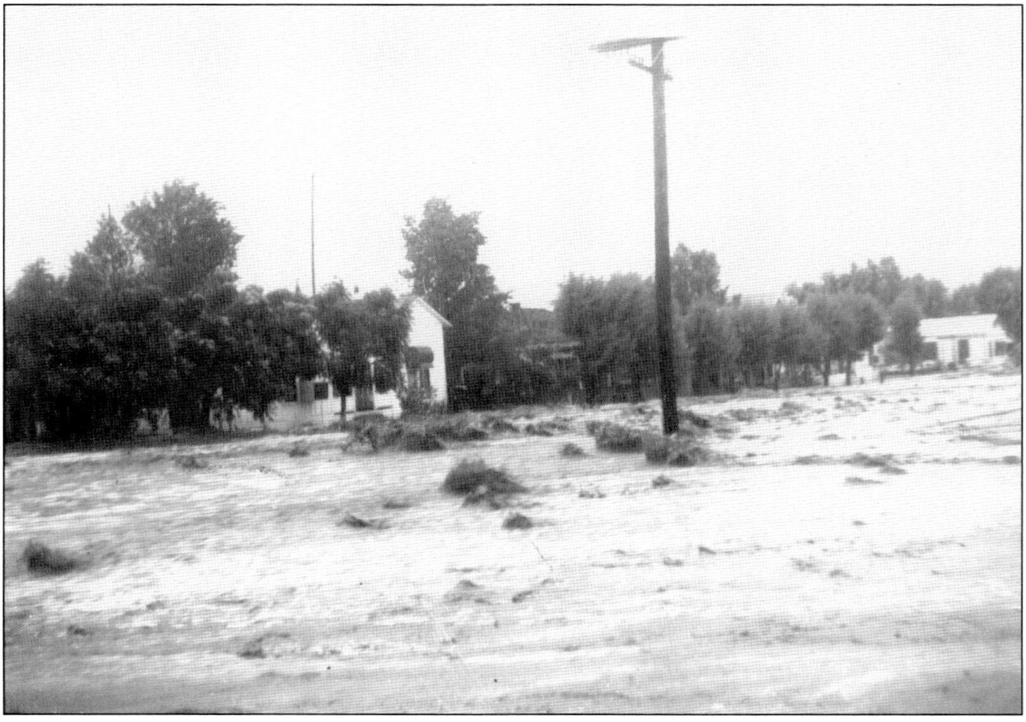

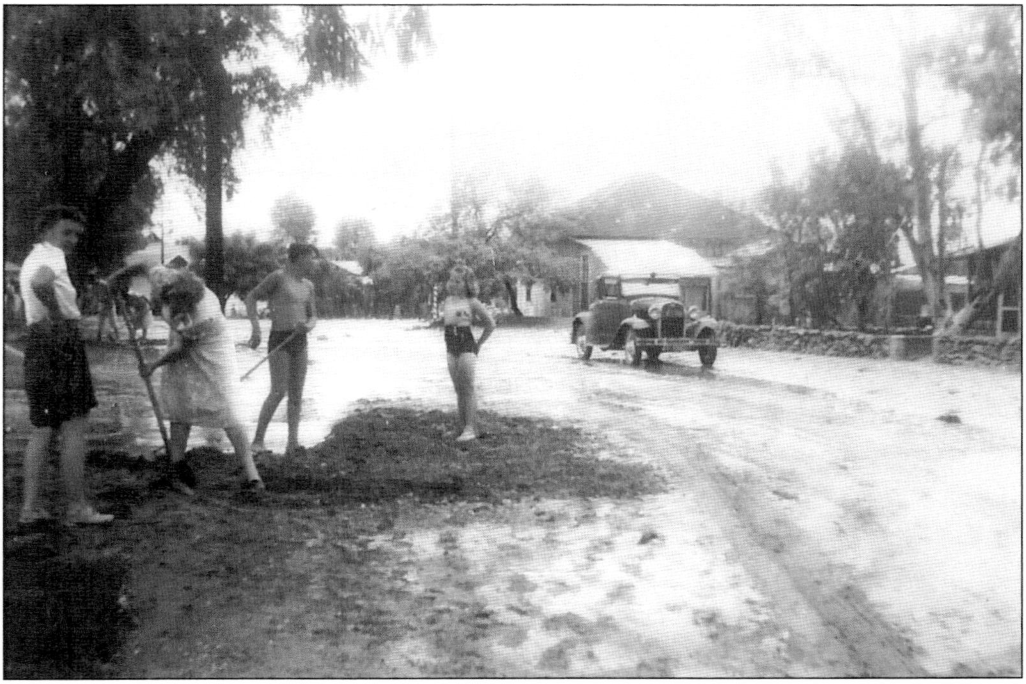

Water and Kids. The flooding of Needles was a serious matter, but some carefree children also saw an opportunity to have some fun. As the water receded, children came out to play. The residents of D Street, however, are seen cleaning up all the mud that was left. (Courtesy of Huge and Anna McCorkle; the Needles Regional Library.)

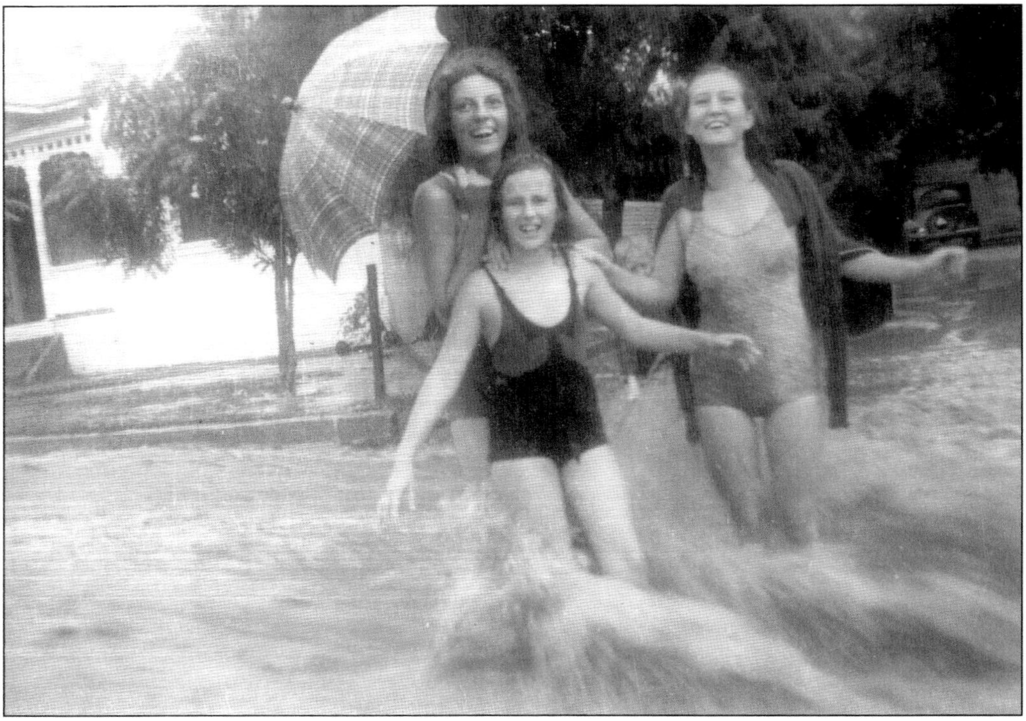

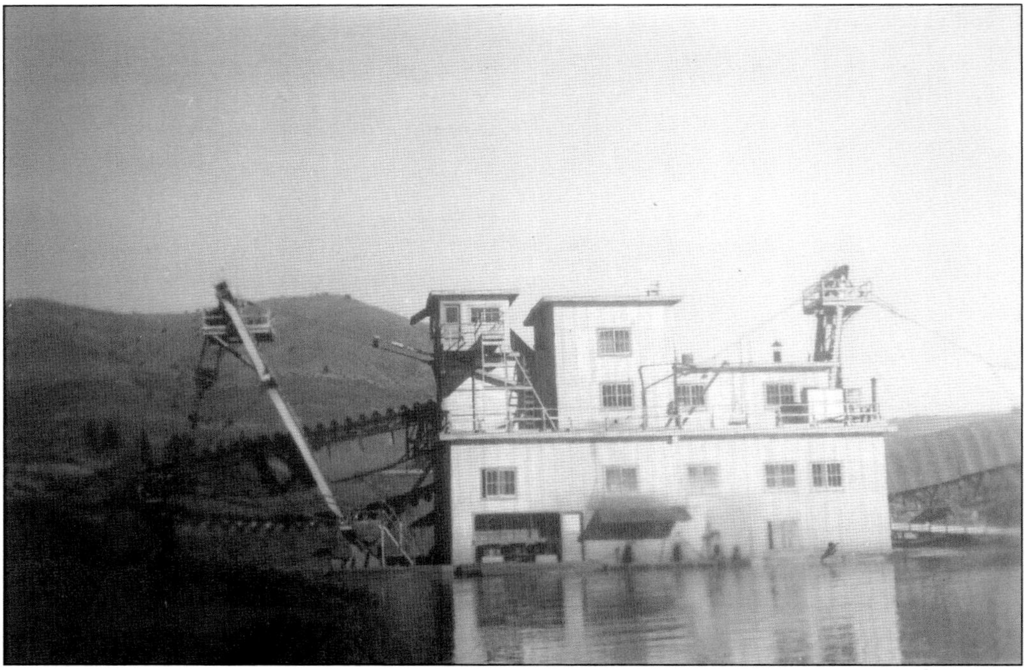

ICEHOUSE. The flood at the Icehouse created problems for the box cars responsible for keeping perishables cool. The railroad shipped perishables in box cars called refers; on top of the box car at the end there were doors where blocks of ice were chopped. The ice was then placed into the top of the car. Because of the flood, perishables in the box cars were lost. (Courtesy of the Needles Regional Library.)

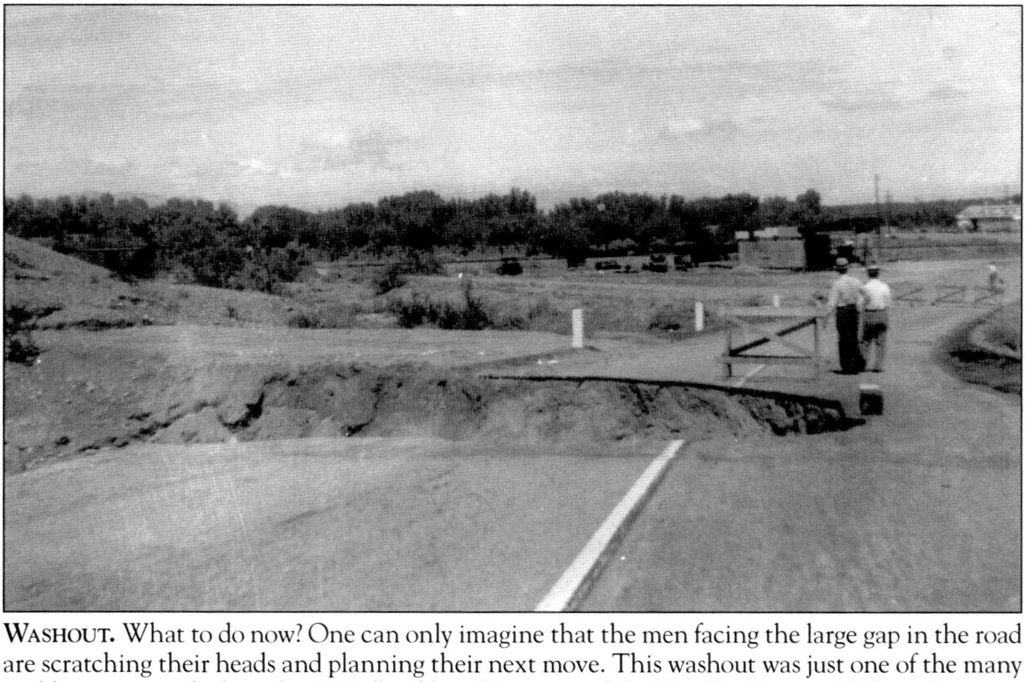

WASHOUT. What to do now? One can only imagine that the men facing the large gap in the road are scratching their heads and planning their next move. This washout was just one of the many problems incurred when the 1938 flood hit. (Courtesy of the Needles Regional Library.)

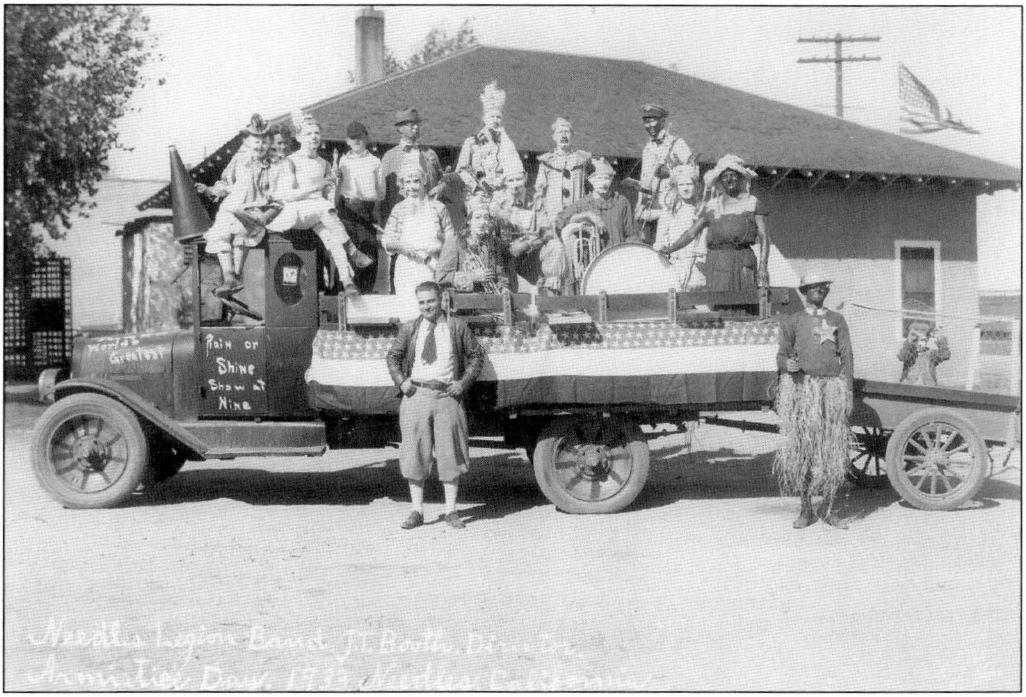

Show at Nine. Come rain or shine, the Needles Legion Band performed at nine. The band is shown here on Armistice Day, 1933. Some members of the band seen above are Louie Welch, Oliver Cox, Red Krober, Sam Thompson, an unidentified band member, Hugh McCorkle, George Blake, Jim Booth, John McCorkle, Neil Sprague, Charles McCorkle, Sam Thompson Sr., Paul Booth, and Arley White. (Courtesy of the McCorkle family.)

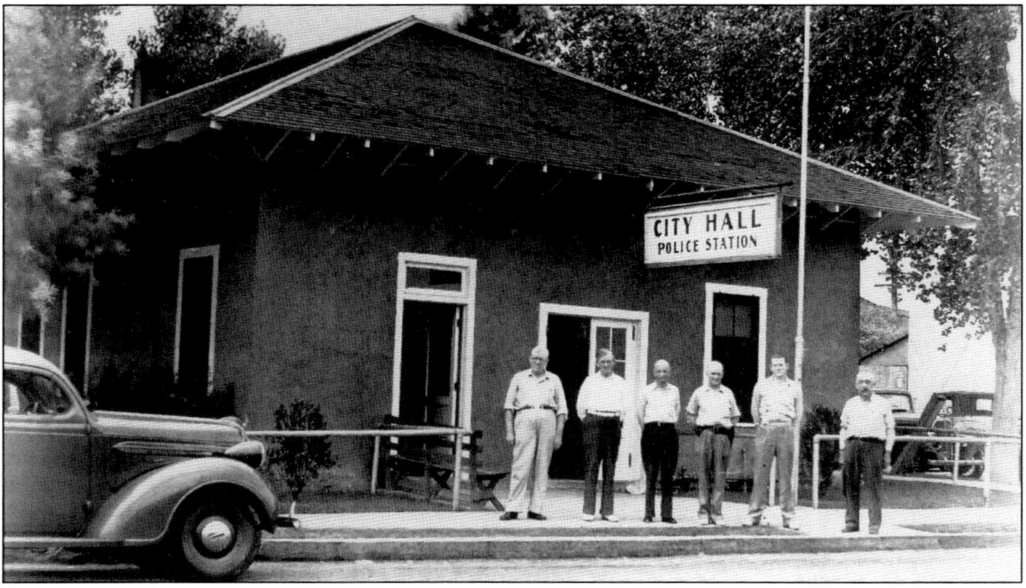

Original City Offices. Pictured is the original city hall in the 1930s, located on the corner of C and Front Streets. From left to right are Frank Kisinger, chief of police; Oliver Cox, head of the Water Department; Faris B. Wilkins, judge; Jack Markum, policeman; Frank Bland, policeman; and George Acuna, constable. (Courtesy of Marilyn Kirchner)

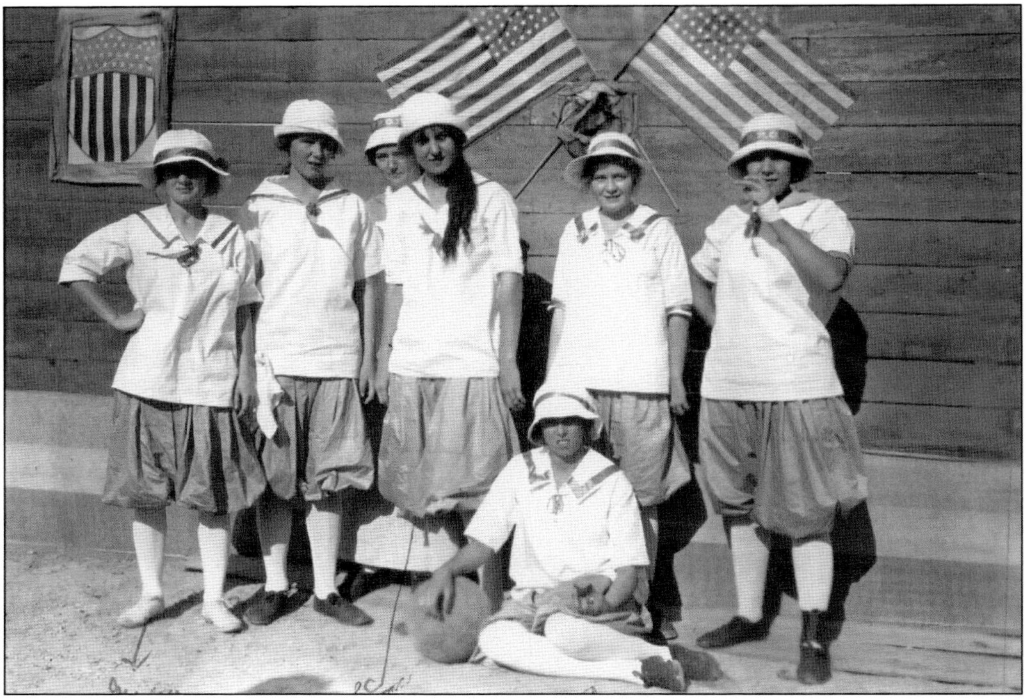

Basketball Team. The Needles women's basketball team is all dressed up in snazzy uniforms. The team enjoys a game during the Fourth of July celebration. From left to right are (sitting) Nellie Thompson; (standing) Winnie Shafer, Edith Thompson, an unidentified player, Emma Mansker, and two more unidentified players. (Courtesy of the McCorkle family.)

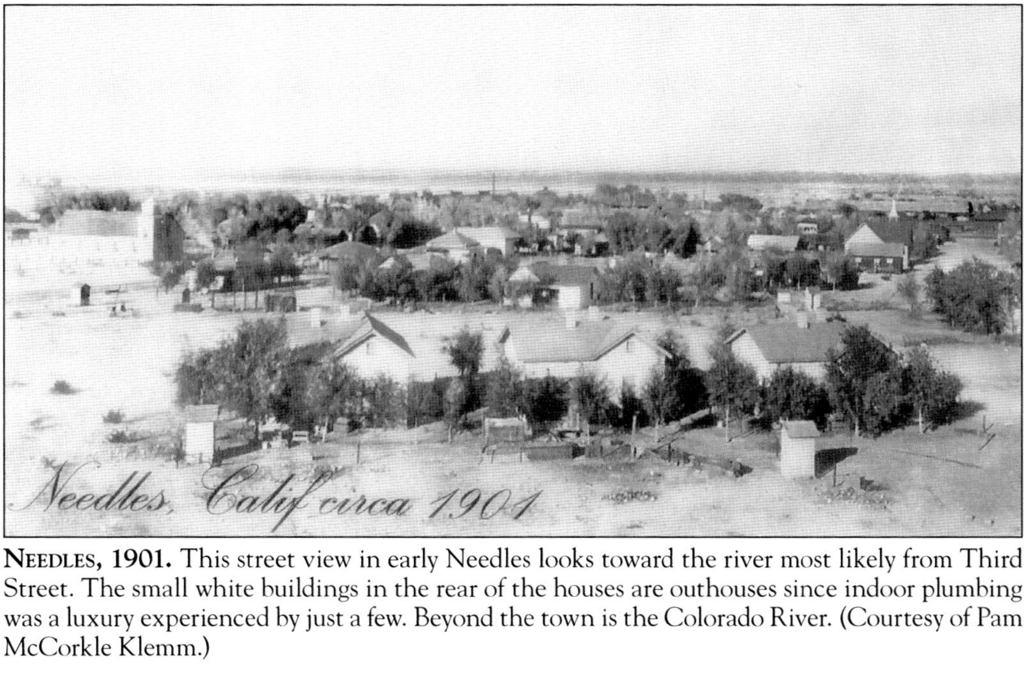

Needles, 1901. This street view in early Needles looks toward the river most likely from Third Street. The small white buildings in the rear of the houses are outhouses since indoor plumbing was a luxury experienced by just a few. Beyond the town is the Colorado River. (Courtesy of Pam McCorkle Klemm.)

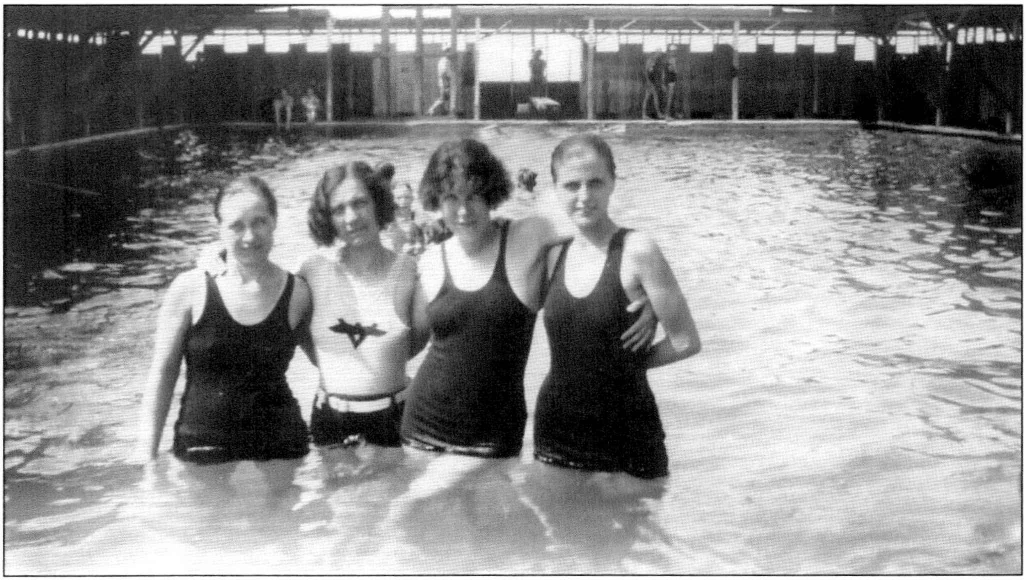

MANSKER POOL. The pool was actually an enormous water tank used for watering a grove of palm trees. When not watering the palm trees, it was used as a swimming pool for the locals. Many children in the 1920s and 1930s learned to swim in the Mansker pool. From left to right, the women are Leona McCorkle, Goldie Duncan, Jean Humiston, and her sister Jean. In the photograph below, from left to right, the children are Bud Duncan, Hugh McCorkle, Paul Humiston, Helen McCorkle, and Dortha Duncan. (Courtesy of the McCorkle family.)

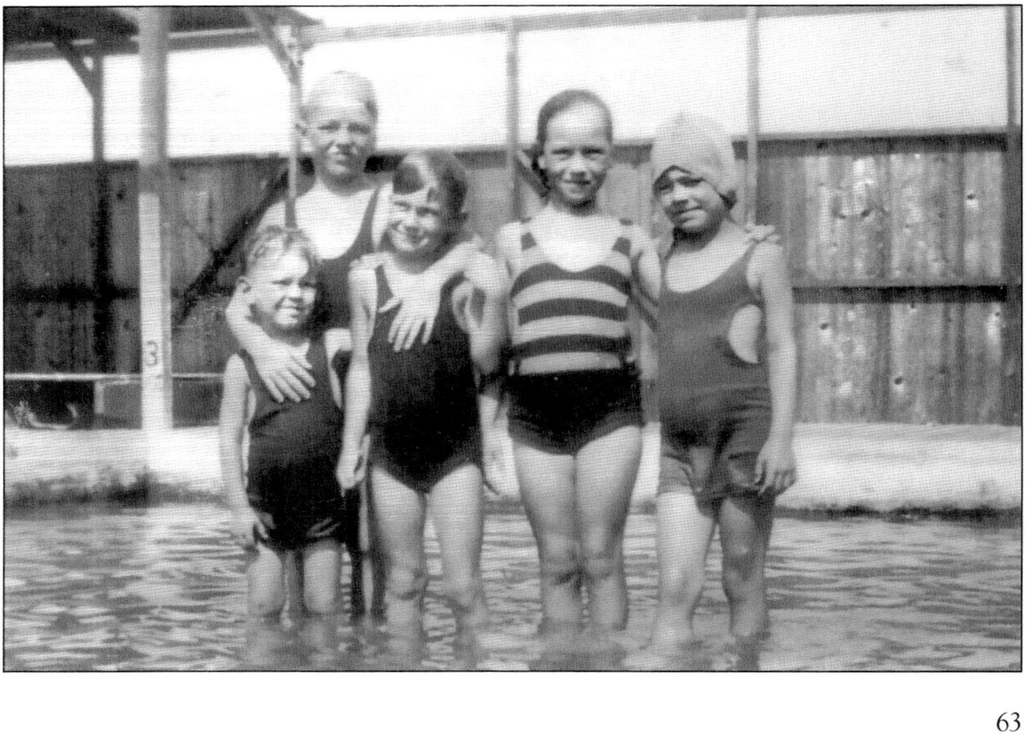

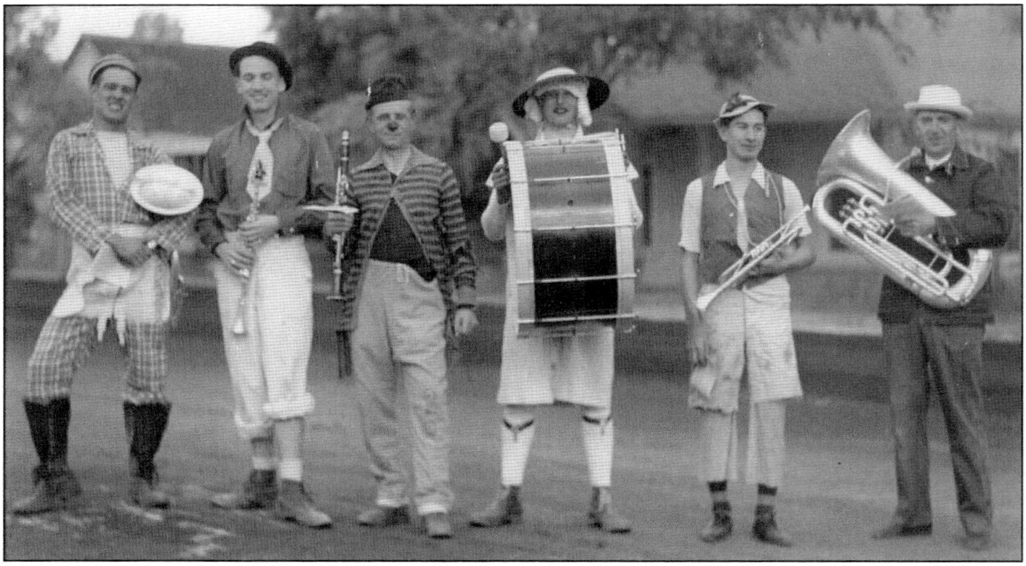

Armistice Day. This was an important day for Needles since many of the residents were serving in the war and it meant a homecoming for many. Here is a group from the Needles Legion Band as they prepared to celebrate Armistice Day. On November 11, a truce was signed with Allies and Germany to signify a cease-fire on the western front. World War I was over, and celebrations flooded the streets. (Courtesy of the McCorkle family.)

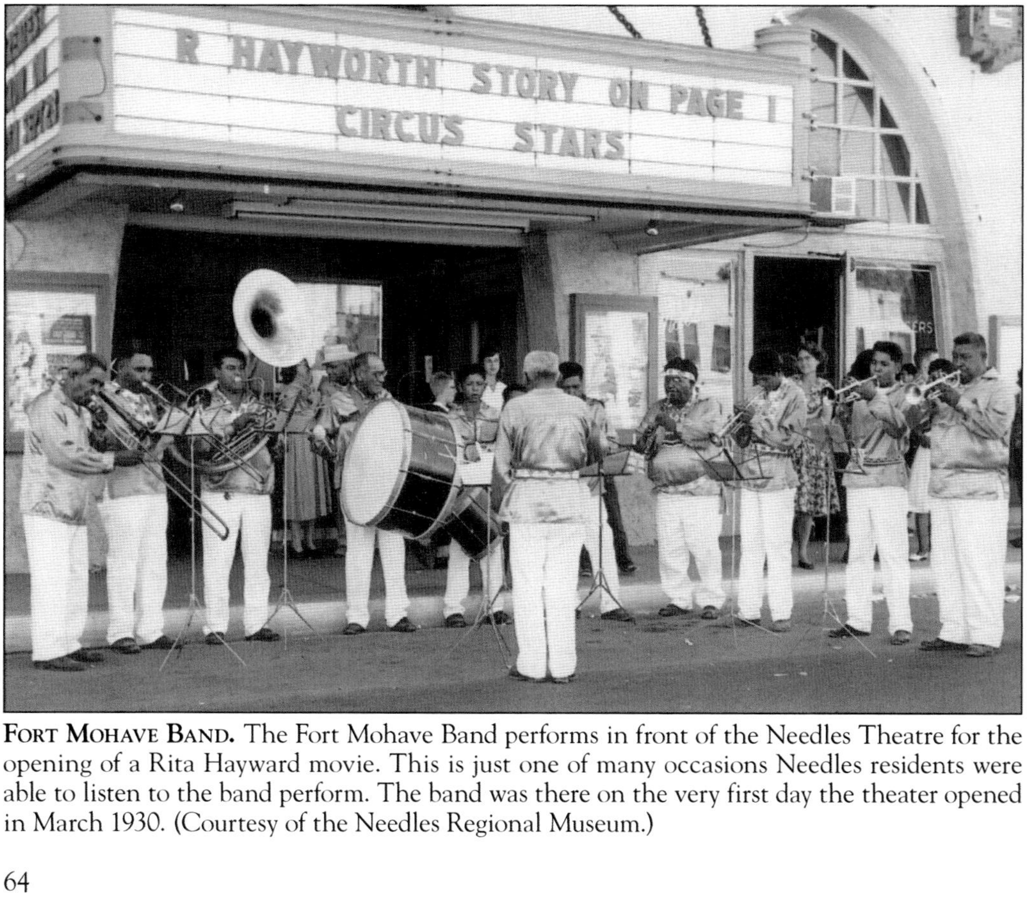

Fort Mohave Band. The Fort Mohave Band performs in front of the Needles Theatre for the opening of a Rita Hayward movie. This is just one of many occasions Needles residents were able to listen to the band perform. The band was there on the very first day the theater opened in March 1930. (Courtesy of the Needles Regional Museum.)

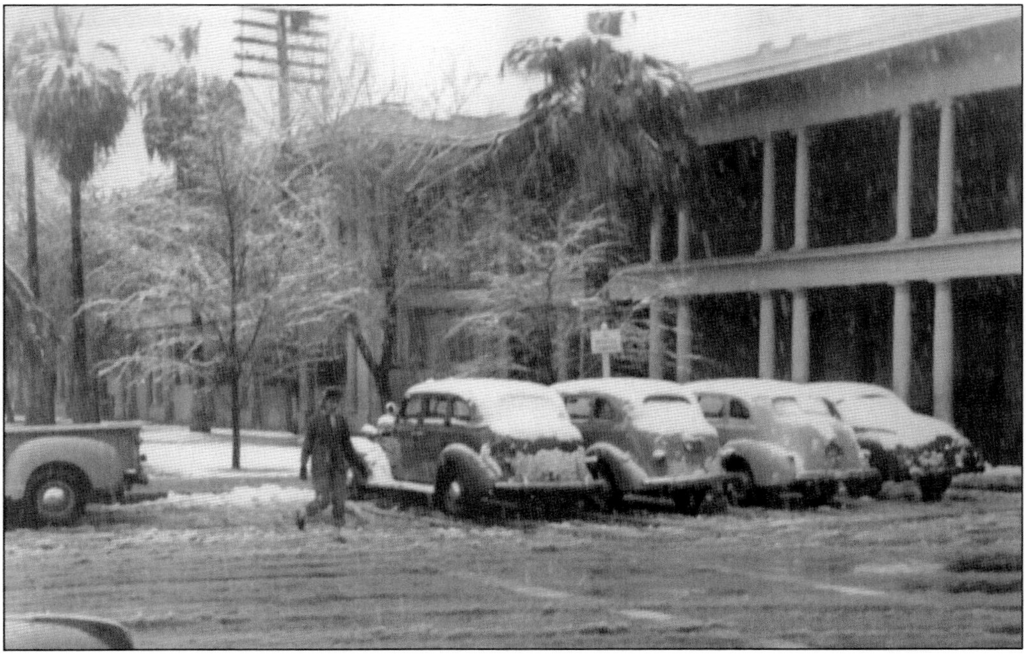

Snow. In 1949, Needles was part of a rare snowstorm hitting the desert all the way to Las Vegas. For many, it was an exciting time; for others not use to driving in snow, it posed a problem. School was cancelled, and children made snowmen and had snowball fights. Here are the cars parked in front of the El Graces train depot covered in snow. (Courtesy of Pam McCorkle Klemm.)

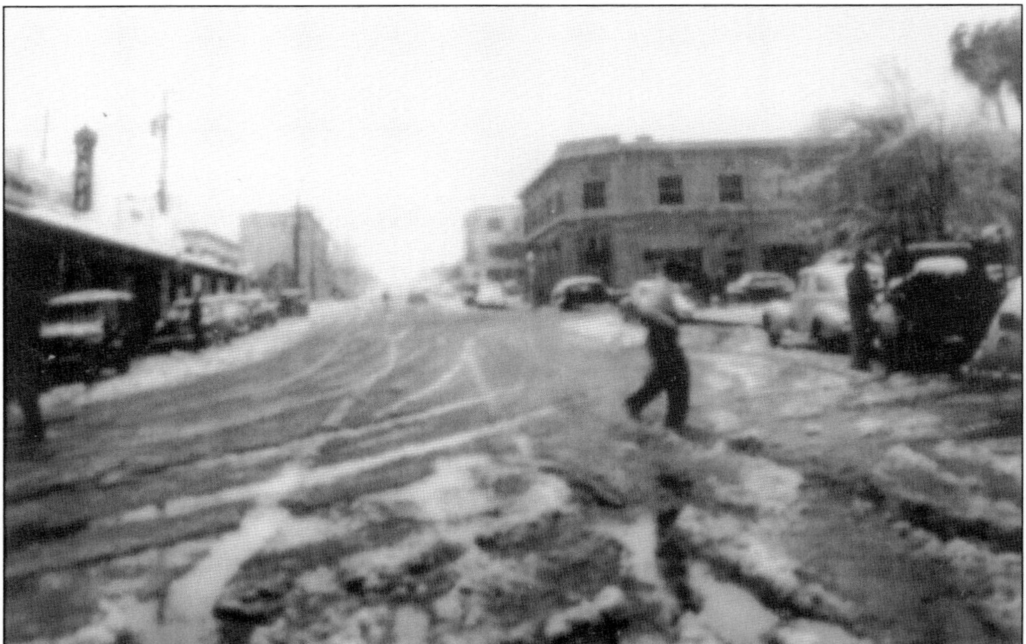

Broadway and F Streets. The snow was everywhere, as the temperature dipped well below the norm for Needles. Those who did not have to go to work were warm and comfortable in their homes. There were those whose job called, and they had to brave the snow-filled streets. This picture looks up F Street to Broadway. (Courtesy of Pan McCorkle Klemm.)

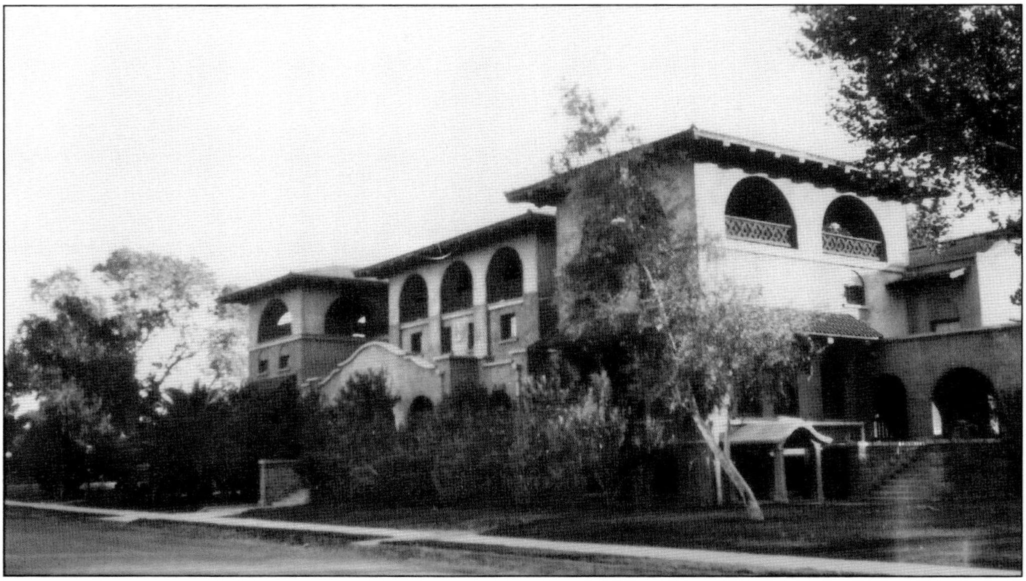

New City Hall and Fire. A newer city hall was built farther down Front Street and included the police station. The upstairs recreation hall was the site of many summer teen dances. Many spirited city council meetings were held there as well. After a fire destroyed the building, city hall was relocated to J Street where it sits today. (Photograph by John Lakner; courtesy Marilyn Kirchner, the Murl Shaver family.)

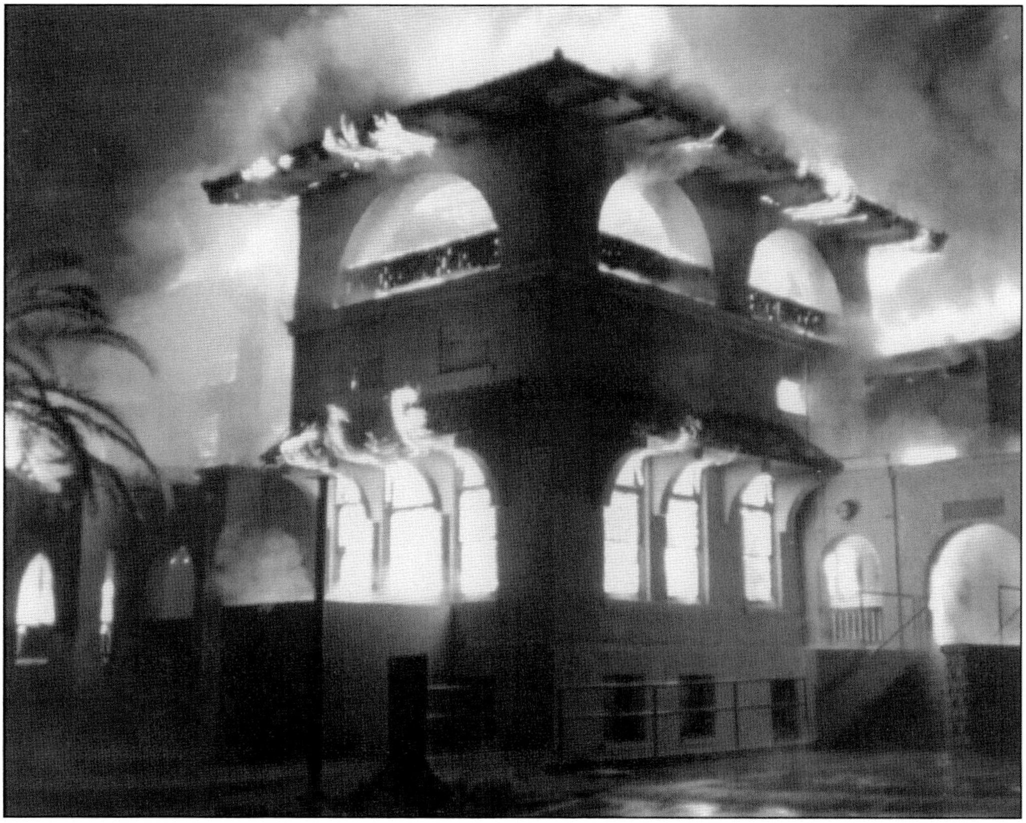

Five

World War II
Needles's Participation

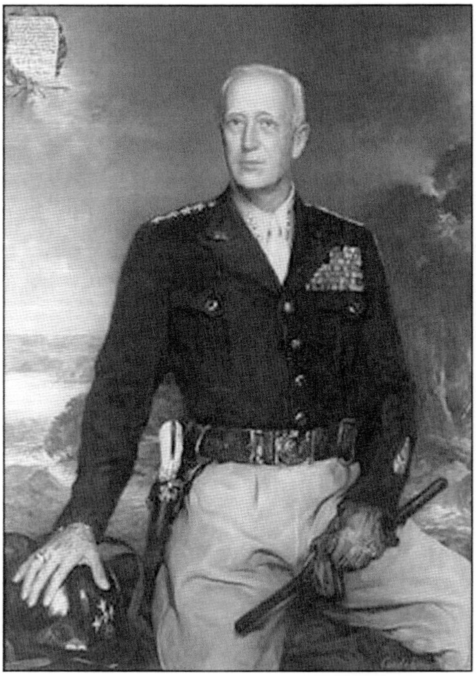

General Patton. Needles participated in World War II as the railroad brought troops and equipment and supplies to Camp Ibis, approximately 21 miles northwest of Needles. In March 1942, the War Department sent Gen. George S. Patton to California to establish a headquarters for the Desert Training Center. The success of the German Army in North Africa led the War Department to focus on a desert site for training. The main headquarters was 20 miles from Indio, California, called Camp Young; more camps were opened throughout the Mohave. Camp Ibis covered 10,215 acres. It included an army airfield, the 53rd (later the 21st) Evacuation Hospital, and a POW camp for Italian prisoners. In 1943, the name of the facilities changed to California-Arizona Maneuver Area (CAMA). When the North African campaign was near its end and the mission for the camps changed, CAMA closed in 1944. General Patton oversaw operations of Camp Ibis. (Courtesy of the U.S. Bureau of Land Management.)

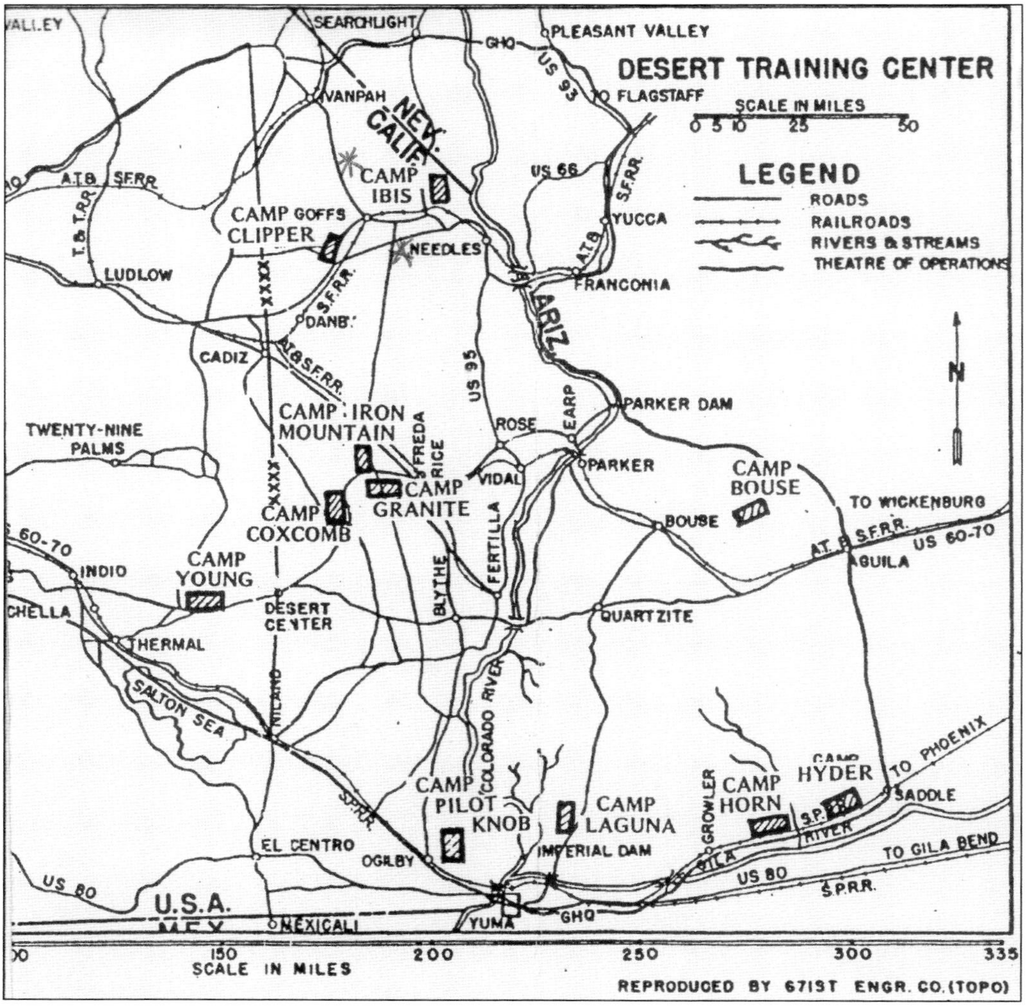

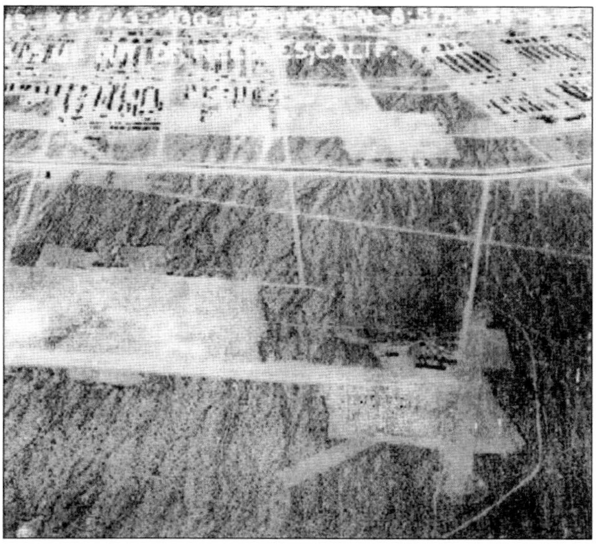

Camp Ibis. The map shows the location of Needles and its proximity to Camp Ibis, approximately 21 miles northwest of Needles. At left is an aerial view of Camp Ibis and adjacent army airfield. The airfield consisted of a single 4,500-foot runway oriented north and south. The Fourth Air Force division was stationed at the Camp Ibis airfield. They trained as bombardment fighters and reconnaissance, flying antisubmarine patrol along the coast until 1942 when that duty was taken over by the Civil Patrol. (Courtesy of the California State Military Museum; San Bernardino County Museum.)

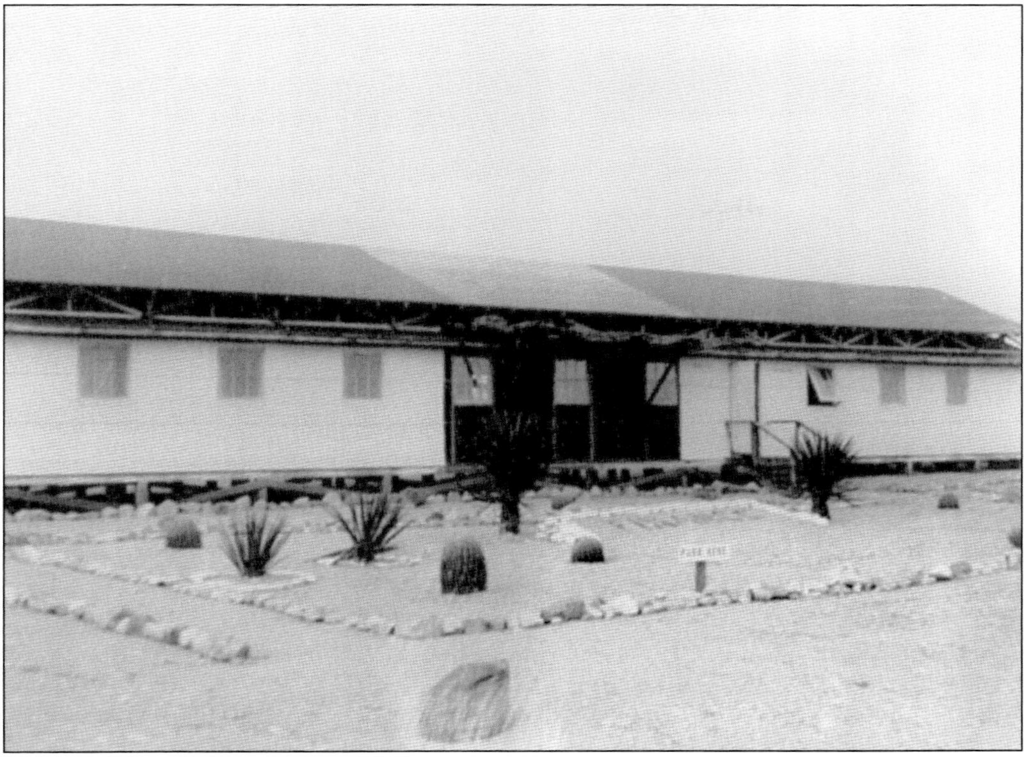

STORAGE WAREHOUSE. These buildings were constructed at Camp Ibis during World War II. The much needed supplies were delivered to the Needles El Garces train depot, unloaded, and trucked to Camp Ibis and the army field hospital. Supplies were stored in these buildings until the war was over and the structures were dismantled. (Courtesy of the U.S. Bureau of Land Management.)

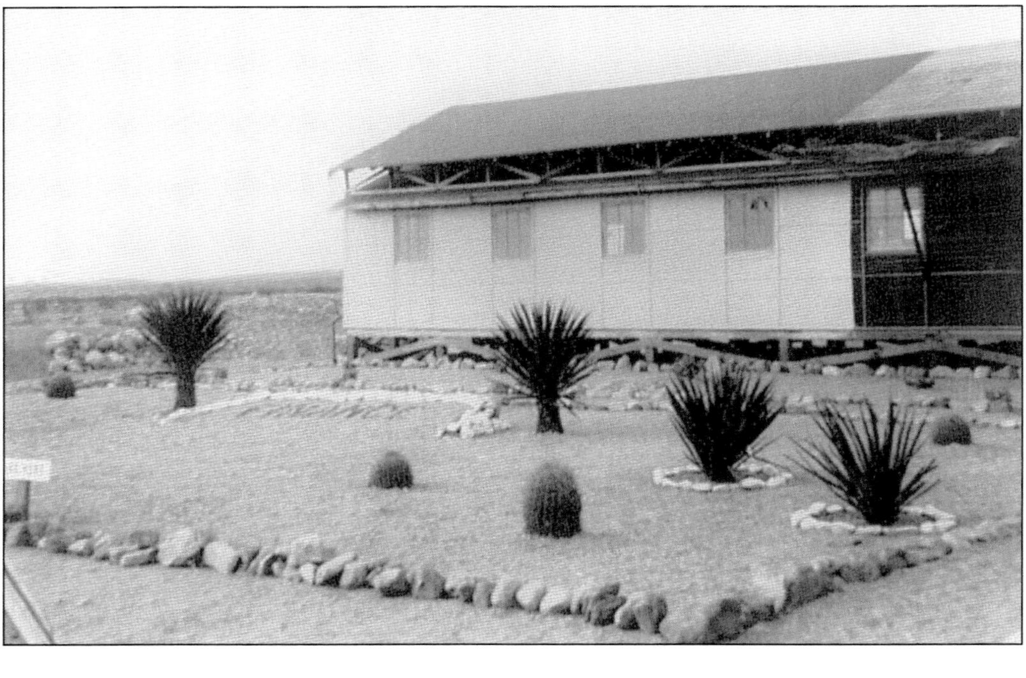

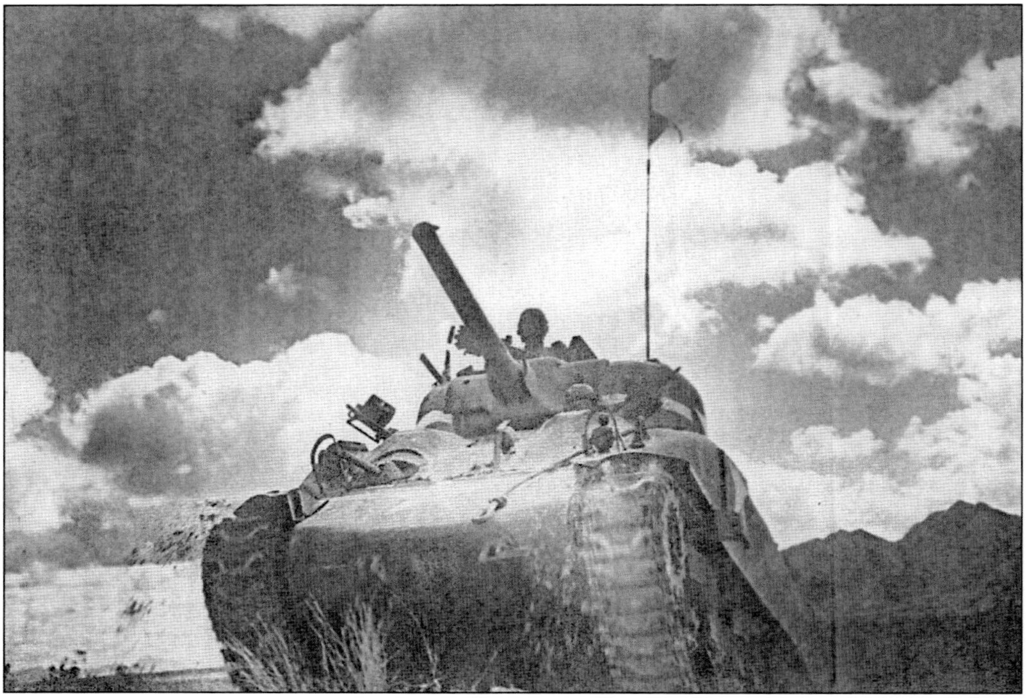

TANK PATROL. At Camp Ibis, armored tanks participated in armored vehicle tactics known as Tank Destroyer School. The 4th and 9th Armored Division, and later the 11th Armored Division, took part in these maneuvers. The desert training prepared the troops for combat in Africa. Many who trained at Camp Ibis joined General Patton on the battlefield. (Courtesy of the U.S. Bureau of Land Management.)

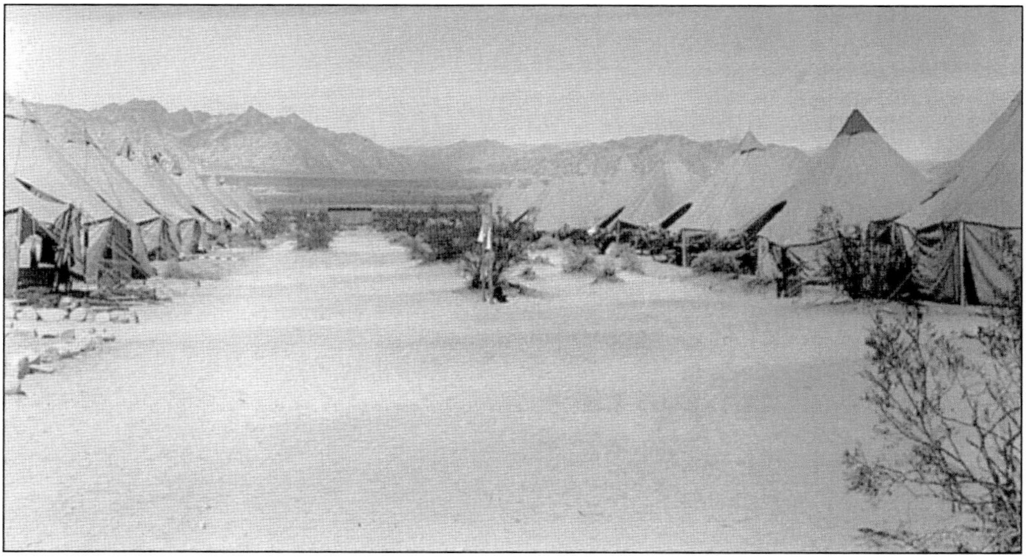

TENTS. Just outside of Needles, multiple rows of cloth barracks line the desert as soldiers make Camp Ibis home. The hot days and cold nights prepared troops for the climate that some would experience on the battlefields of North Africa. In order to protect the men from scorpions, rattlesnakes, and tarantulas, diesel fuel was poured around the tents. (Courtesy of the U.S. Bureau of Land Management.)

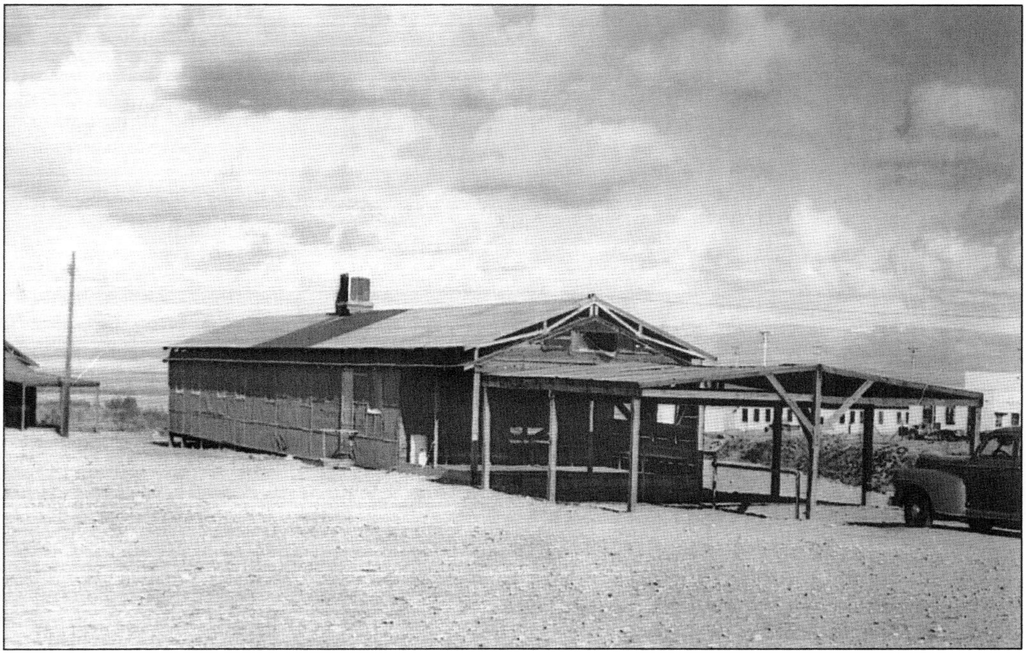

Army Barracks. During World War II, the town of Needles was called upon to help support the war. The railroad transported troops and machinery to Camp Ibis. In addition, U.S. Army facilities were located in several parts of town. These barracks are believed to be remnants of the army hospital once located at Bailey and Washington Streets. After the war, some of the children attended early grades in the barracks, which had become a school. This site is where Vista Elementary School sits today. (Courtesy of the Herb Bender family.)

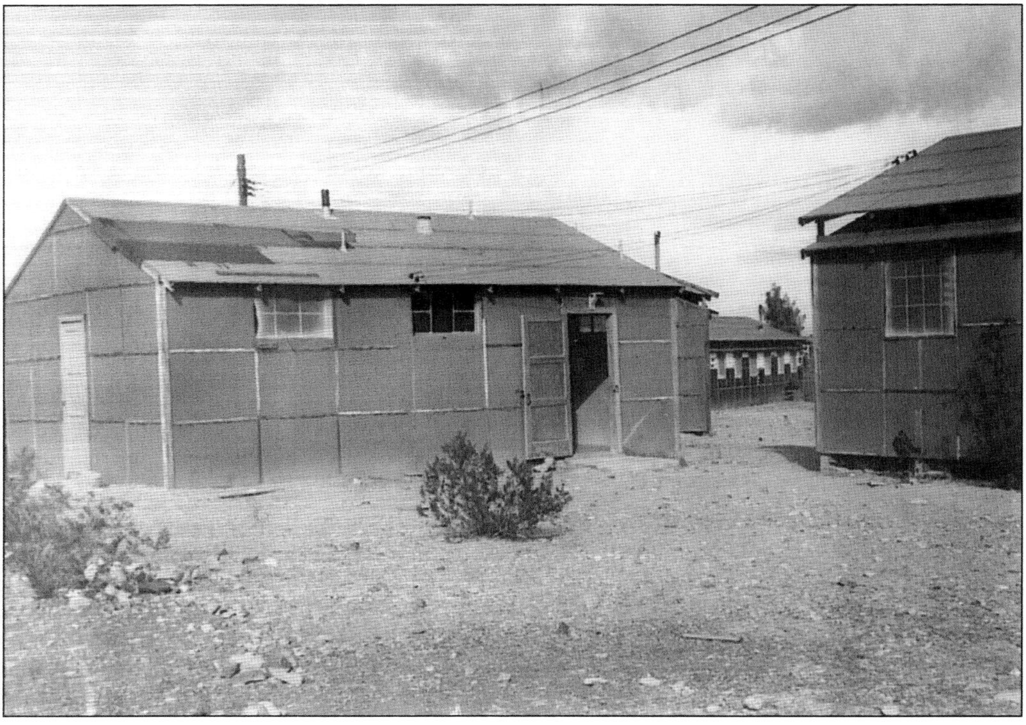

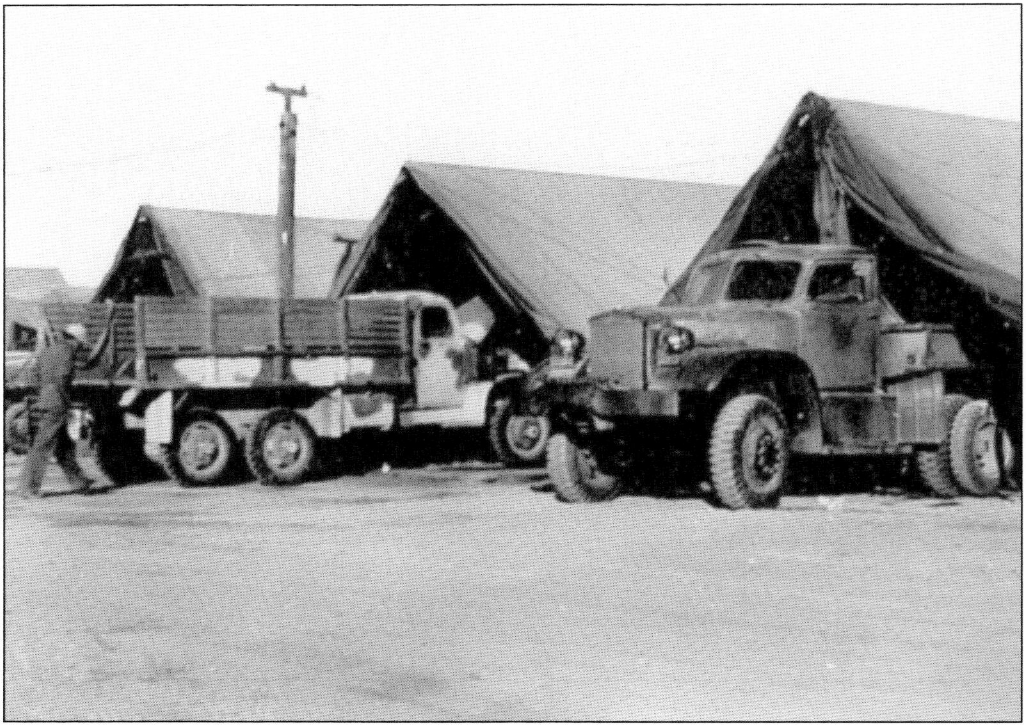

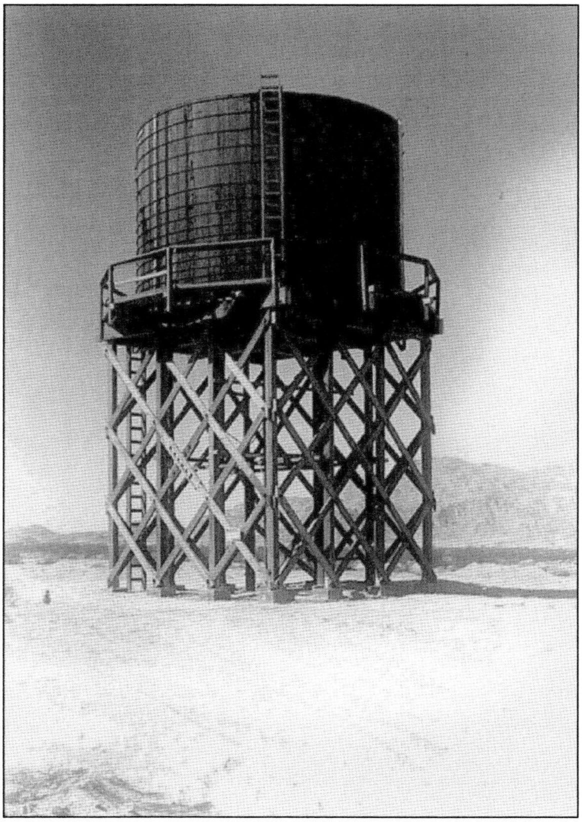

Truck Service. Military trucks vital to carrying materials, food, and soldiers throughout Camp Ibis were serviced at the tented "garage." The Needles desert sand was a problem for all of the equipment, which required constant maintenance. Sand was a condition that would be met on the battlefield, and the conditioning done in the desert was vital to the success of the troops. (Courtesy of the U.S. Bureau of Land Management.)

Water Tank. Besides the need for drinking water, there was a need for water for the vehicles and hygiene. A full 28 shower buildings were constructed on the training site for enlisted men, as well as 14 officer showers and 173 latrines, all supported by a 50,000-gallon water tank built on a elevated wooden platform. (Courtesy of the U.S. Bureau of Land Management.)

Stuck Truck. This picture shows the problems experienced with sand dunes in the desert. A military supply truck gets stuck in the desert sand and provides the troops with a first-hand lesson, one better learned at Camp Ibis than on the battlefield. The Needles desert proved to be a worthy training camp. (Courtesy of the U.S. Bureau of Land Management.)

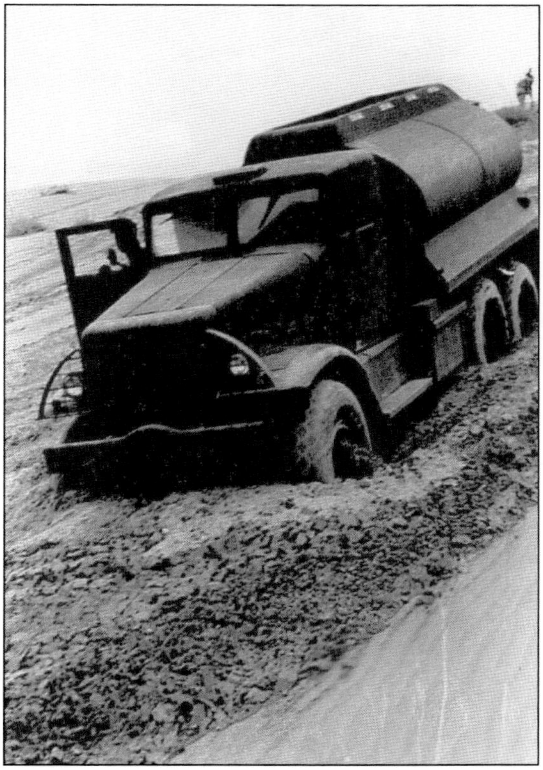

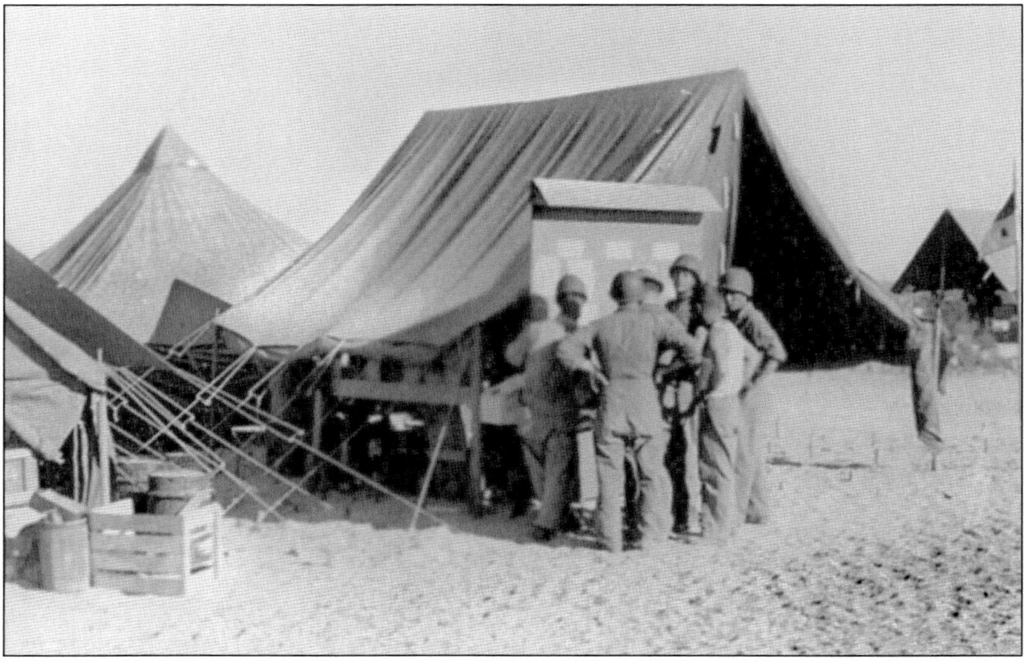

Bulletin Board. Getting ready for another day of training, the troops at Camp Ibis stand in front of the bulletin board that usually held orders of the day, instructions, and messages destined for the troops. The board stands in front of a tent that can also be used to store supplies. (Courtesy of the U.S. Bureau of Land Management.)

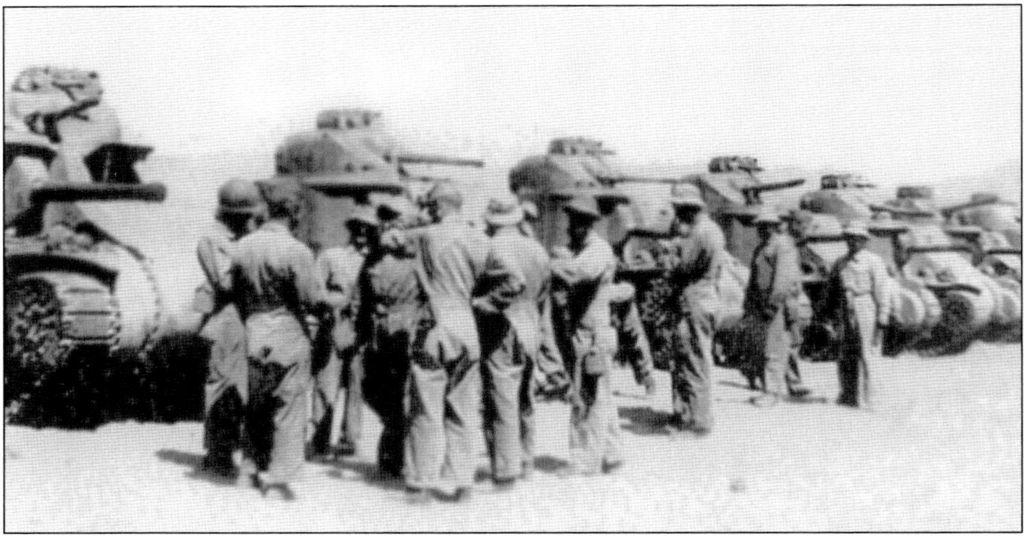

TANK TROOP. This group of soldiers is waiting for instructions prior to mounting their armored vehicles. The exercise is part of the Tank Destroyer School, which is carried out daily at Camp Ibis just outside Needles. The terrain is typical of the location that they will experience once deployed. (Courtesy of the U.S. Bureau of Land Management.)

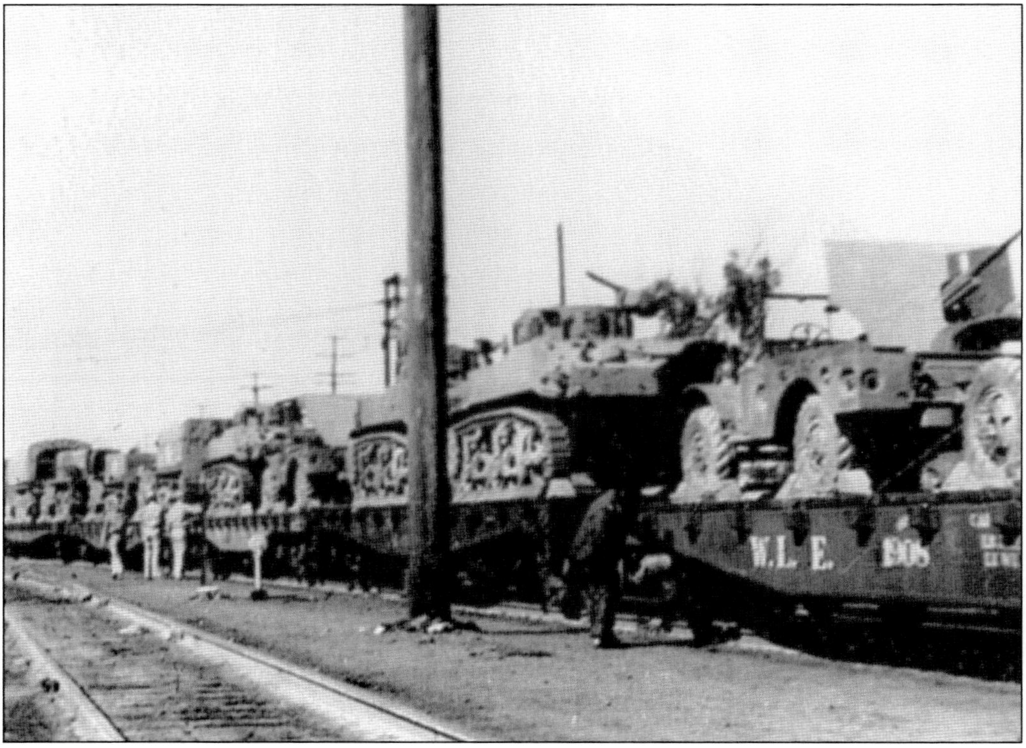

TANKS ON A TRAIN. The Needles train depot regularly received military supplies and troops. These half-tracks on railroad flatcars were off loaded and sent to Camp Ibis just outside Needles. These tanks were used in the tank destroyer maneuvers that were part of the daily activities in the desert, preparing troops for activities on the battlefield. (Courtesy of the U.S. Bureau of Land Management.)

Six

Through the Years
Events, People, and Places

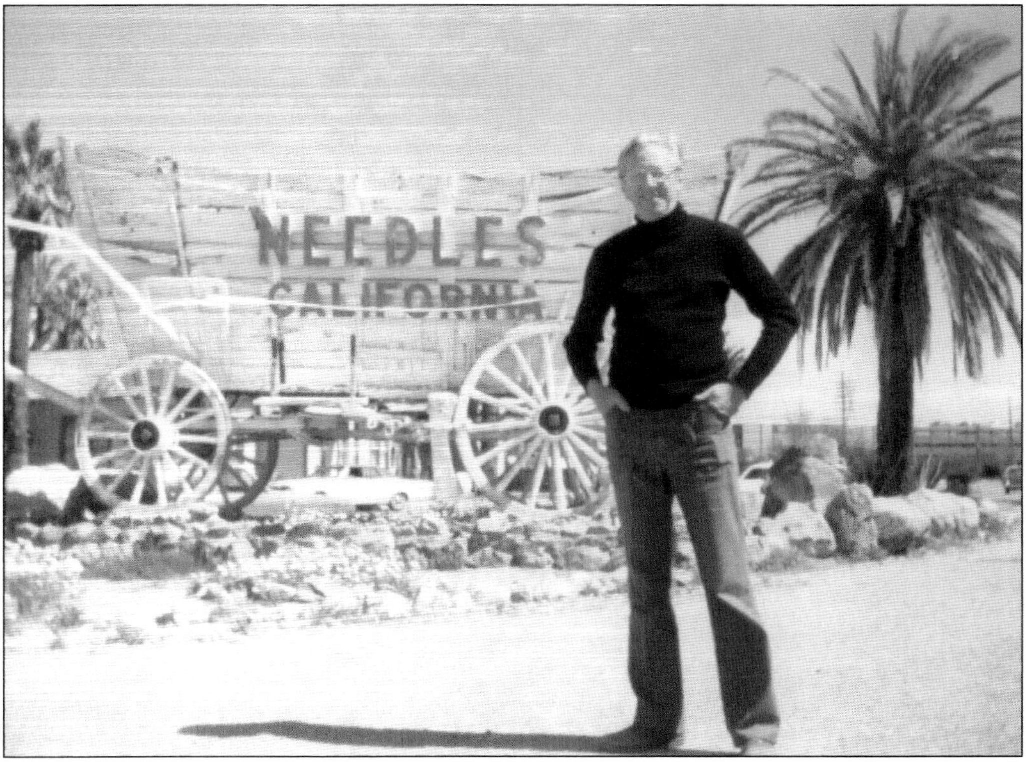

Charles Schulz. Famous cartoonist Charles Schulz, as a small boy, enjoyed Needles for just a brief time. In 1929, he moved to Needles with his family and his dog, Spike. Charles, also known as "Sparky," was just seven years old then, but the town made an impression on him. As an adult, he and his family visited Needles several times. His father and his uncle Monroe opened a barbershop in Needles, which was located across from Santa Fe Park. Charles attended the newly built D Street School with another young boy who became a prominent businessman in Needles, Bill Claypool. This picture was taken on one of his visits in 1980. (Courtesy of the Charles Schulz Museum.)

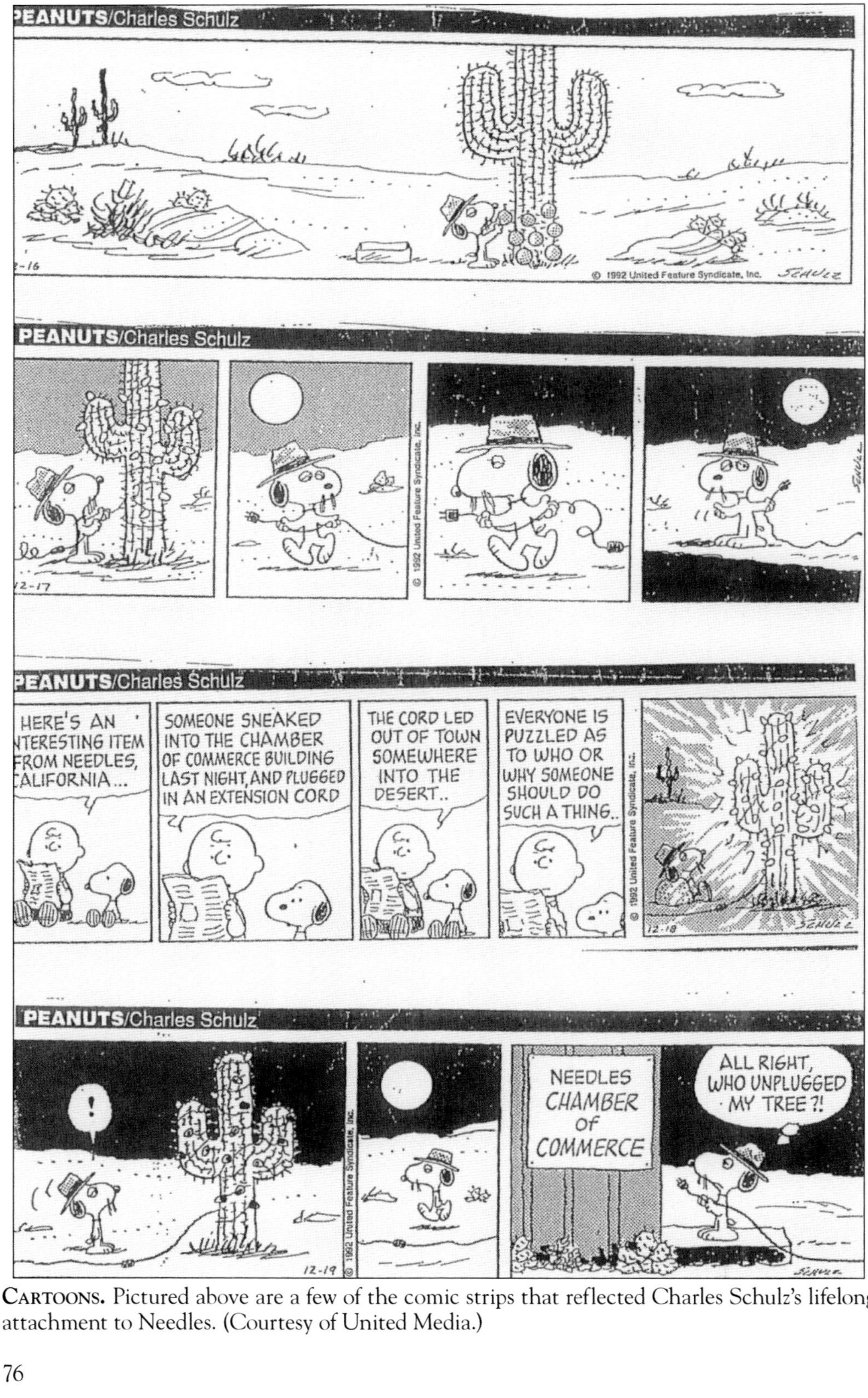

Cartoons. Pictured above are a few of the comic strips that reflected Charles Schulz's lifelong attachment to Needles. (Courtesy of United Media.)

THE GRAPES OF WRATH. Several of the scenes in the movie *The Grapes of Wrath* were filmed in Needles. One of the scenes shows a family seeking a new beginning in California as they crossed the bridge from Arizona to California traveling on Route 66. The cast stayed at Carty Camp while filming scenes in Needles. (Courtesy of the Route 66 Corridor Preservation Program; National Park Service.)

THE CAST. The main characters of *The Grapes of Wrath* are pictured in this promotional photograph. From left to right, they are Grandpa Joad (Charley Grapewin), Rose-of-Sharon (Dorris Bowden), Ma (Jane Darwell), Pa (Russell Simpson), Tom (Henry Fonda), Winfield (Darryl Hickman), Noah (Frank Sully), Ruthie (Shirley Mills), John (Frank Darien), Al (O. Z. Whitehead), Connie (Eddie Quillan), and Casey the preacher (John Carradine). (Courtesy of the Victorville Route 66 Museum.)

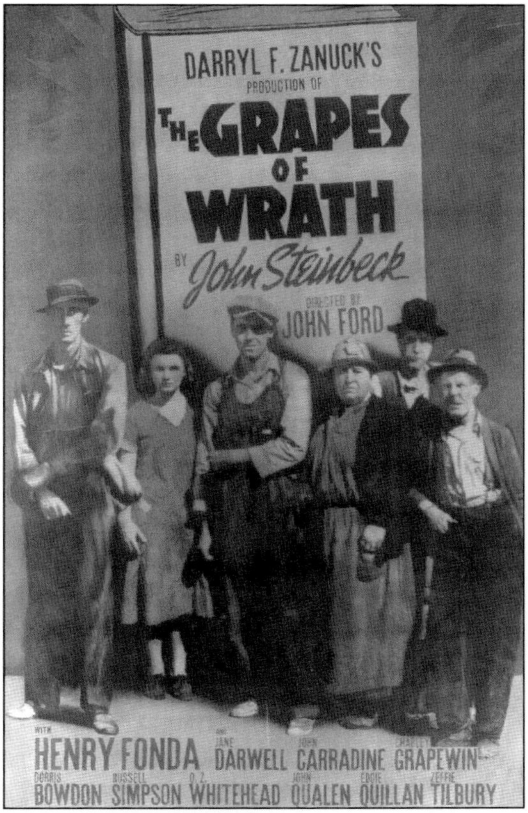

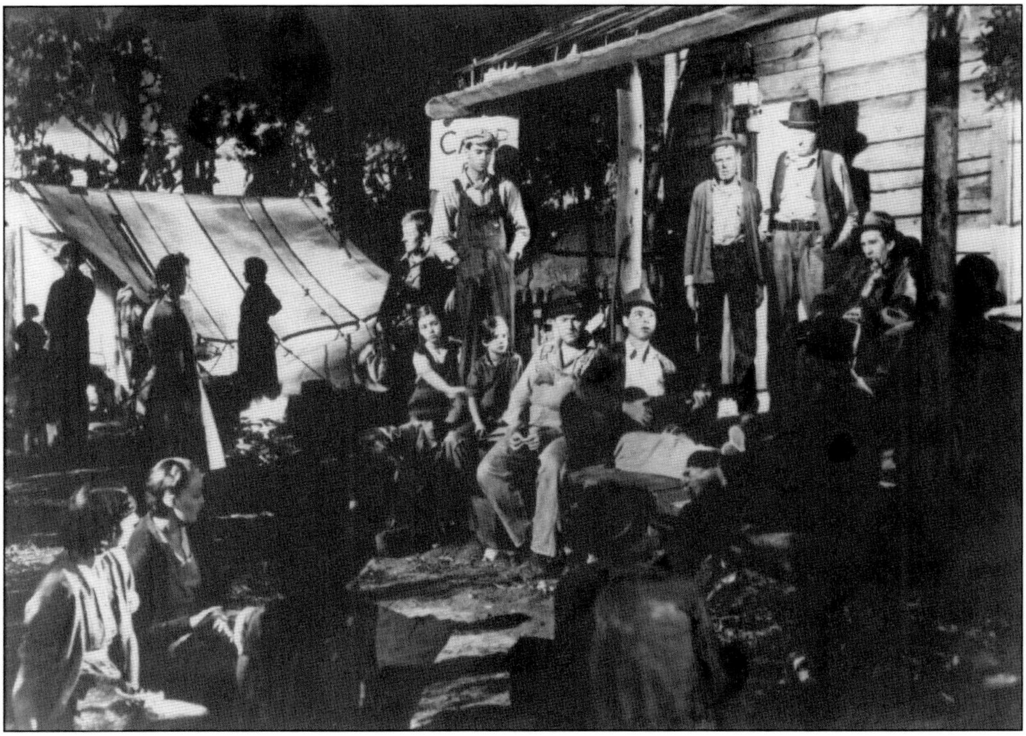

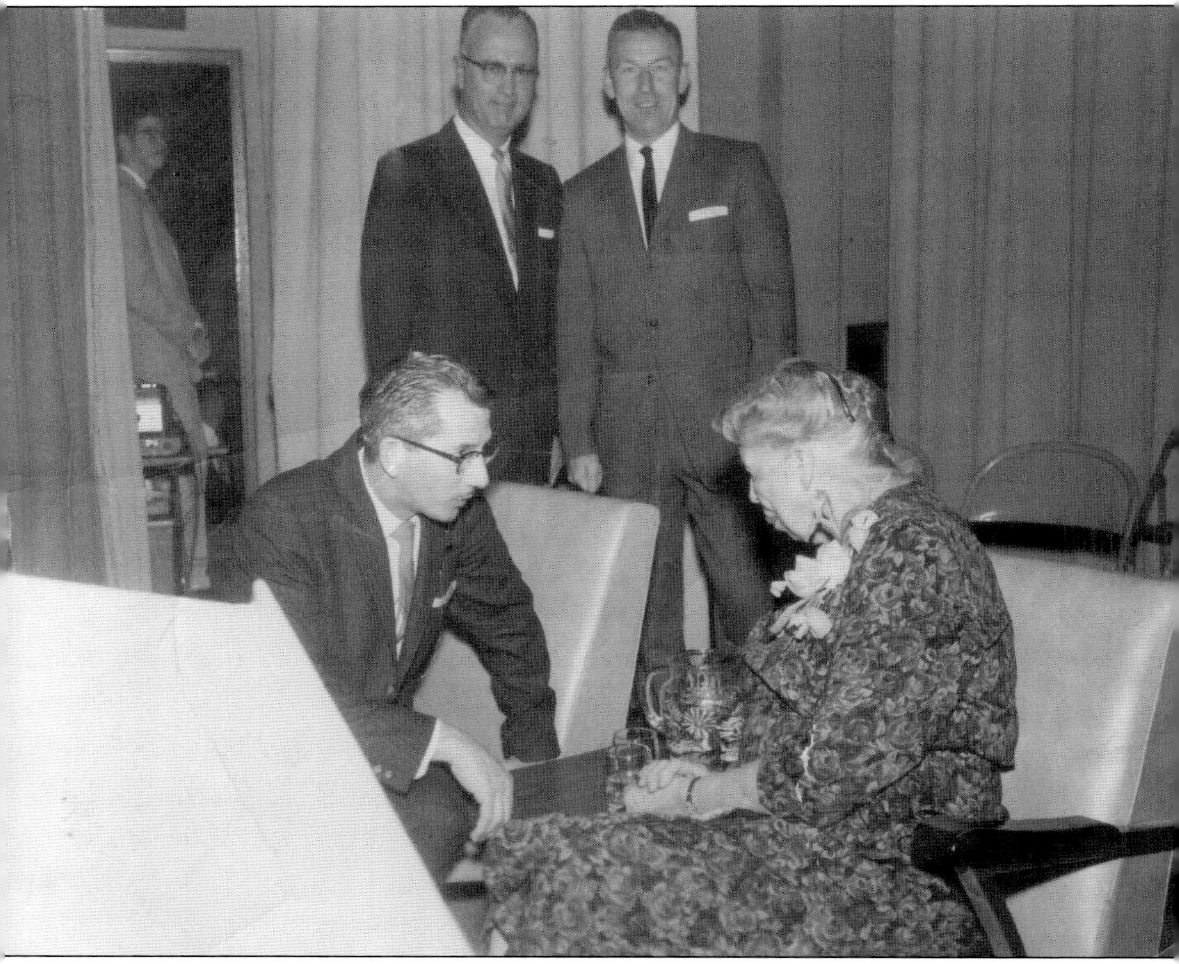

ELEANOR ROOSEVELT. Needles High School hosted a number of prominent speakers in a variety of fields. Former first lady Eleanor Roosevelt participated in an adult forum with a lecture entitled, "Russia, the People and Country as I See It." Pictured from left to right are (first row) B. J. "Barney" Fitzpatrick and Roosevelt; (second row) Dr. Max Rafferty, superintendent of the Needles Unified School District and later California's superintendent of public instruction, and vice principal Wallace Coon. (Courtesy of Kathleen Rafferty.)

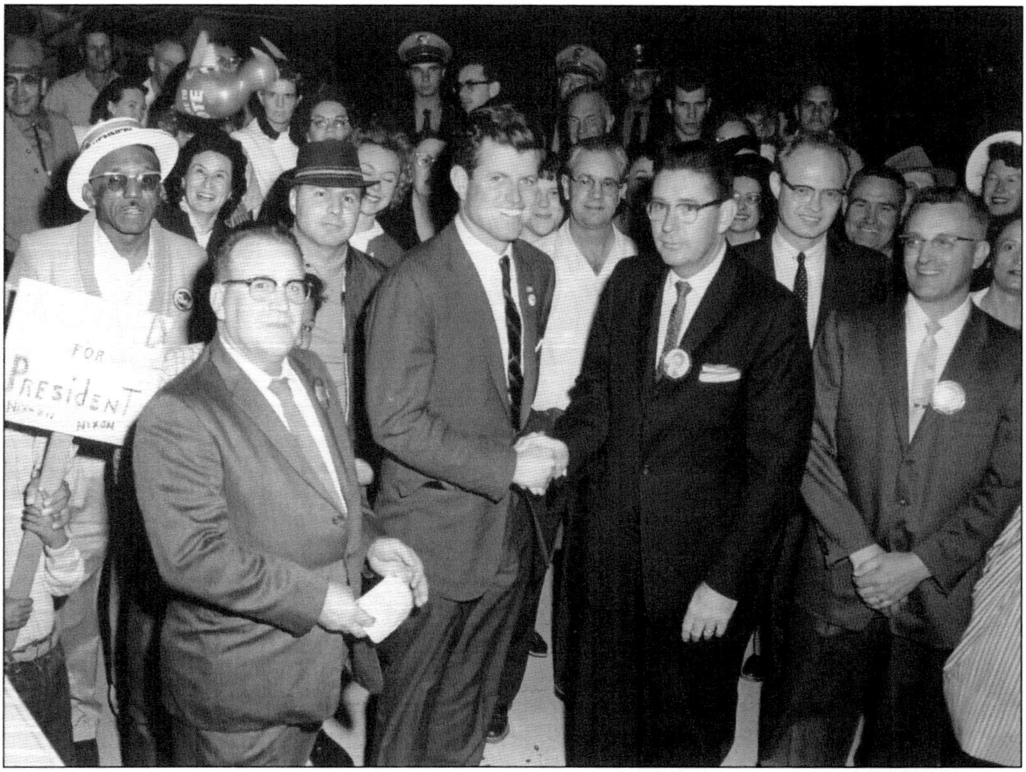

Ted Kennedy. Future longtime Massachusetts senator Edward Kennedy made a stop in Needles as he campaigned for his brother John F. Kennedy in the 1960 presidential race. Shown here from left to right gathered to greet Kennedy are Hugh O'Dell, Henry Smith, and Wendell Sneed. In the background is a crowd of Needles residents, including Duke Watkins, owner of the local barbershop (behind the sign at left). The Fort Mohave Band played at the reception, where Kennedy spoke about the importance of electing his older brother. The picture was taken by Henry Orzel. (Courtesy of Judy Orzel Browder and Dottie Orzel Hutcherson.)

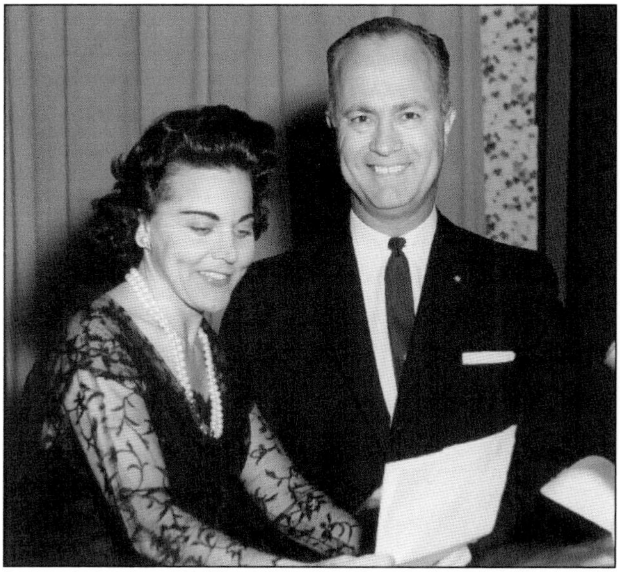

Ann Landers. Also participating in one of the adult forums held at the high school was Esther Pauline Lederer, better known as Ann Landers, the famous advice columnist. Her lecture was both informative and humorous. She spoke about her early childhood and how she became an advice columnist. She is pictured here with Dr. Max Rafferty, superintendent of the Needles Unified School District. This picture was also taken by Henry Orzel. (Courtesy of Judy Orzel Browder and Dottie Orzel Hutcherson.)

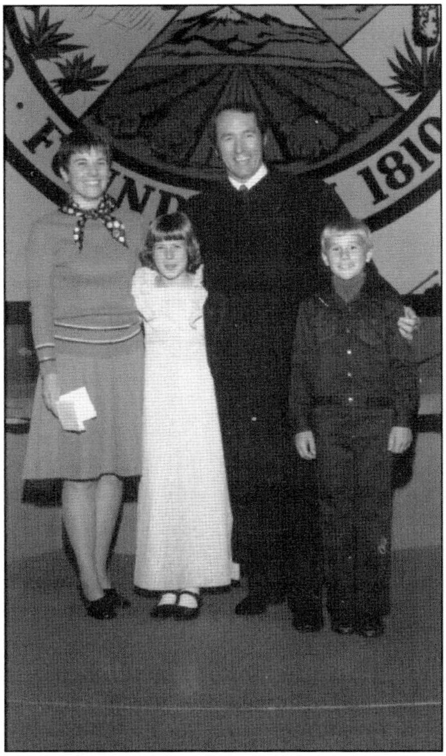

Mayor Morris. A young Pat Morris arrived in Needles with his family at the age of four. After graduating from Needles High School, Pat attended the University of Redlands, graduating cum laude. He then graduated from Stanford University School of Law. In 1976, Pat was sworn in as Superior Court judge where he served until being elected to an unprecedented three terms as Superior Court presiding judge. In 1981, he was named Inland Southern California Trial Judge of the Year. From 1991 to 1993, he served as chief justice of the Judicial Council. The National Council of Juvenile and Family Courts of America awarded him the highest award for meritorious service. The photograph at left shows him with wife Sally, daughter Katie, and son Jim. (Courtesy of the Morris family.)

Swearing In. The photograph below shows Morris during his swearing in for his first term as mayor of San Bernardino in 2006. His brother Phillip Morris, also a judge, officiated in the ceremony as Pat's wife, Sally, looked on. Pat's strong anti-crime platform won him a second term as mayor.

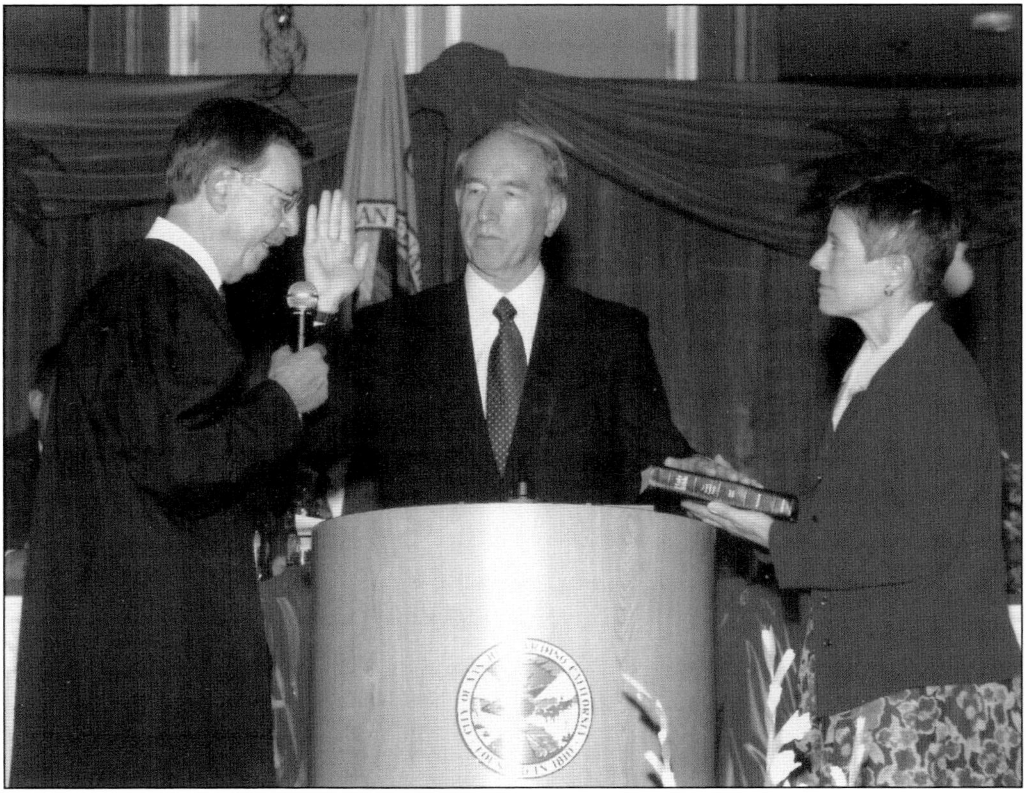

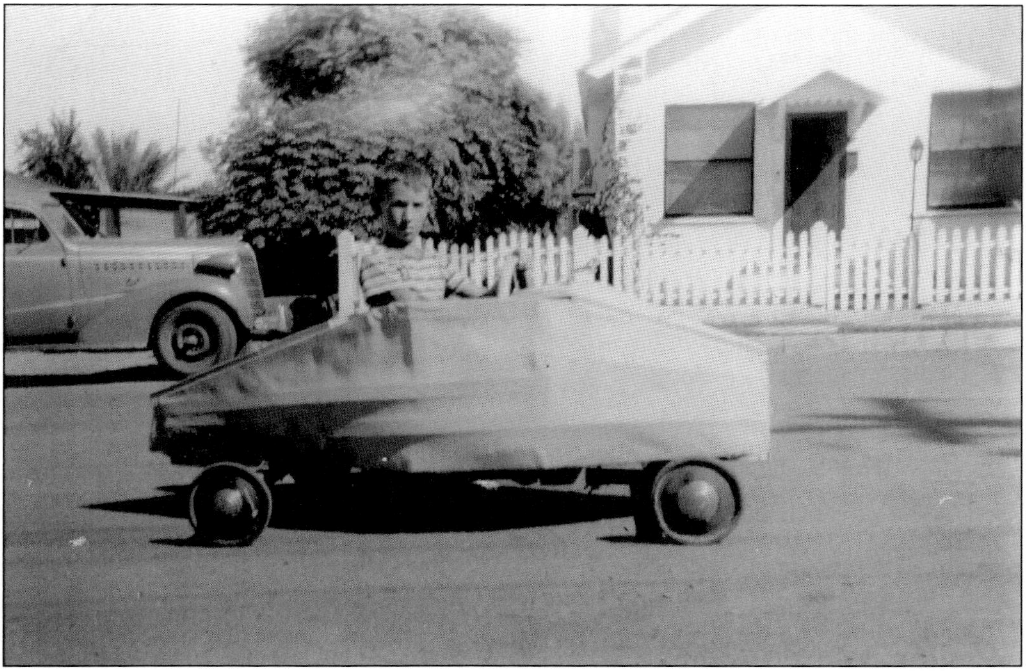

Patrick Morris. Young Pat sits in front of his home in Needles with his soapbox derby entry. Using the wheels off his Radio Flyer wagon, he soon realized that it was all in the wheels: those with special soapbox derby wheels carried the day, no matter what their racers looked like. Though Pat had constructed his homegrown cart with great care and ingenuity, he was out in the first heat. At right is Pat running distance for the Needles High School track team. (Courtesy of the Morris family.)

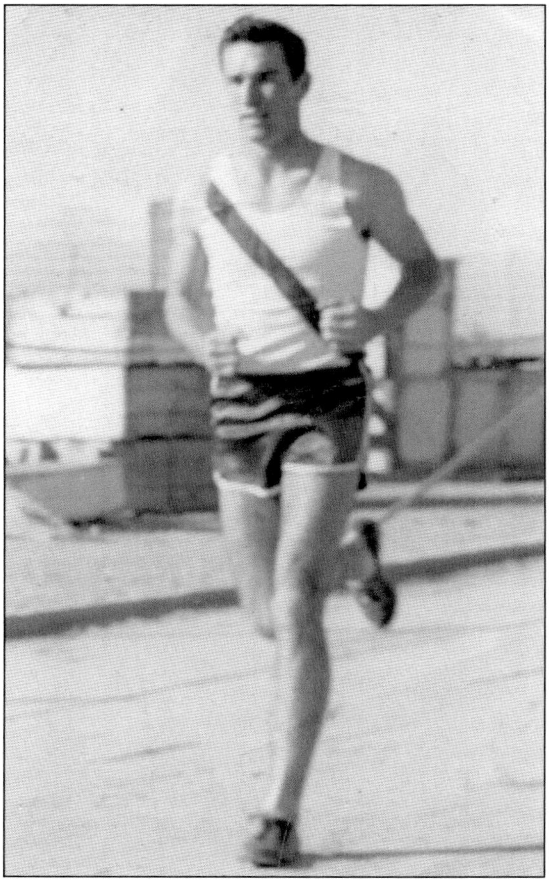

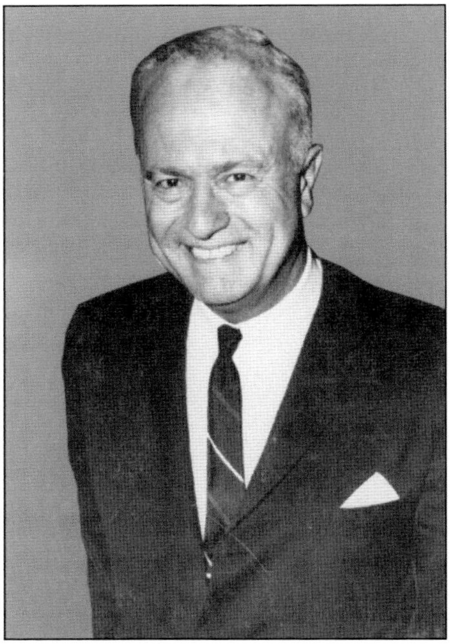

Dr. Max Rafferty. Max Rafferty was the superintendent of the Needles Unified School District from 1956 to 1961. Rafferty installed a system of programs for gifted students, scholars, and athletes that gained national attention. Later, in 1961, he was superintendant of schools for La Cañada and delivered a rousing speech, "The Passing of a Patriot," which received considerable public attention. A movement began to draft Rafferty to run for California State Superintendent of Public Instruction. He ran and he won, serving in this position from 1963 to 1971. Rafferty held strong beliefs in basic education as a solid foundation for learning. He was the author of books on education and later wrote a syndicated column espousing his educational views. Below is a picture of Rafferty at a campaign rally. (Courtesy of Dennis Rafferty.)

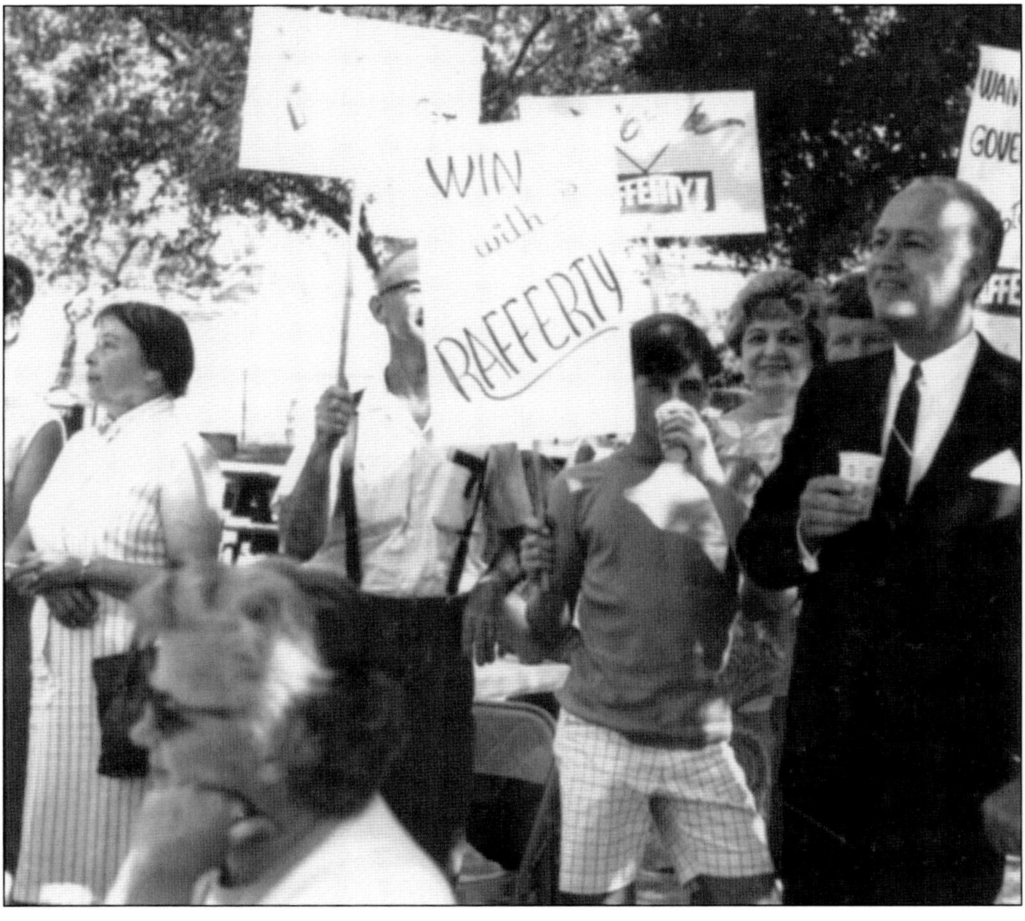

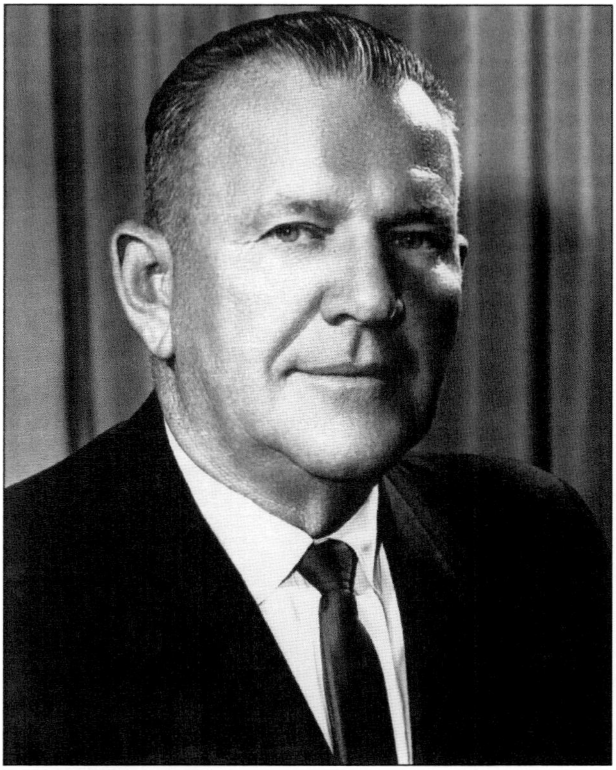

Frank Bland. After three years as a marine in the Pacific theater during World War II, Frank Bland began his civilian law enforcement career as police chief of Needles, where he served until his election as San Bernardino County sheriff in 1955. He then held the sheriff's position for seven terms, from 1955 to 1983. Numerous institutions and scholarships have been named for him. Below is a picture of Bland as Needles often saw him, with his horse in one of the Marathon Parades. (Courtesy of the San Bernardino County Sheriff's Department.)

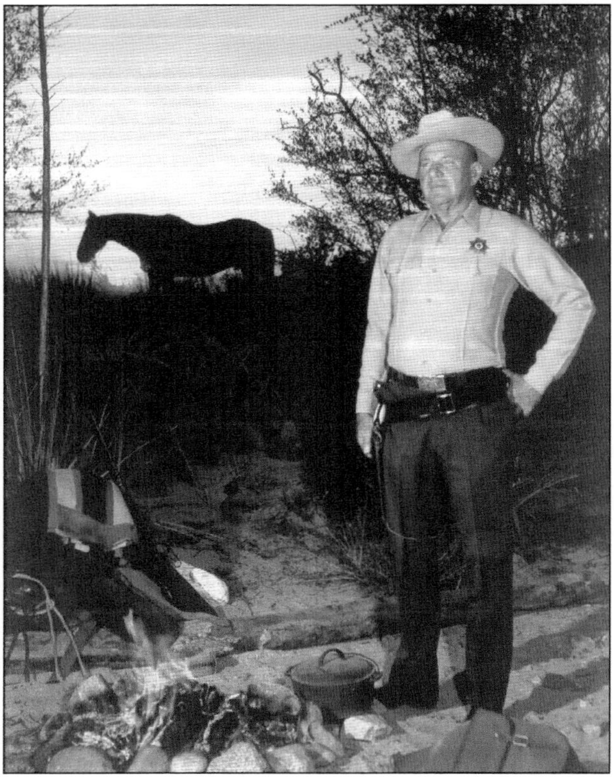

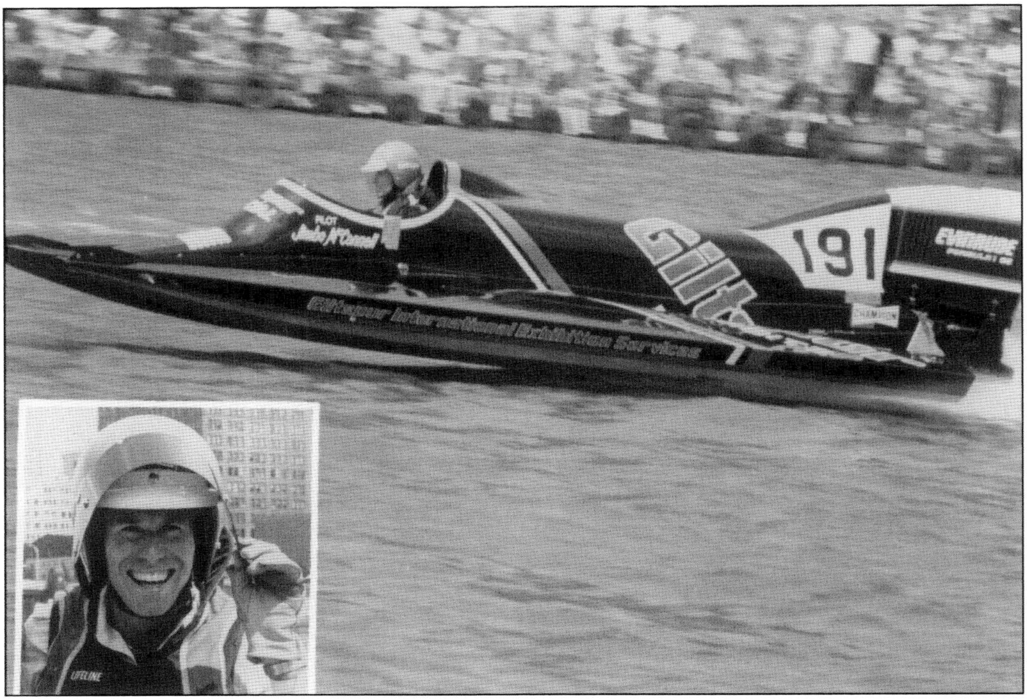

Needles Champion. World and National Outboard Boat Racing champion Jimbo McConnell was born and raised in Needles. In 1958, at the age of 14, Jimbo competed in the Needles Marathon Boat Race, and his career in the sport began. After winning a number of Marathon races, Jimbo became a product development test driver and racer for Evinrude Motors. Throughout his racing career in the United States, Canada, South Africa, Germany, France, Italy, Holland, Norway, and other locations, he never failed to mention his hometown of Needles, California. After winning races around the world and setting numerous records (many of which stand today), he suffered a career-ending racing accident in 1985. Jim and his wife, Cathy (also from Needles), retired to their beloved town on the Colorado River, making Needles their home once again. (Courtesy of Jimbo and Cathy McConnell.)

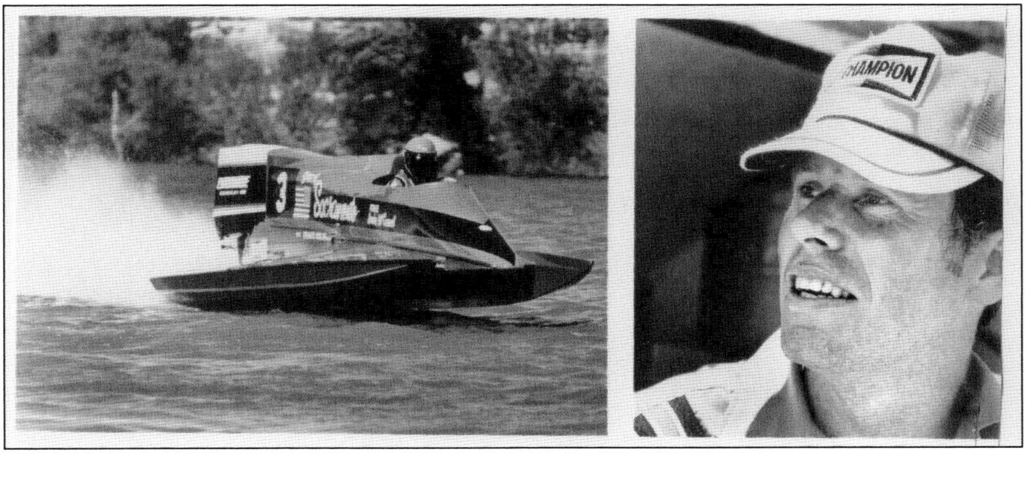

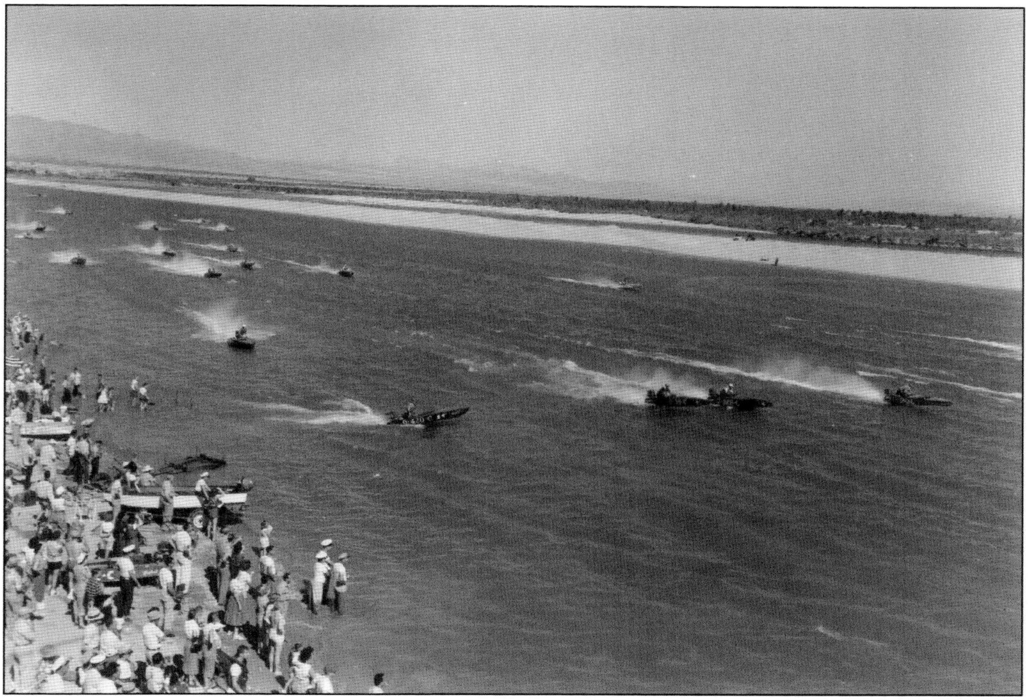

MARATHON BOAT RACES. Two local residents, L. A. Andrews and Sam Cord, read about the boat races in New York's Hudson River and were inspired to create the Marathon Boat Race event in Needles. The first race was held in 1948 and sponsored by the Lions Club. In later years, the event drew as many as 5,000 people to watch the outboard classic of the West. Entries came from as far away as New York. The races were eventually sanctioned by the American Power Boat Association. In the photograph below, Marathon racers crouch on their knees for balance as they fight for first place. About a third of the racers failed to finish the race, which took two hours and 33 minutes. The winner of the Class-A division was John Drake, who set a new world's speed record. The day ended with a deep-pit barbecue and the presentation of trophies. (Courtesy of Judy Orzel Browder; the Needles Regional Museum.)

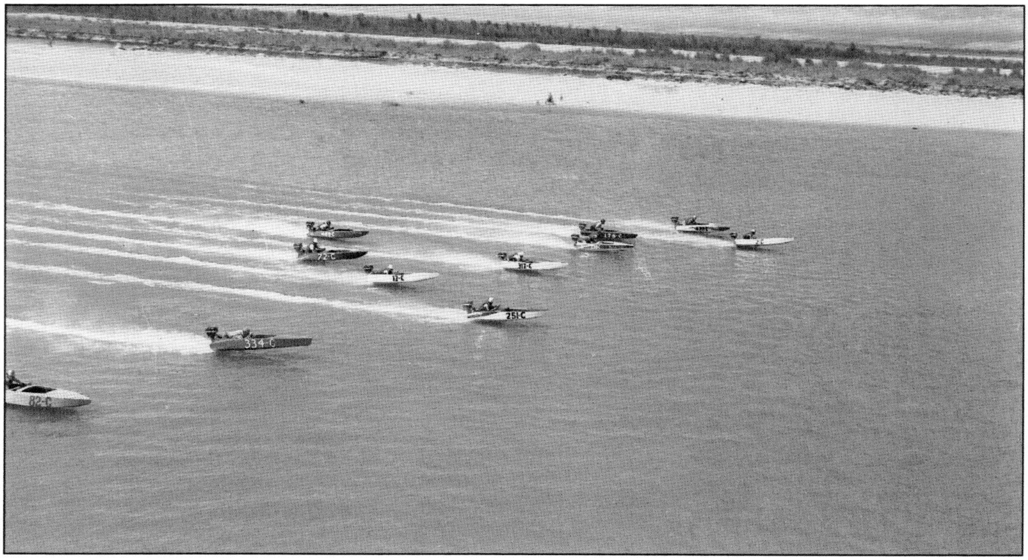

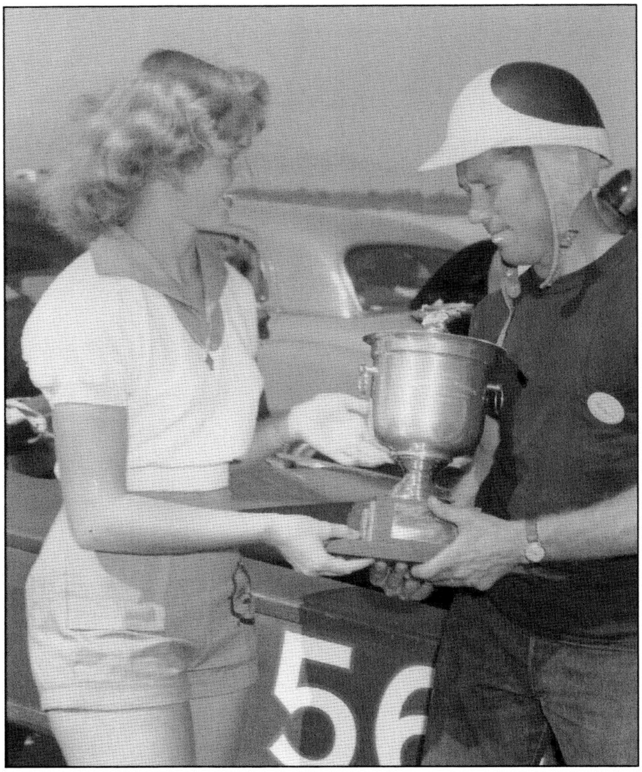

MARATHON QUEENS. Patricia Stolfus was voted the 1953 Marathon Queen. Part of her duties on Marathon Weekend included riding on the queen's float and presenting a trophy to the winner of the Marathon Boat Races. In 1953, the winner of the 115-mile round-trip race was Dr. William E. Schiefer from San Diego. Below, 1956 Marathon queen Ann Castle makes a trophy presentation to Johnny Drake. (Courtesy of the Needles Regional Museum).

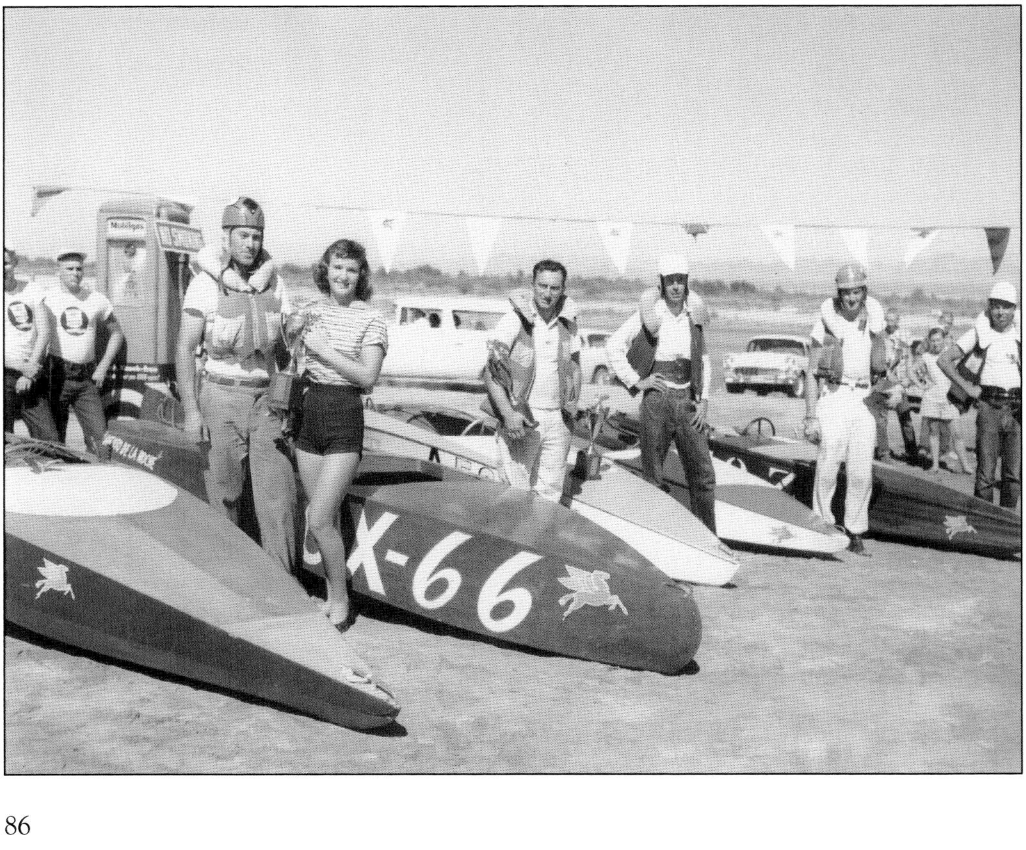

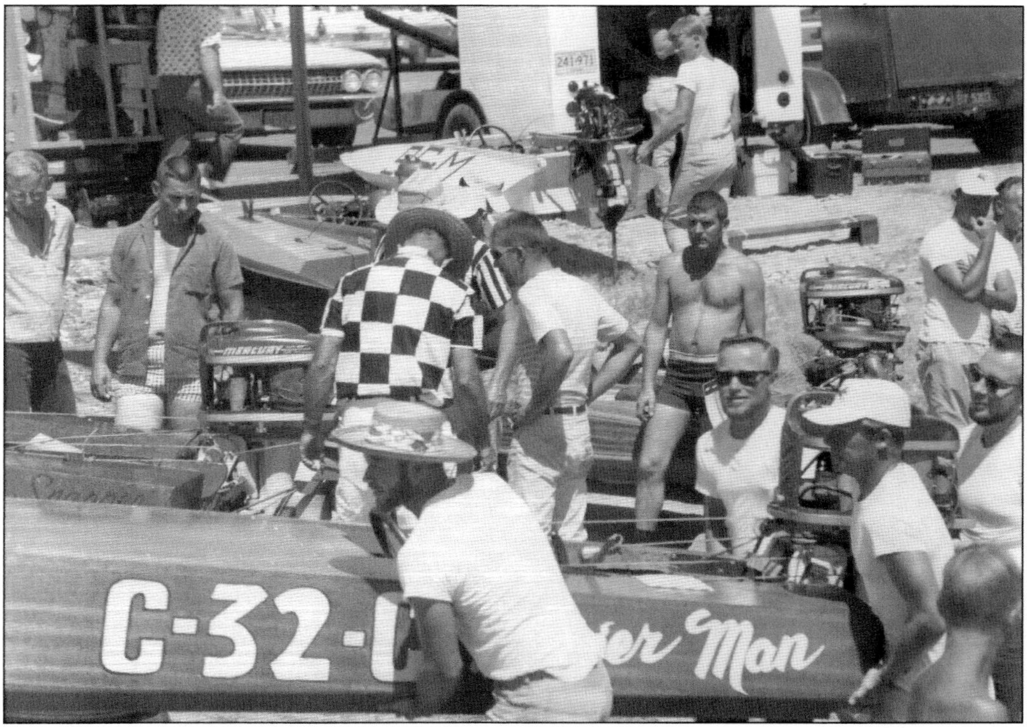

BOAT INSPECTION. Getting ready for the Marathon Boat Race, these entries prepare to have their boats weighed as part of the qualifying. The man in the black-and-white checkered shirt is an official looking over the engines. The winner of the 1949 Marathon Boat Race Class-A division, John Drake, stands to the right in the white cap. (Courtesy of Art Horn.)

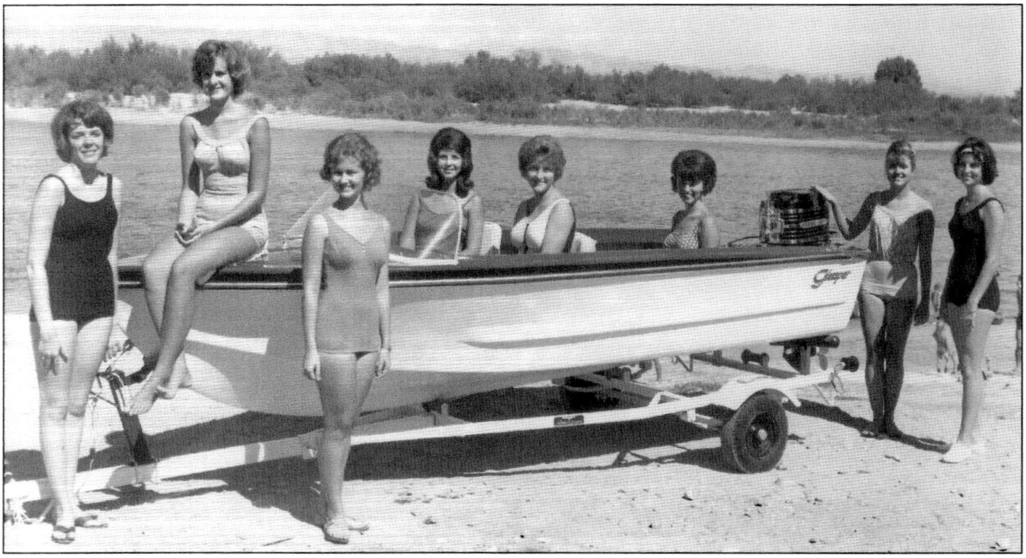

MARATHON RAFFLE. The 1962 Marathon committee sold tickets for a raffle to raise money for the race. Pictured is the raffled boat and that year's Marathon pageant contestants. From left to right, they are Sandra Hall, Mary Rowen, Carolyn Reiman, Annette Sheridan, Diane Thompson, Sheri Dudley, Joyce Coffey, and Rowena Lyons. Not pictured are Marathon queen Wilma Jenkins, princess Sheri Dudley, and second princess Kathy Lenox. (Courtesy of Art Horn.)

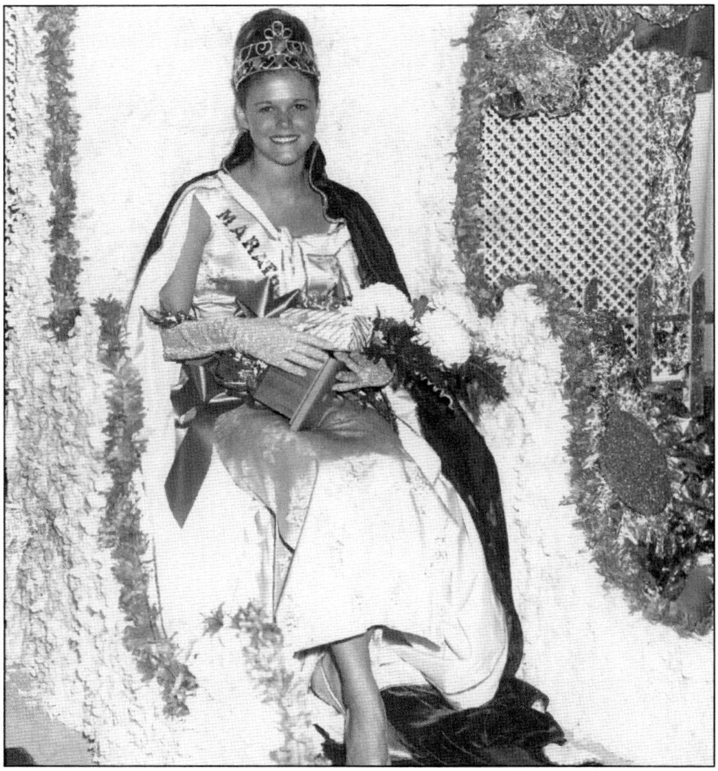

Crowning. Janis George is crowned Marathon Queen in the photograph at left. Below, Janice cuts the ribbon to signify the opening of the Needles Inspection Station. With her are Jack Lambert (left) and Herb Martin (right). (Courtesy of the Janis George family.)

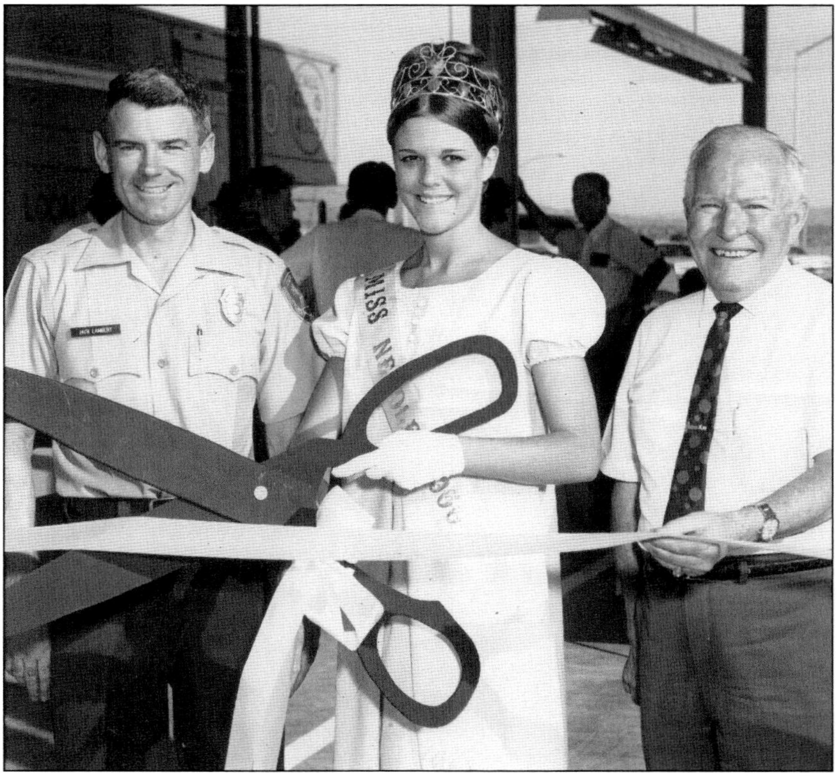

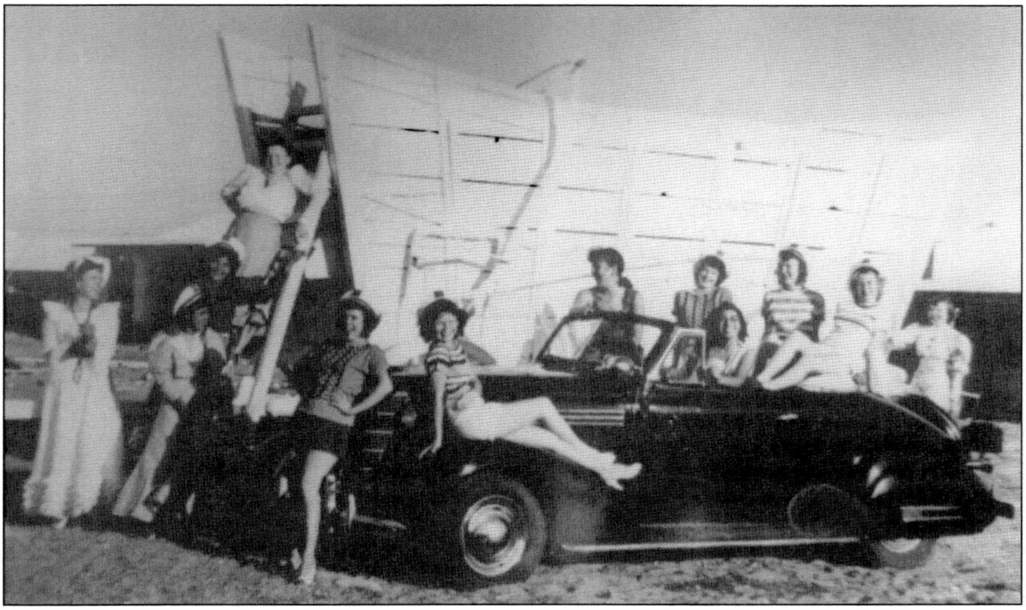

Wagon Wheel. Needles beauties grace a vintage convertible in front of a wagon that is under construction and now sits on Route 66 in downtown Needles. From left to right, the young women on the car in this *c.* 1951 photograph are Beverly Powell, Linda Lacy, Twyla Trotter, Annabel Skinner, Charlotte Johnson, Harriet Hoble, and Patsy Gutierrez. The rest are unidentified. (Courtesy of the San Bernardino Public Library.)

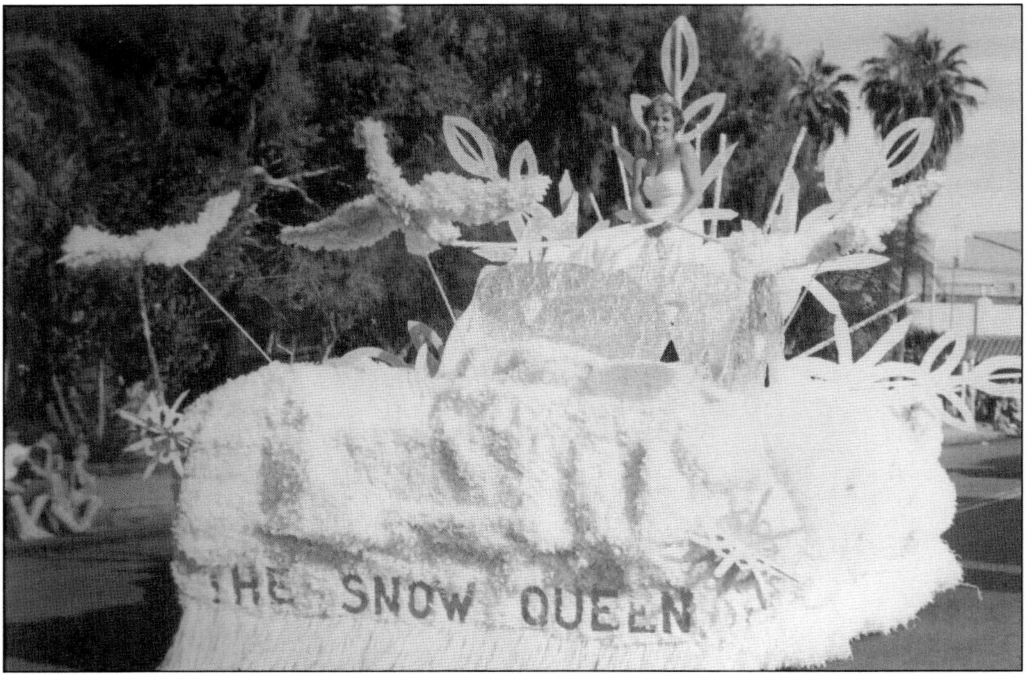

Snow Queen. The 1954 Marathon Parade's theme was "Fairy Tales." The first-place winner was the California Pacific Utilities float, "Hansel and Gretel." The "Snow Queen" float, pictured here, took second place. The floats were made with different colors of crepe paper instead of flowers. (Courtesy of Linda Daniel Andrews.)

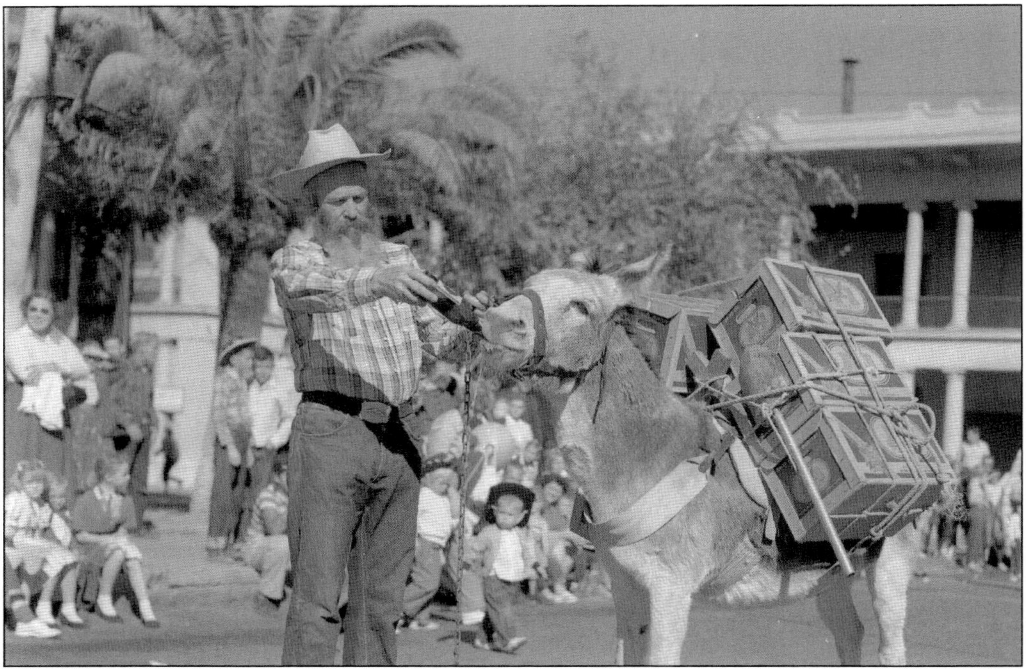

"MAN AND THE DONKEY." Shown here is another entry from an early Marathon Parade; apparently this prospector is packed up and ready to go, but the donkey appears not so willing. The pack on the donkey's back is full of A-1 Pilsner Beer, and the prospector is feeding the beer to the donkey as encouragement. History does not record whether or not the donkey finished the parade. (Courtesy of Judy Orzel Browder.)

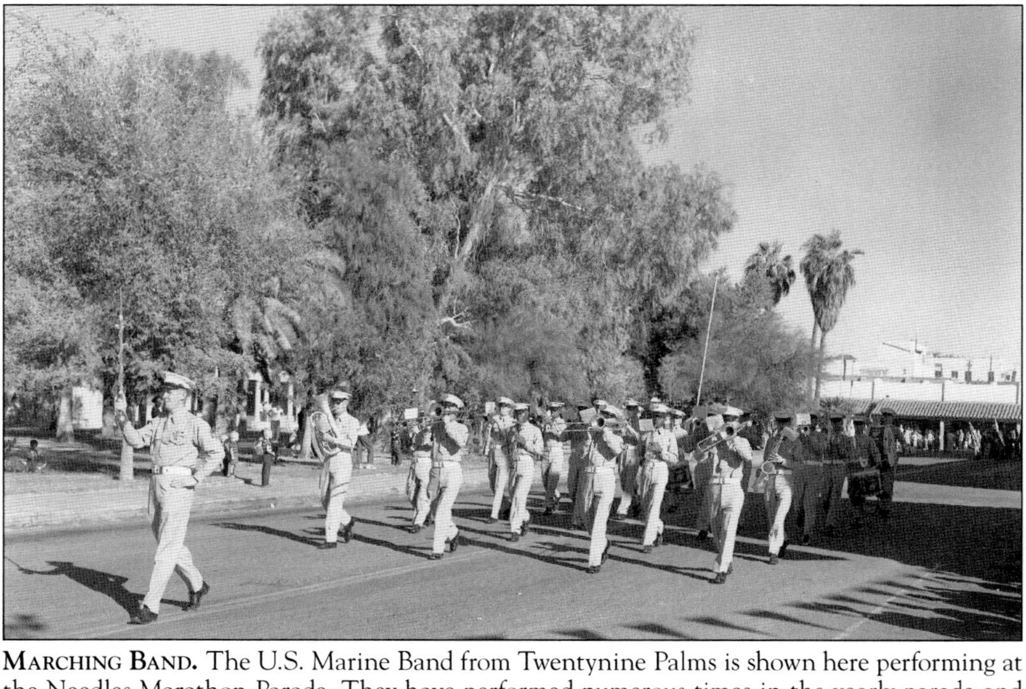

MARCHING BAND. The U.S. Marine Band from Twentynine Palms is shown here performing at the Needles Marathon Parade. They have performed numerous times in the yearly parade and have taken home many trophies. (Courtesy of Judy Orzel Browder.)

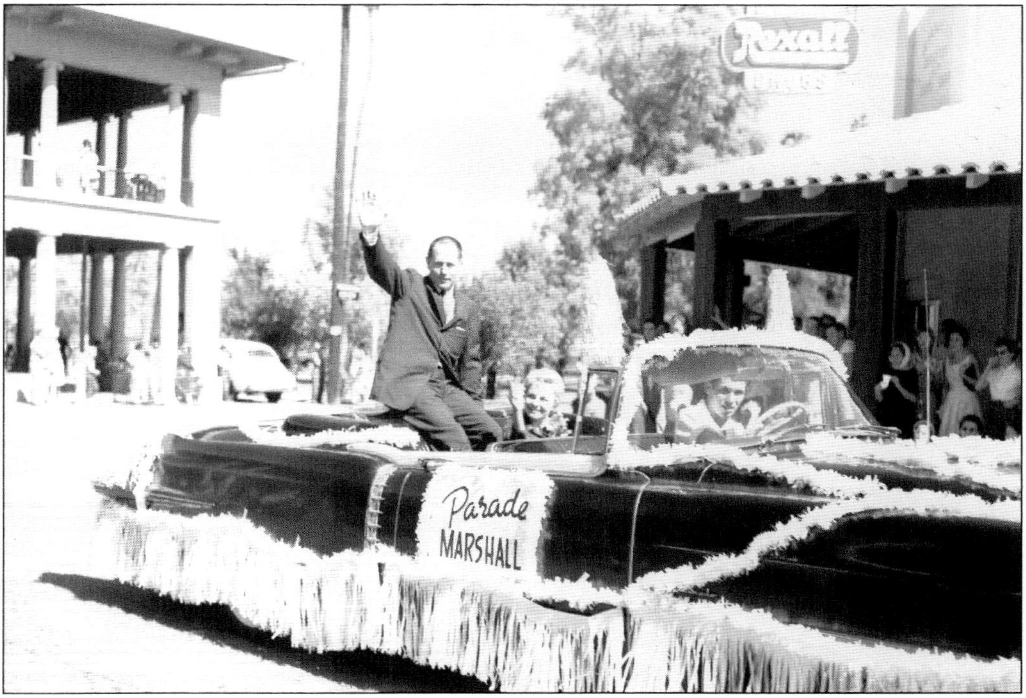

GRAND MARSHAL. The grand marshal for the Marathon Parade in 1961 was California lieutenant governor Glenn M. Anderson. Riding with Anderson is his wife, Lee. In the background is the El Garces Harvey House as they round the corner onto F Street. Driving the grand marshal's car is Jimbo McConnell. (Courtesy of Judy Orzel Browder.)

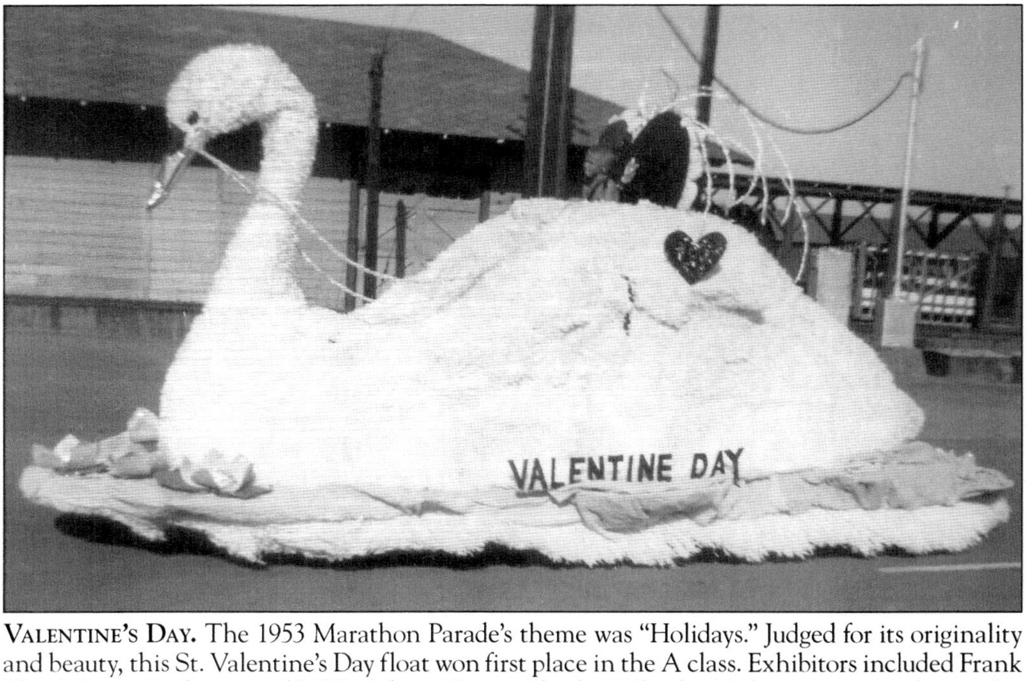

VALENTINE'S DAY. The 1953 Marathon Parade's theme was "Holidays." Judged for its originality and beauty, this St. Valentine's Day float won first place in the A class. Exhibitors included Frank Bland, L. A. Andrews, and J. W. Nelson. Young Charles "Chuckie" Johnson is seen playing the role of Cupid. (Courtesy of Linda Daniel Andrews.)

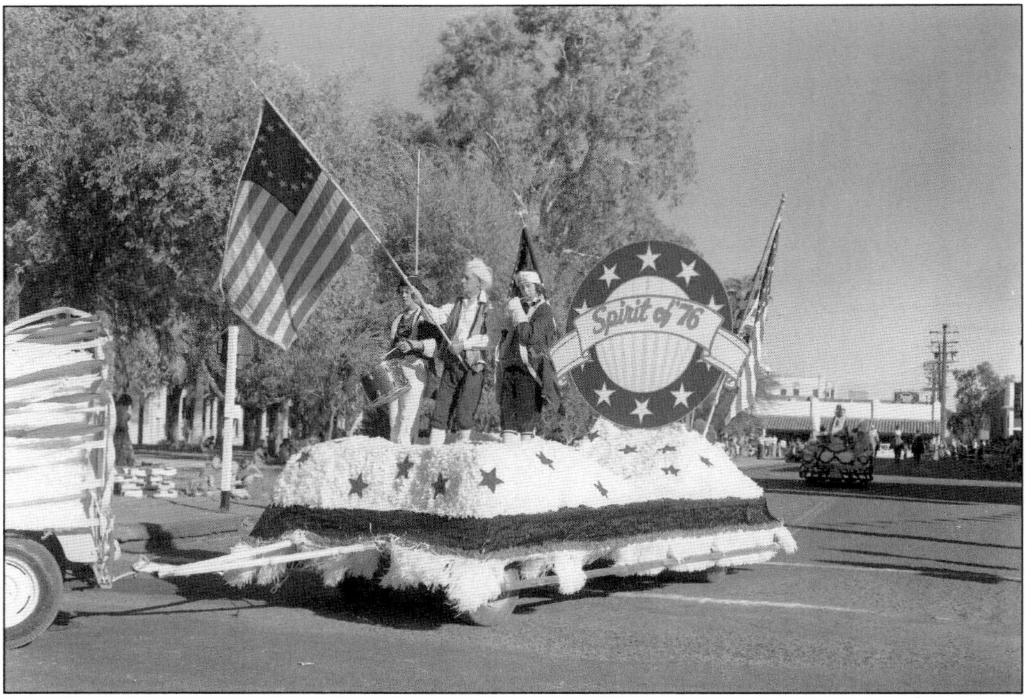

Patriotic. "Spirit of '76" and "Right to Vote" are two of the floats depicting a patriotic theme for one of the annual Marathon Parades. These beautiful floats were made with different colors of crepe paper and required hours of hard work. Different businesses and organizations sponsored each float. In the photograph below, Linda Daniel Andrews is seen riding the "Right to Vote" float. (Courtesy of Linda Daniel Andrews.)

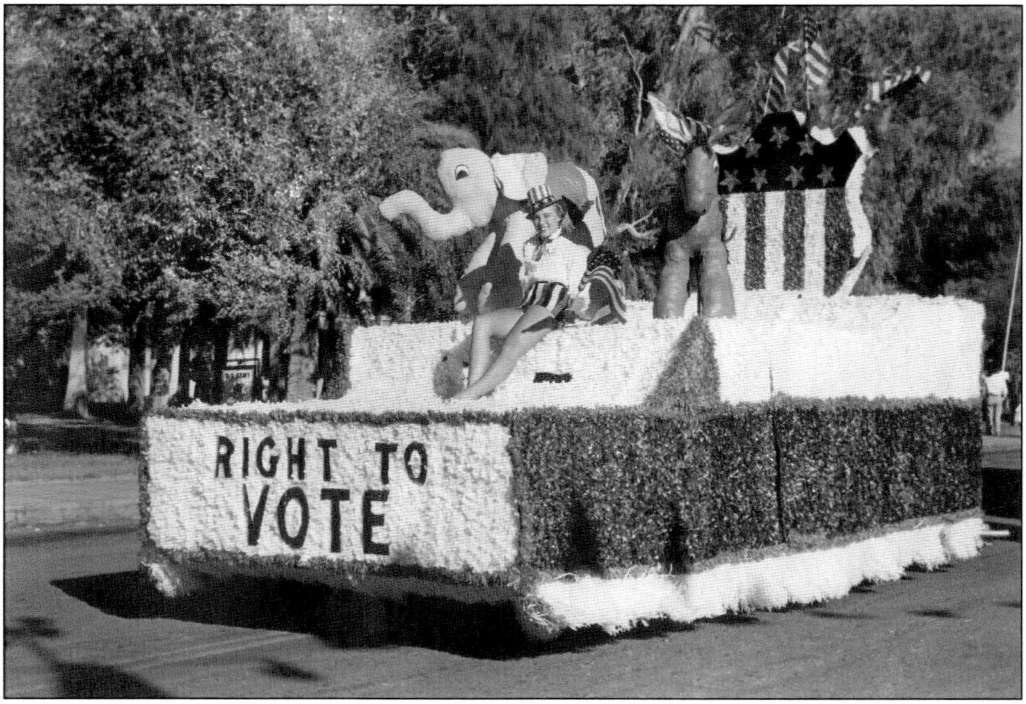

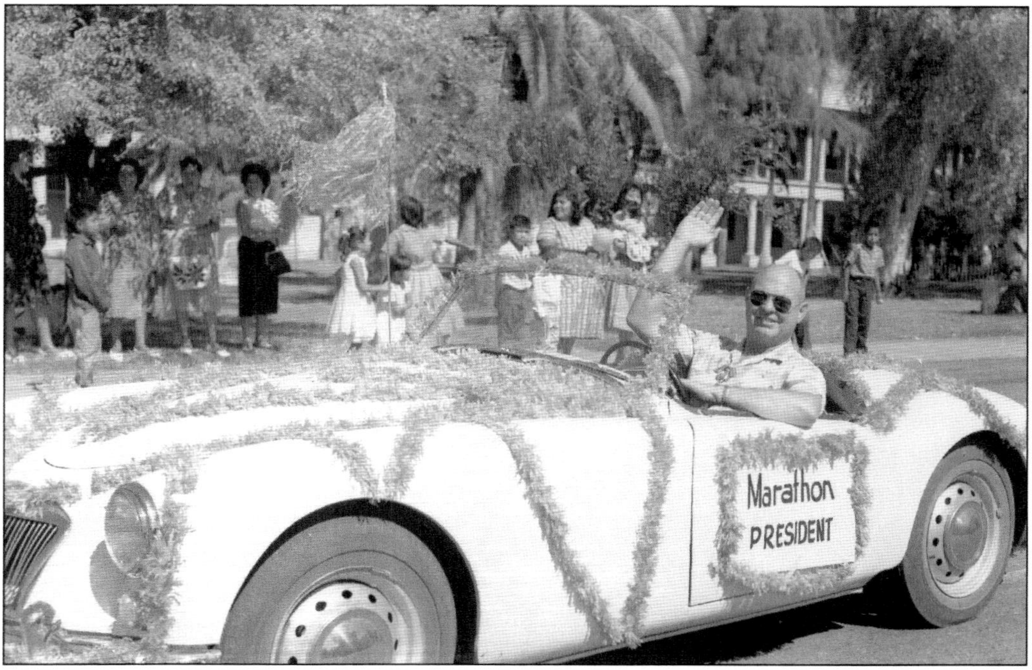

MARATHON PRESIDENT. Parade president Jack Soden of the Southern California Gas Company is shown here as he drives by Santa Fe Park and waves to the crowds. (Courtesy of Judy Orzel Browder.)

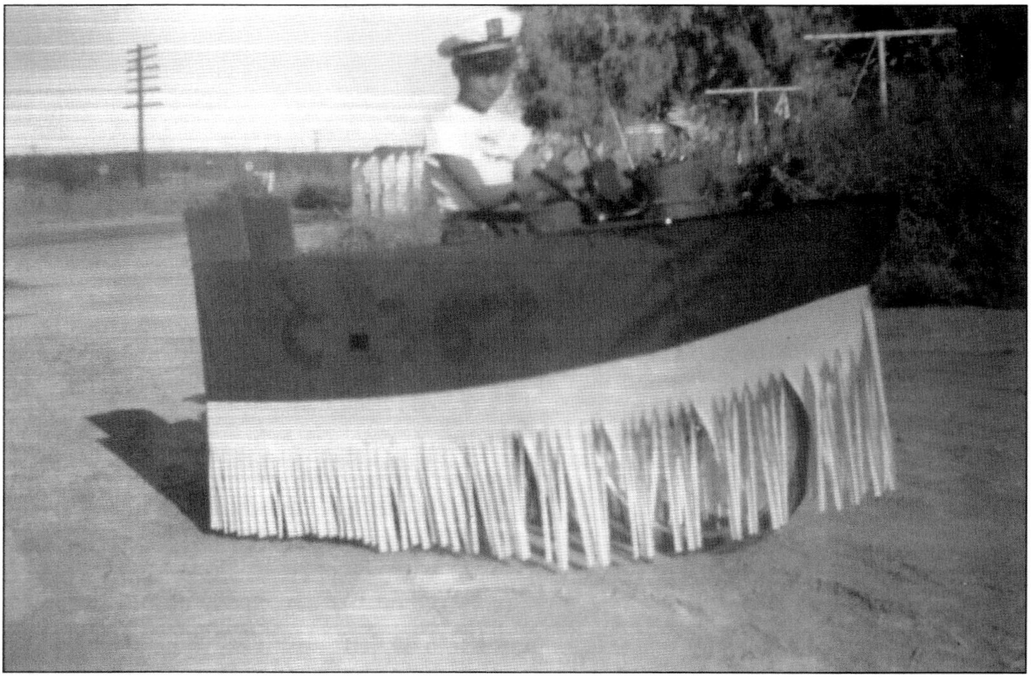

FUTURE CHAIRMAN. Young Art Horn is seen in his navy hat as he rides a float in the 1948 Marathon Parade. This was the beginning of a long history of participation in the event; as a teen, he worked with the pit crew and later was chairman of the Marathon for a number of years. (Courtesy of Art Horn.)

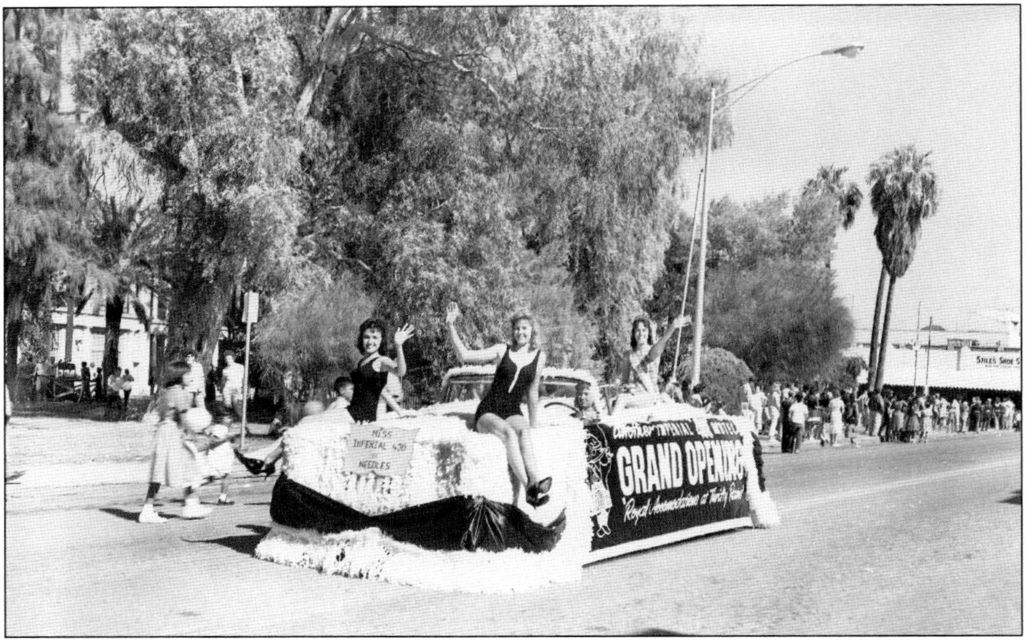

Beauty Pageant. In 1962, a beauty pageant kicked off the opening of the Imperial 400 Motel. The winner and her court are pictured on the Imperial 400 Motel float entered in the annual Marathon Parade. The queen is Trisha Roarke. On the front of the float are, from left to right, Sylvia Diaz and Nancy Cox. (Courtesy of Judy Orzel Browder)

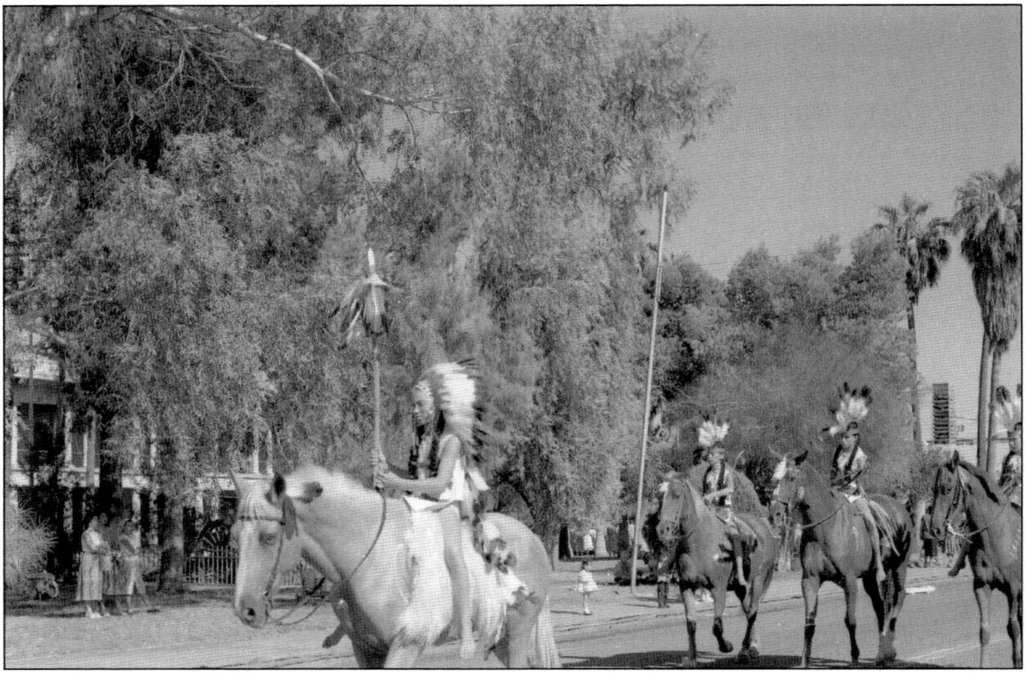

Native American Children. The annual Marathon events drew people from all over the country. Of special interest to those visiting from the East Coast were the Native Americans entries. This group of children are showing off their bareback riding skills as they ride through town in their headdresses. (Courtesy of Judy Orzel Browder.)

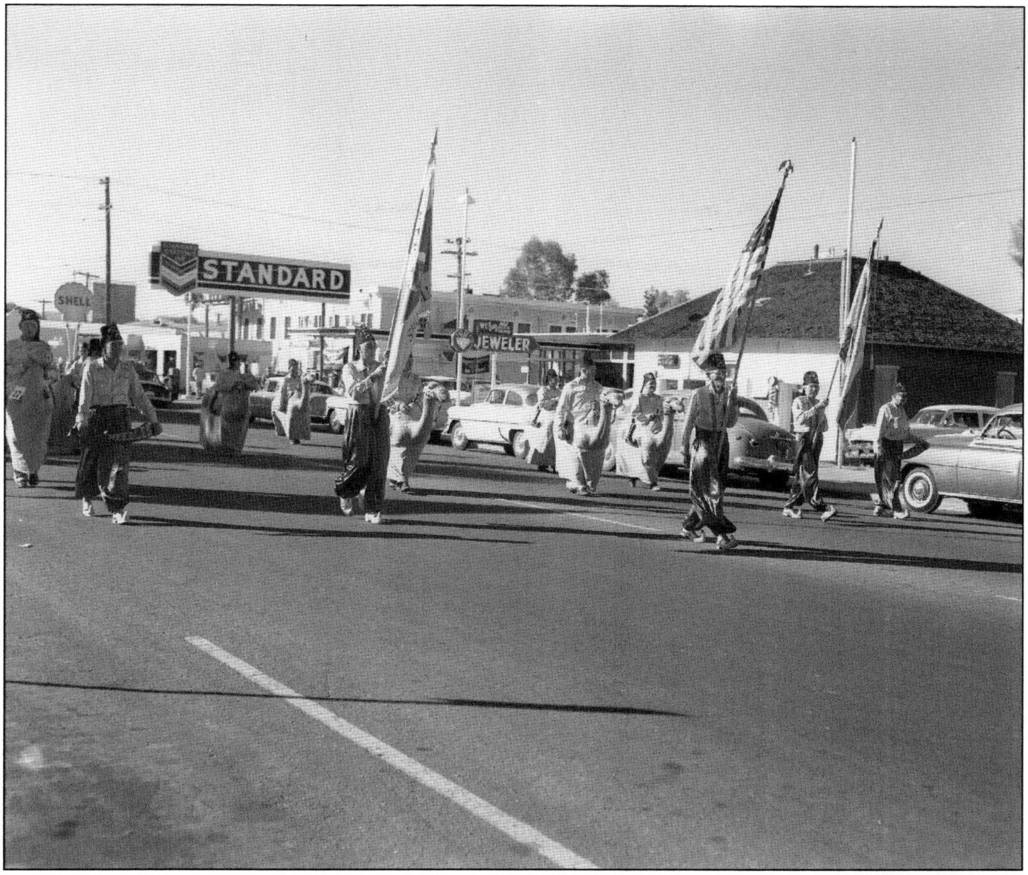

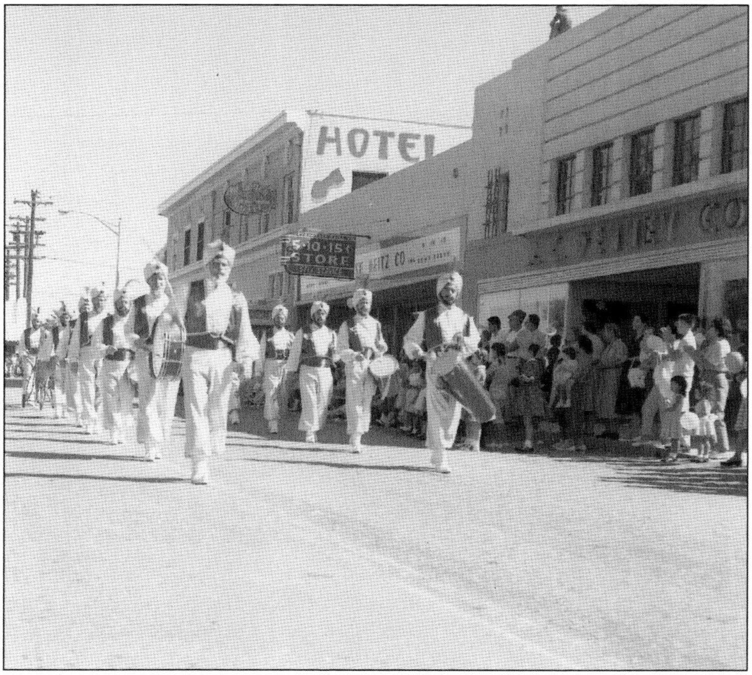

Shriners. The Shriners from Barstow participated on a regular basis in the Marathon Parade with their special marching band. The significance of the camels depicts a part of Shriner tradition representing their "Journey in the Sand." At right is another part of the Shriners called the "Mossafer Arabic Band." This order is a parade chapter and performs in parades around the country. (Courtesy of Judy Orzel Browder.)

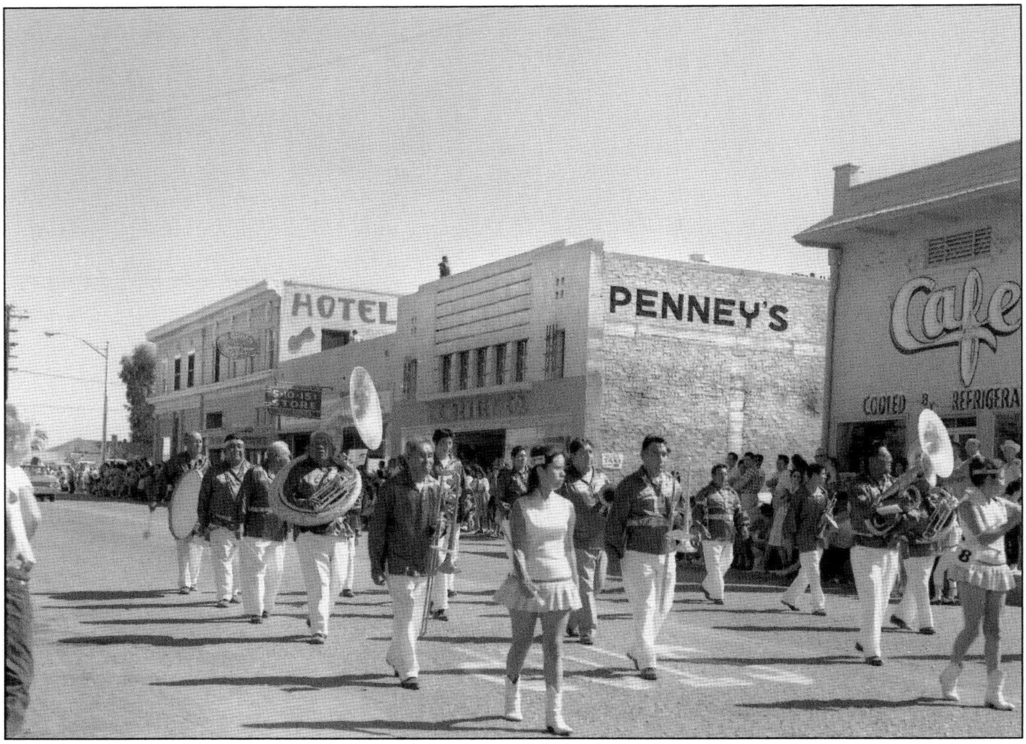

Fort Mohave Band and Twirlers. As crowds line the street, the background shows many businesses that are no longer there such as J. C. Penney's, the Monarch Hotel, and Jackson's Café. (Courtesy of Judy Orzel Browder.)

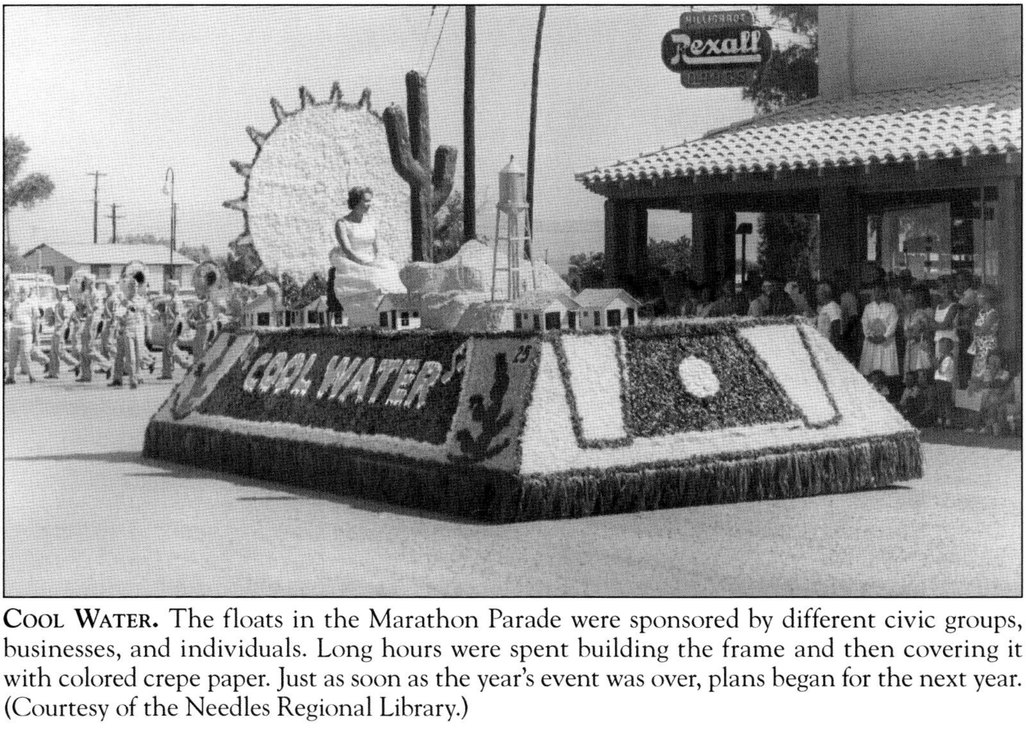

Cool Water. The floats in the Marathon Parade were sponsored by different civic groups, businesses, and individuals. Long hours were spent building the frame and then covering it with colored crepe paper. Just as soon as the year's event was over, plans began for the next year. (Courtesy of the Needles Regional Library.)

Seven

BUSINESSES

HISTORIC ROUTE 66

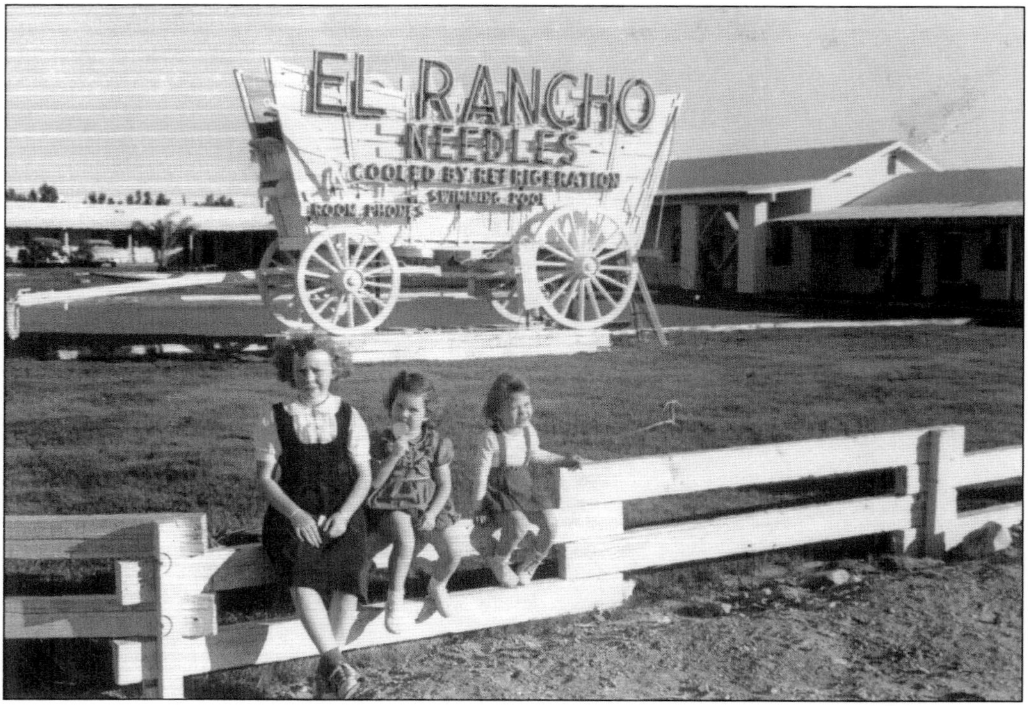

WELCOME. The famous "Welcome to Needles" wagon was originally displayed on the grounds of the El Rancho Motel. The El Rancho Motel was located on Route 66 and enjoyed a stream of travelers going to all points east and west. The motel is gone and the welcome wagon sits farther down the road; however, Route 66 remains alive and well. Seen here from left to right posing with the wagon are Judy Orzel, Nancy Opinsky, and Nancy Walters (Courtesy of Judy Orzel Browder and Dottie Orzel Hutcherson.)

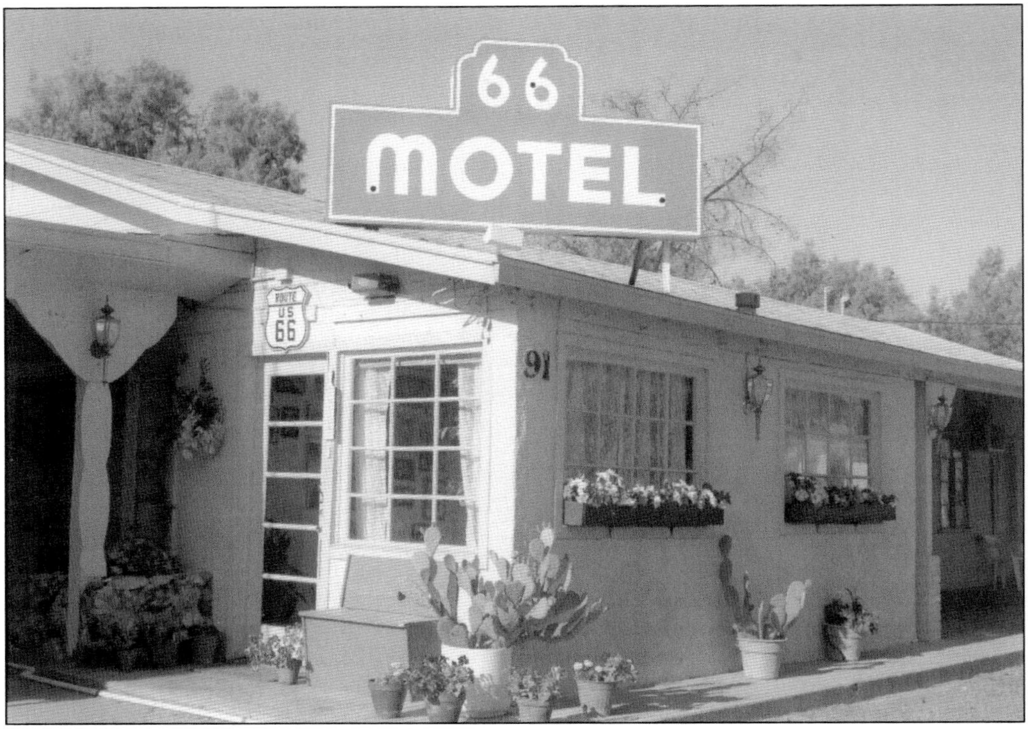

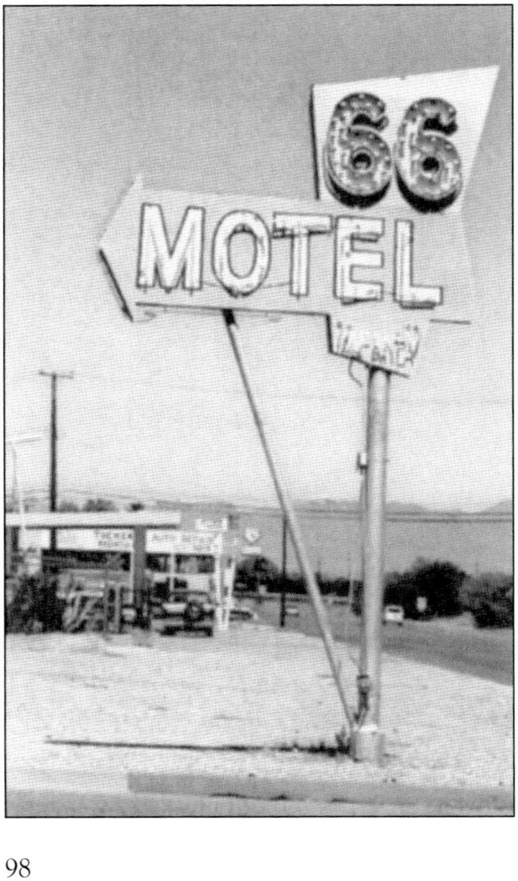

Motel 66. One of the best-known sites in Needles is Motel 66. The sign appears on many Route 66 Web sites and in a variety of publications. Dating back to the mid-1920s, this motel once stood next door to Carty Camp. The camp has come and gone, but Motel 66 is still home to regular guests. Some have been coming to visit for years. (Courtesy of Marjut Baakkanen.)

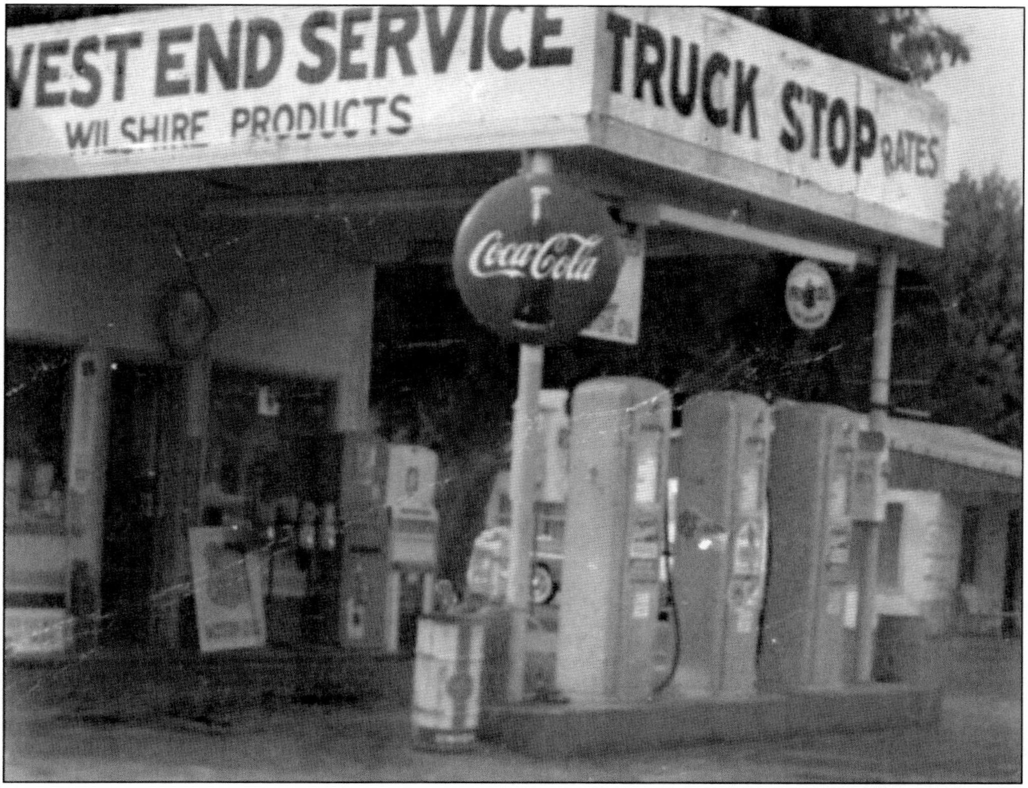

GAS AND LODGING. During the heyday of Route 66, it might cost motorists 27¢ a gallon to fill up their gas tanks. Station attendants would do the actual pumping; the driver and passengers sat and watched, or got out to stretch their legs, use the rest room, and maybe purchase a cold drink. Attendants would also clean the vehicle's windshield, check its oil and water, and ensure that its tires were properly inflated. The West End Truck Stop was one of many gas stations that prospered as tourists traveled from coast to coast by way of Needles. At right is a picture of the Desert Inn on Broadway Street (Route 66), owned by Winnie Schaffer in the 1950s. (Both photographs courtesy of Linda Bailey Starr.)

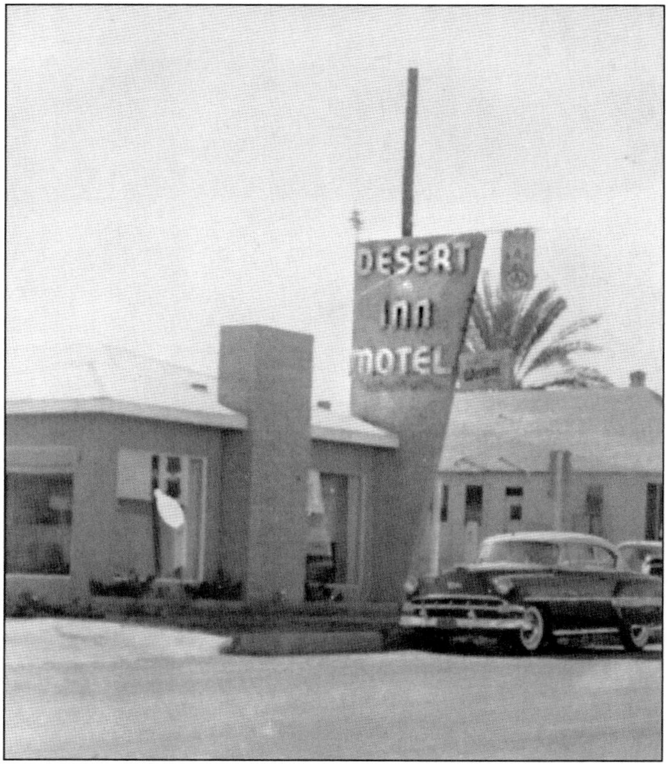

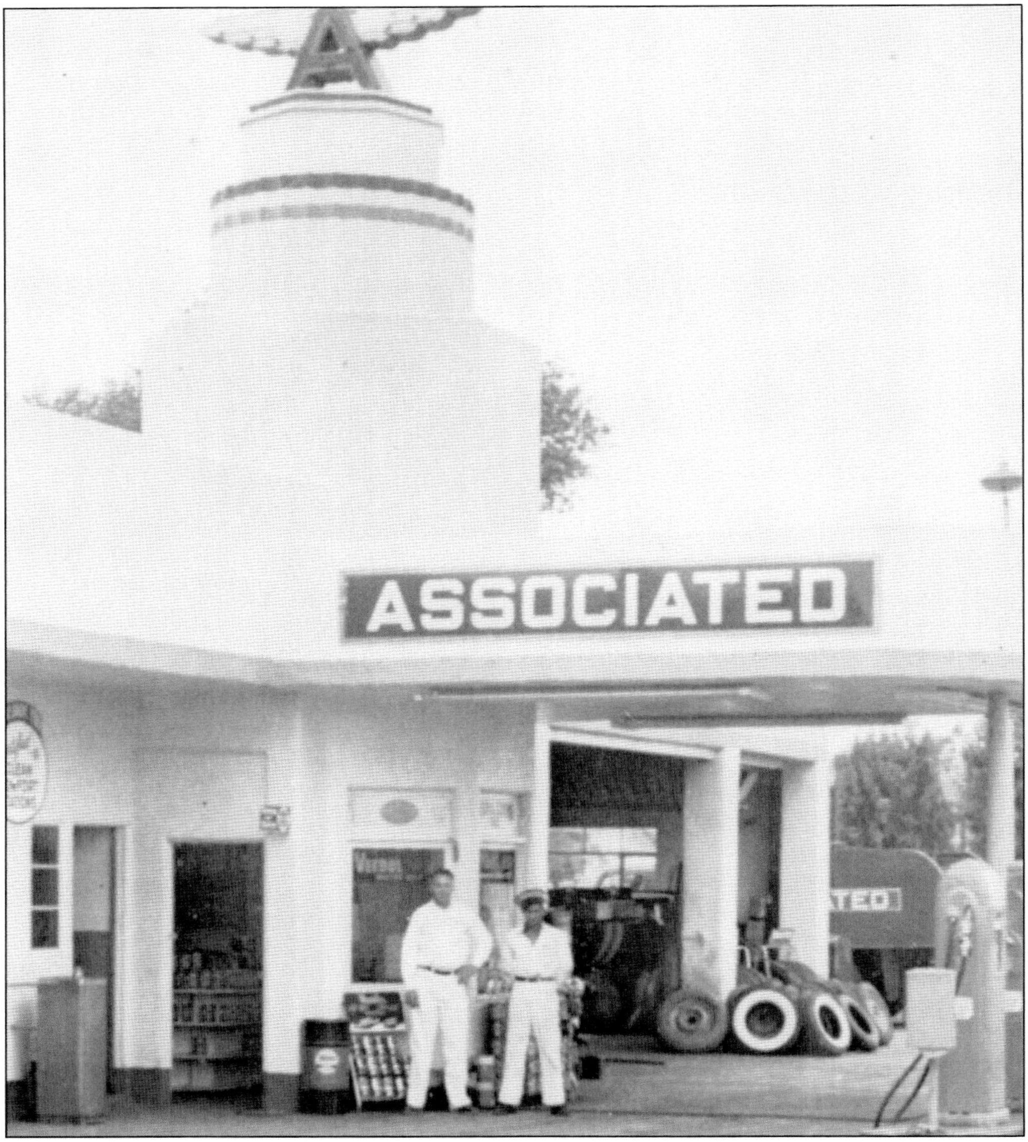

Flying A. Associated Oil was founded in 1901. In 1932, they named their premium gas "Flying A." The tall Flying A emblem could be seen on all of the company's service stations. The Needles Flying A, located on the end of town, provided gas, clean windshields, and a sympathetic nod as travelers talked about the summer heat. In 1966, Phillips Petroleum purchased the network and renamed the gas stations Phillips 66.

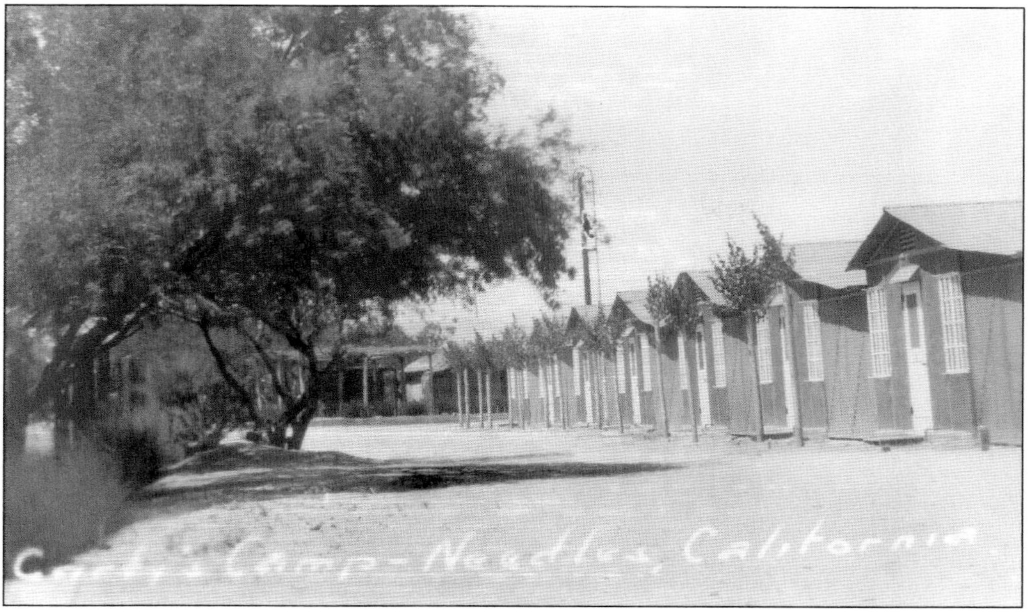

Carty Camp. R. Carty and Ernest Mansker built Carty Camp in 1925. They originally offered just 14 bungalows, but later added a service station and a store. The now-dilapidated bungalows and gas station still stand east of town on Route 66. The cast of *The Grapes of Wrath* famously stayed in the bungalows while shooting exteriors in Needles, but many thousands of lesser-known travelers also had memories of a stay in this historic landmark. (Courtesy of Marilyn Kirchner.)

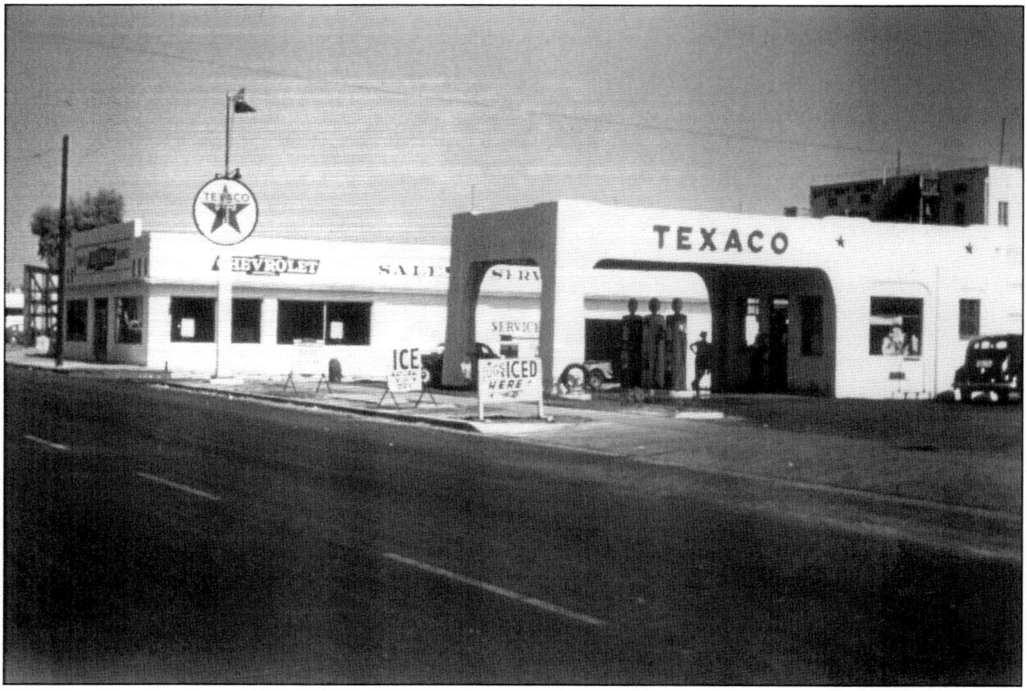

Texaco Gas Station. Russell and Jack Weart purchased this gas station in the late 1940s, one of the many that handled the busy Route 66 traffic through Needles. The brothers operated the station until the mid-1970s. (Courtesy of Rosemary Weart.)

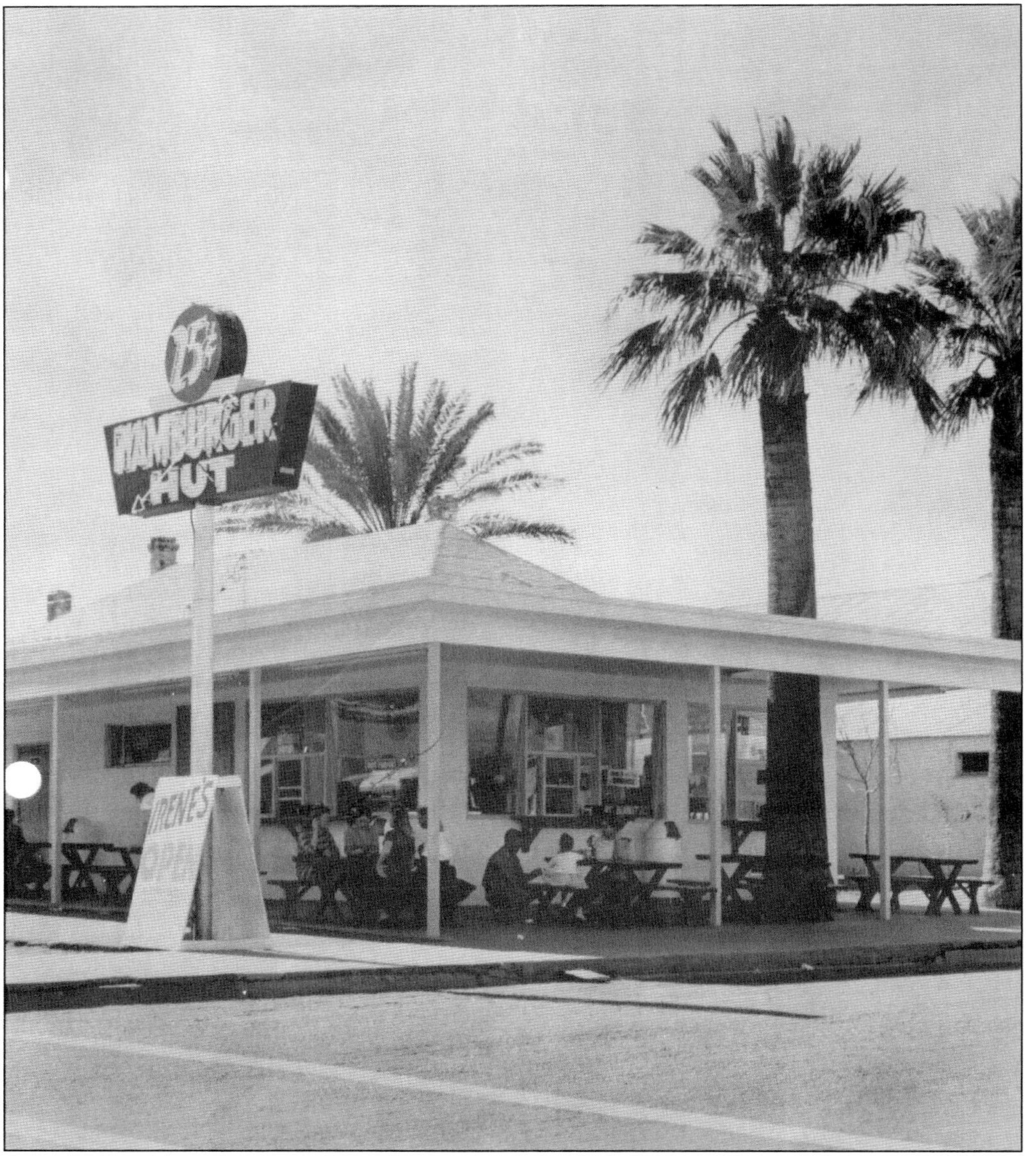

ANOTHER HANGOUT. Sitting along Route 66, this historic landmark was a favorite for the entire community. Just 25¢ purchased a great hamburger and a chance to get caught up on the Needles news. Irene's later became the Burger Hut and still operates today—much to the delight of Route 66 enthusiasts. (Courtesy of the Needles High School.)

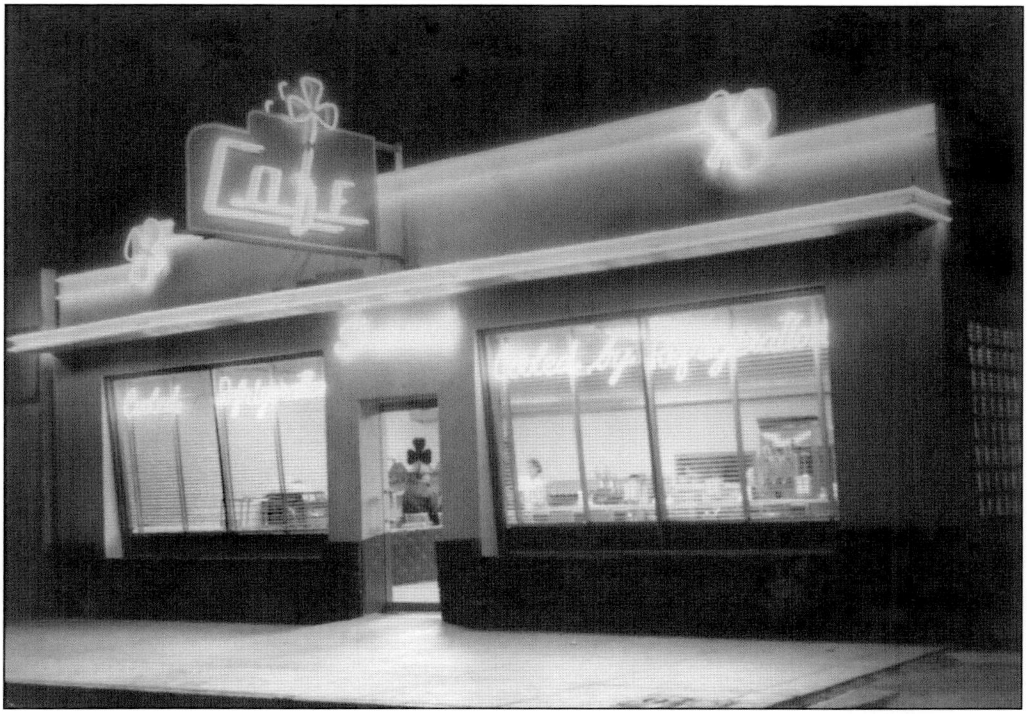

The Shamrock Café. Who else would own the Shamrock Café but the McConnells? This popular eatery opened in 1949 and served hundreds of travelers as they drove through Needles on Route 66. The neon signs were typical of businesses along the famous highway. Many residents started their day at the café before heading off to work, and the dinner crowd was a mix of tourists and locals. (Courtesy of the McConnell family.)

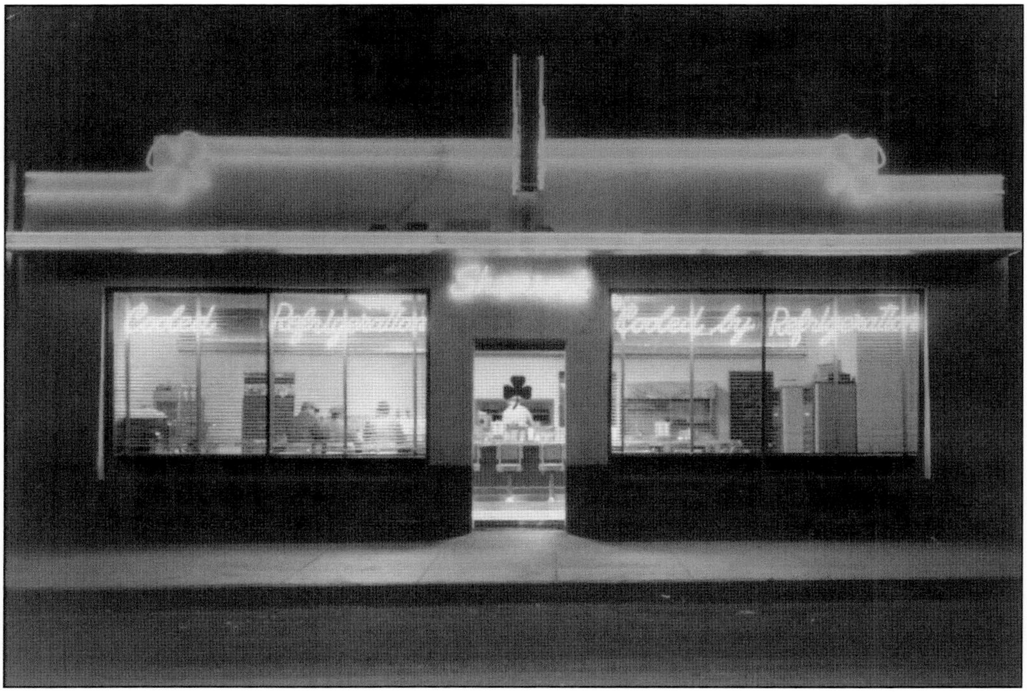

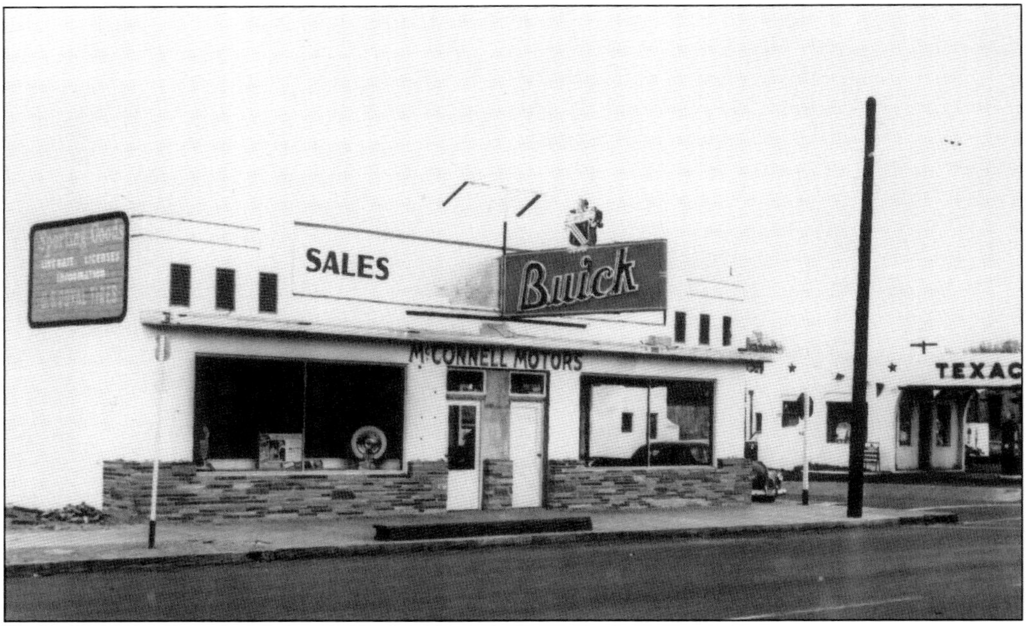

McConnell Buick. This business was another of the ones that lined Route 66. Built in the early 1950s, people came to Needles from surrounding communities to purchase a car or get it serviced. It later became a Chevrolet dealership, which serviced local residents for many years. (Courtesy of the McConnell family.)

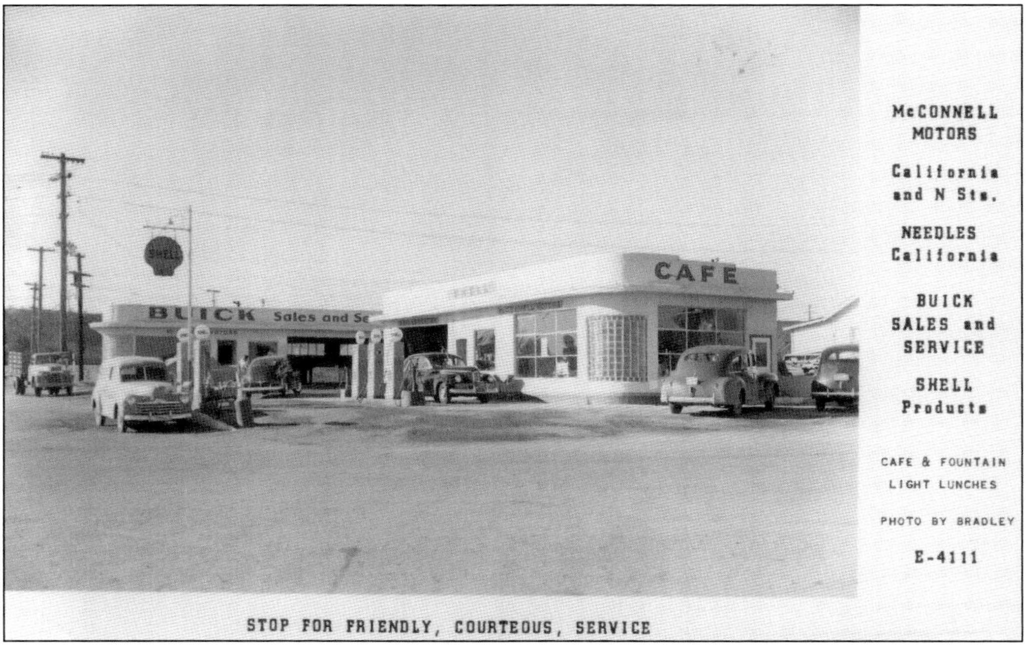

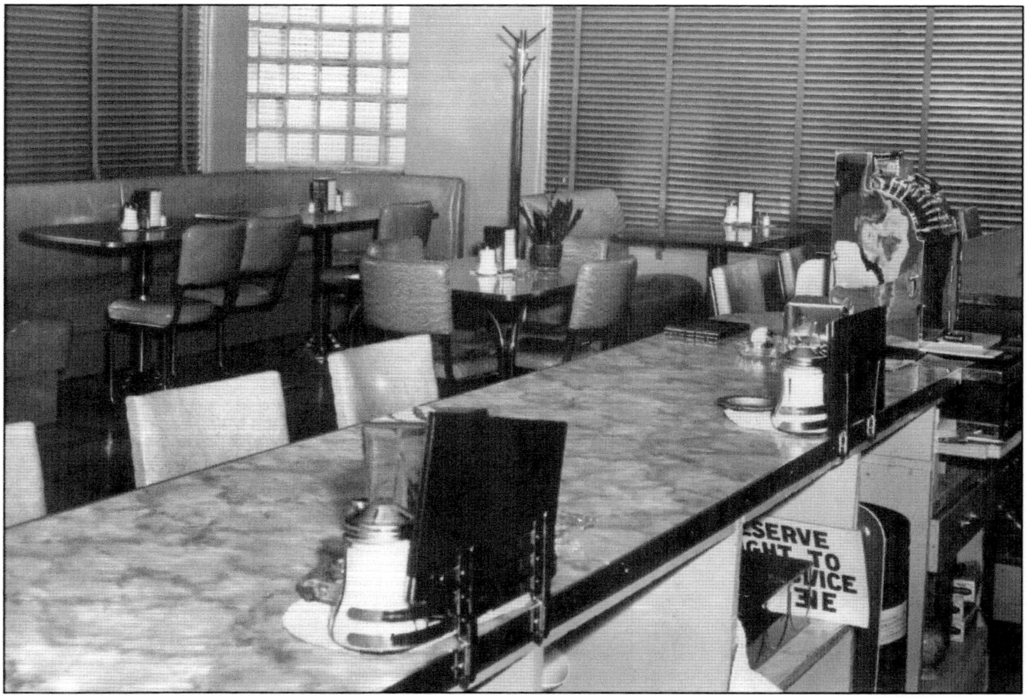

Inside the Café. McConnell Motors Café had the typical Formica countertops and vinyl upholstery one would expect to see in a 1940s diner. The café was later torn down and rebuilt on another section of Route 66. In the photograph below are the new restaurant and truck stop built in the early 1950s. The café featured a new lunch counter; hungry truckers found this a great place to gas up and grab something to eat. (Courtesy of the McConnell family.)

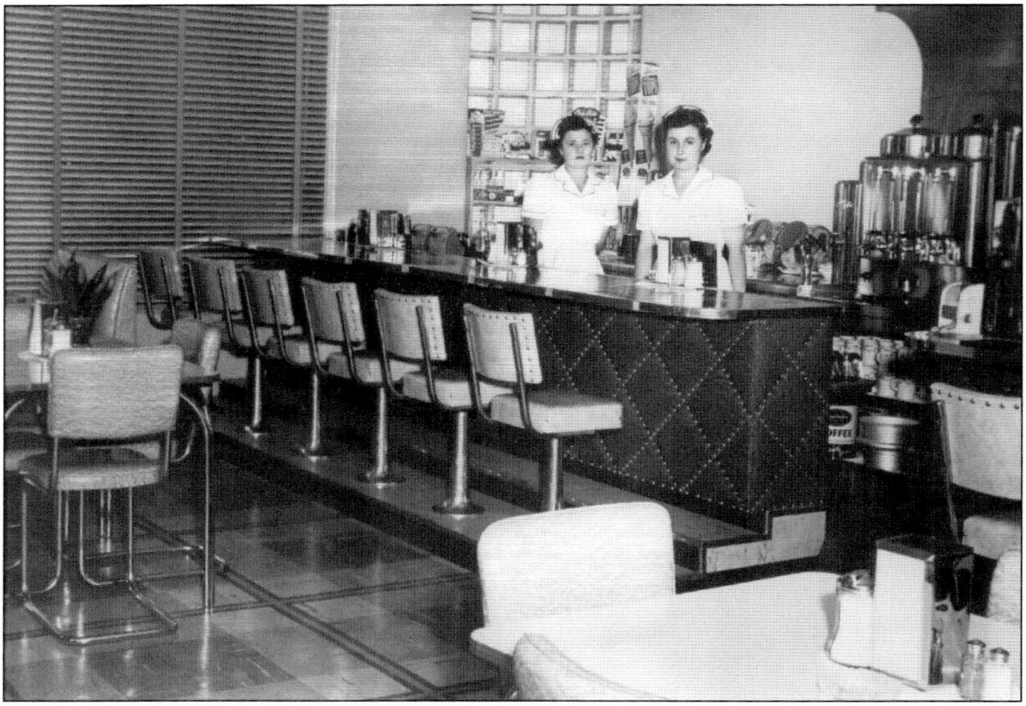

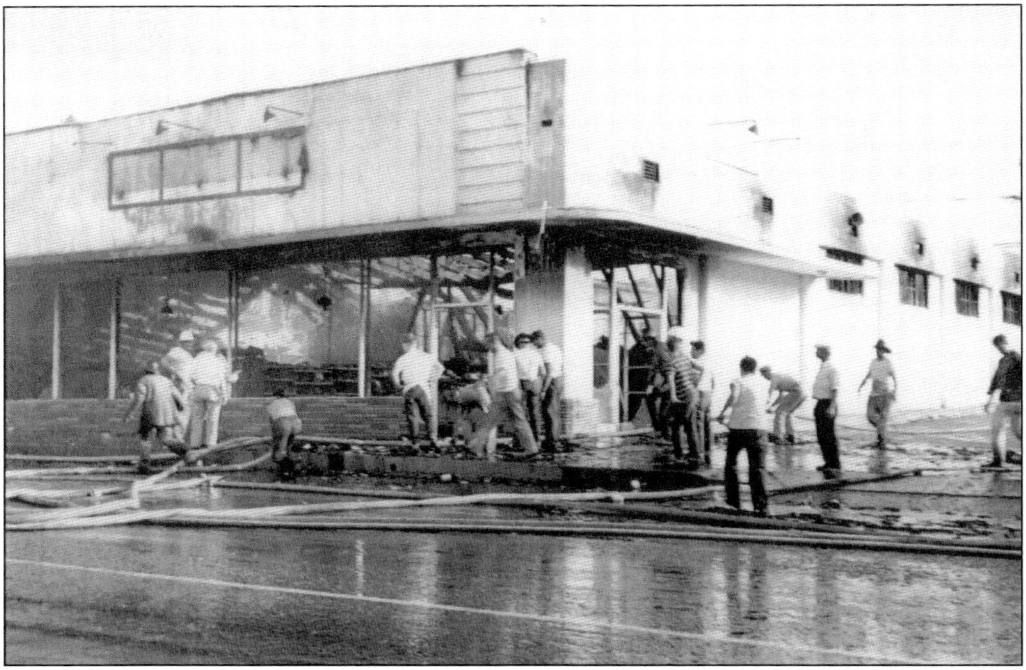

Sunshine Market. The Shaver family bought out their partners and in 1956 held a grand opening for the Sunshine Market, seen in the photograph above. The following year, however, the market suffered a devastating fire. Seen below are community members and firemen battling the blaze. Though fire damage caused it to close for several months, the Shavers' Sunshine Market reopened and went on to serve the community until the early 1980s. (Courtesy of the Murl Shaver family.)

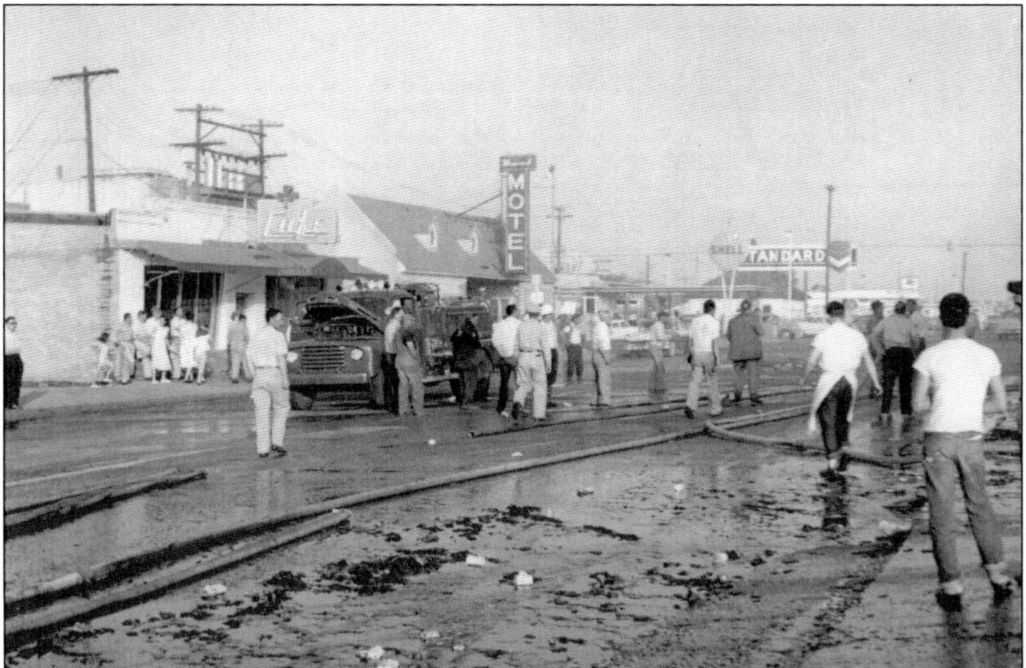

Eight

1950s School Days
End of an Era

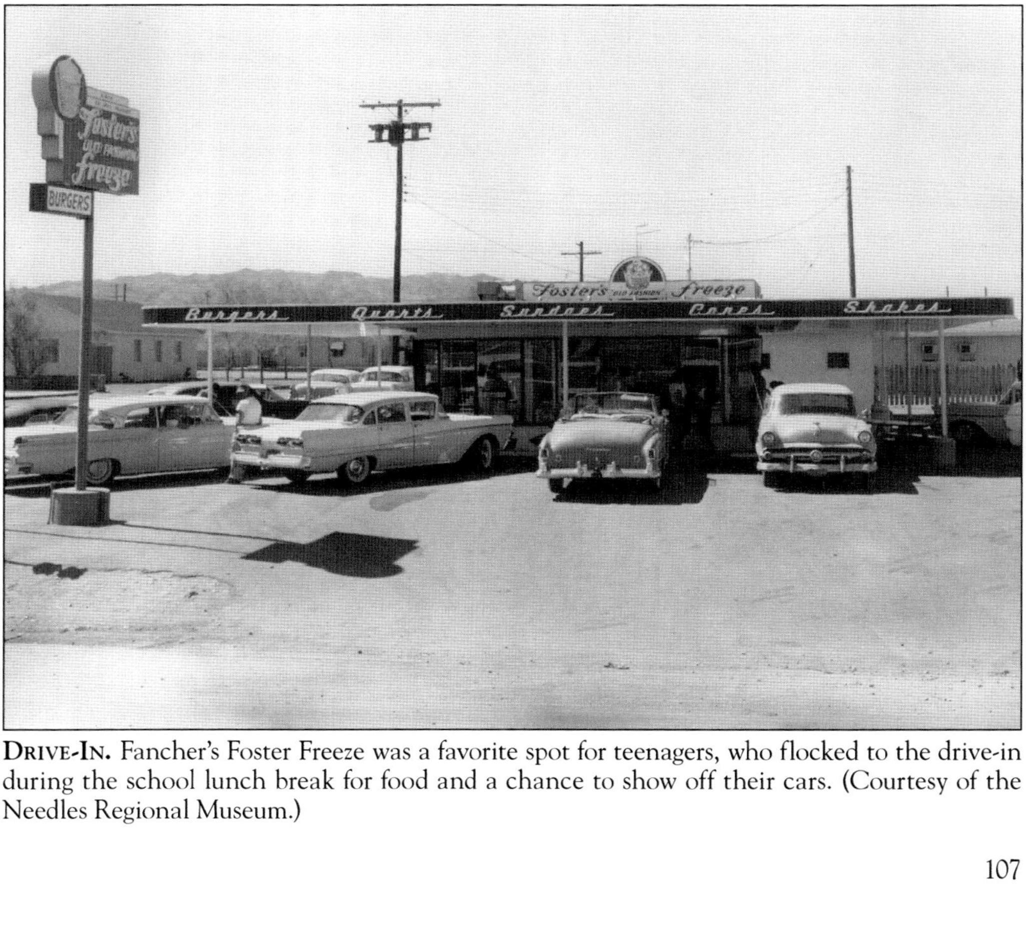

Drive-In. Fancher's Foster Freeze was a favorite spot for teenagers, who flocked to the drive-in during the school lunch break for food and a chance to show off their cars. (Courtesy of the Needles Regional Museum.)

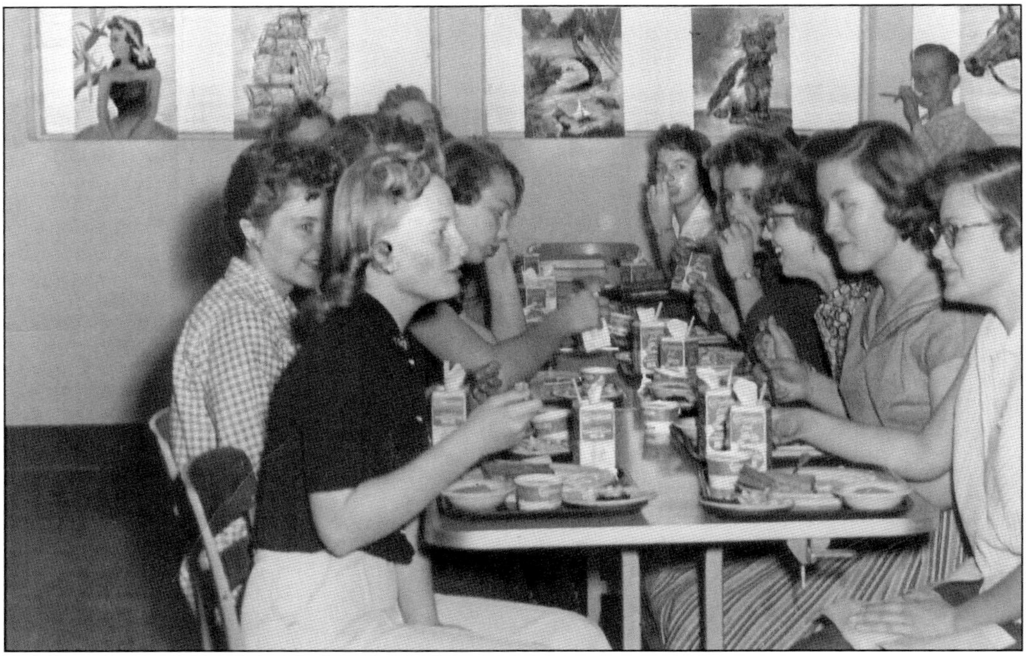

LUNCHTIME. The high school caféteria at lunch was not only a time for nourishment but also served as a place to get caught up on the latest news. The group at this table is posing for a photographer from the high school annual. Pictured in the forefront from left to right are Karen Moore, Wanda Driskell, Nancy Morris, and Anita Pickens. Below is the loyal caféteria staff that put up with the lunchroom antics. (Courtesy of Carolyn Brown Holman.)

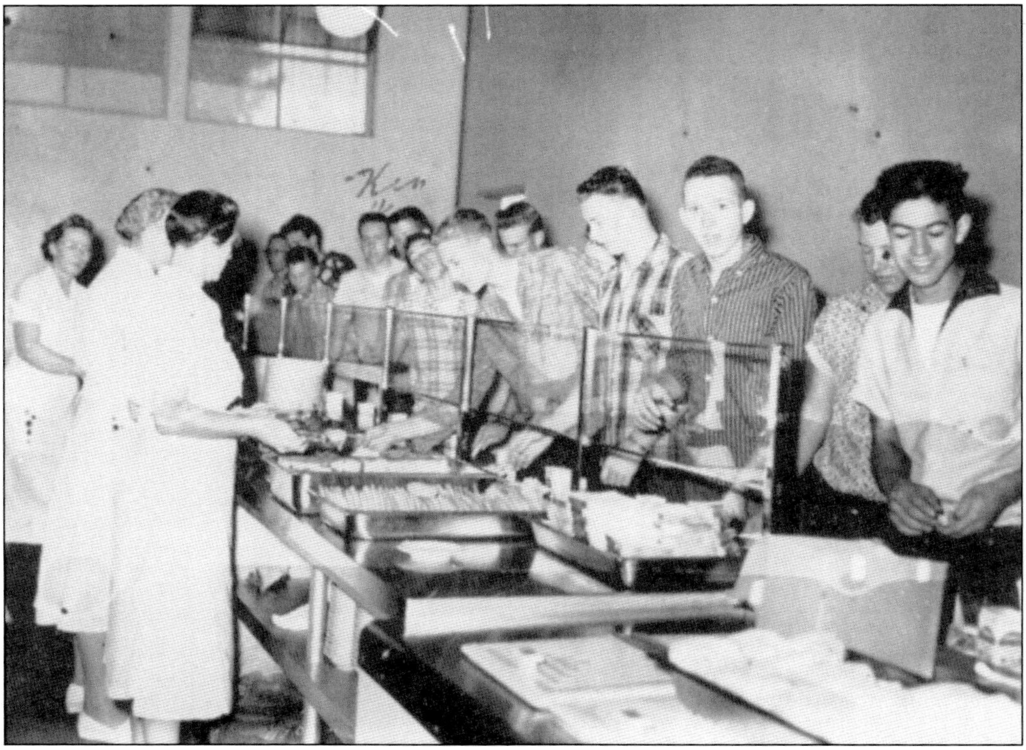

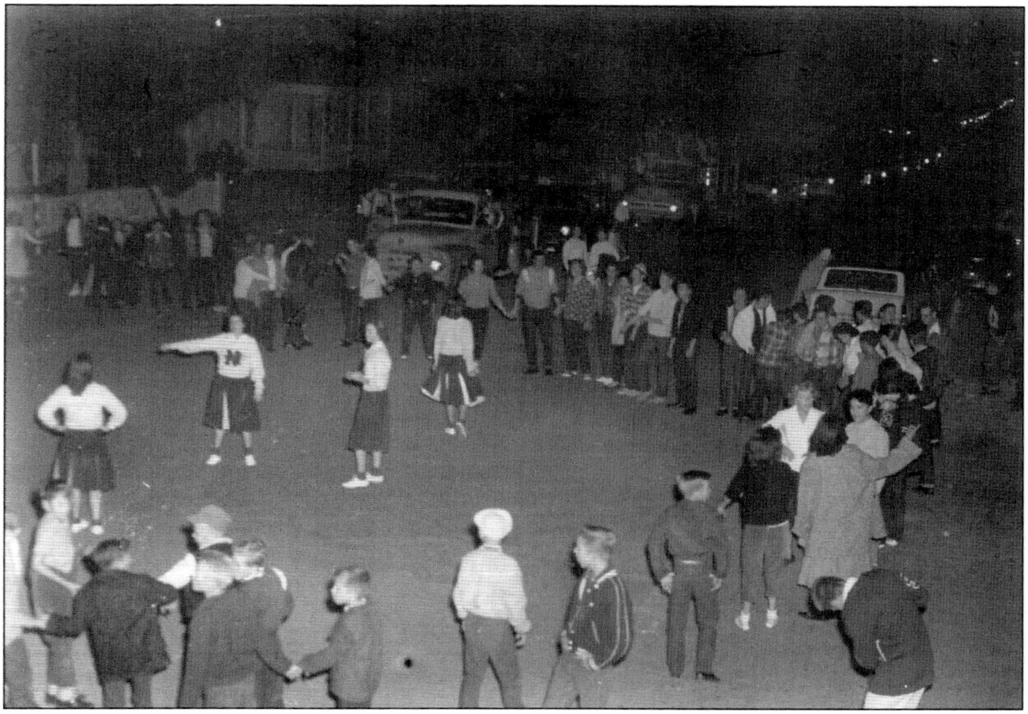

Snake Dance. Needles enjoyed all of the high school athletic events, turning out for home games as well as those out of area. As preparation for a football game, the song leaders, cheerleaders, and students gathered behind Claypool's and wound their way up Broadway Street towards the high school. This event was known as a "Snake Dance," and it culminated in a roaring bonfire. (Courtesy of Dona Schulz Wyzlic.)

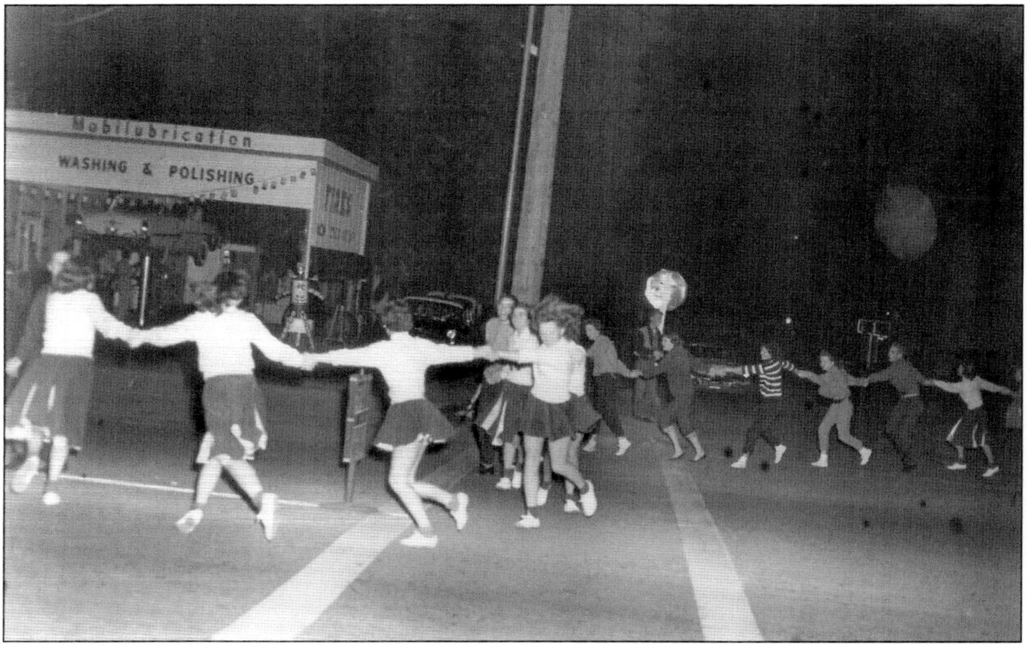

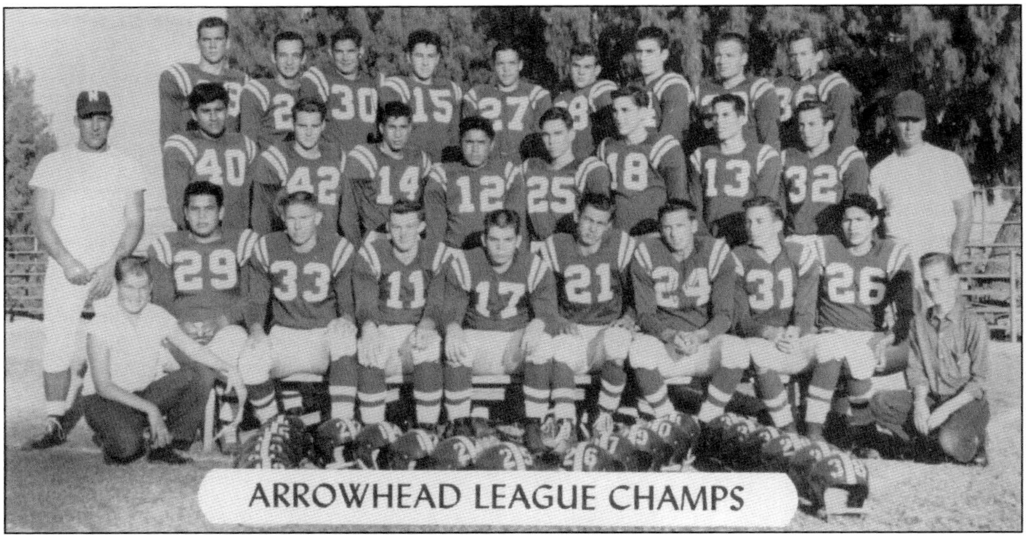

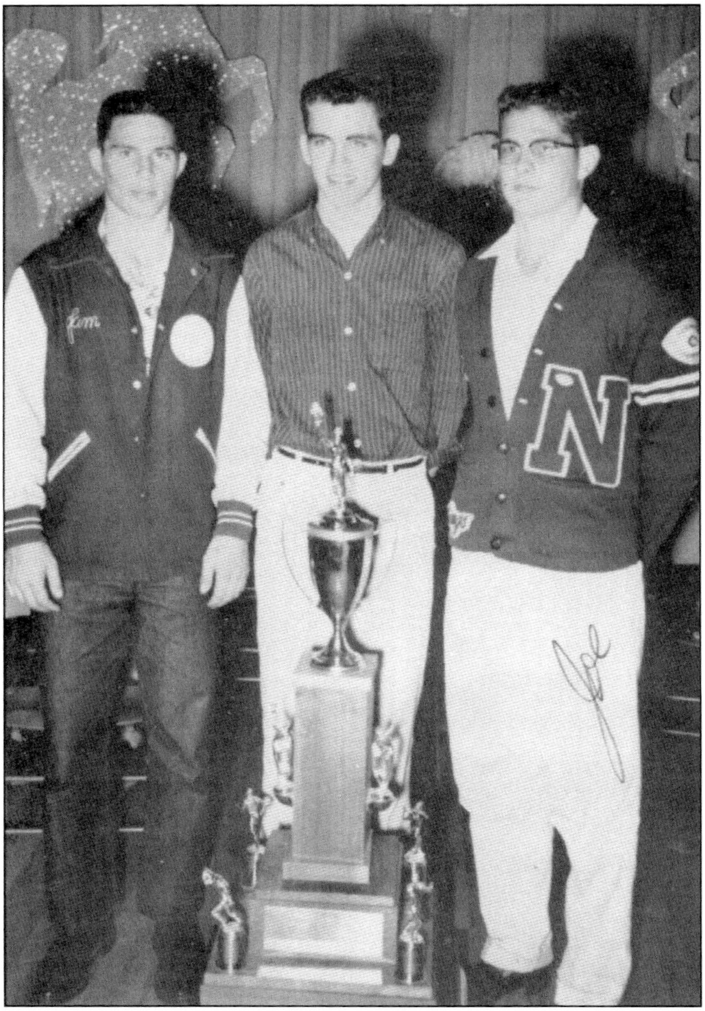

ARROWHEAD LEAGUE. The 1958 Needles Mustangs went 10-0 and were the Arrowhead League champions. Most of the team members were juniors, still looking forward to their senior year and what would be another great season. In the picture at left, shown from left to right are Jim Shephard, Danny King, and Joe Spaulding. Jim and Joe were voted Most Valuable Players of the Year, and Danny was chosen Sportsman of the Year. (Courtesy of Needles High School.)

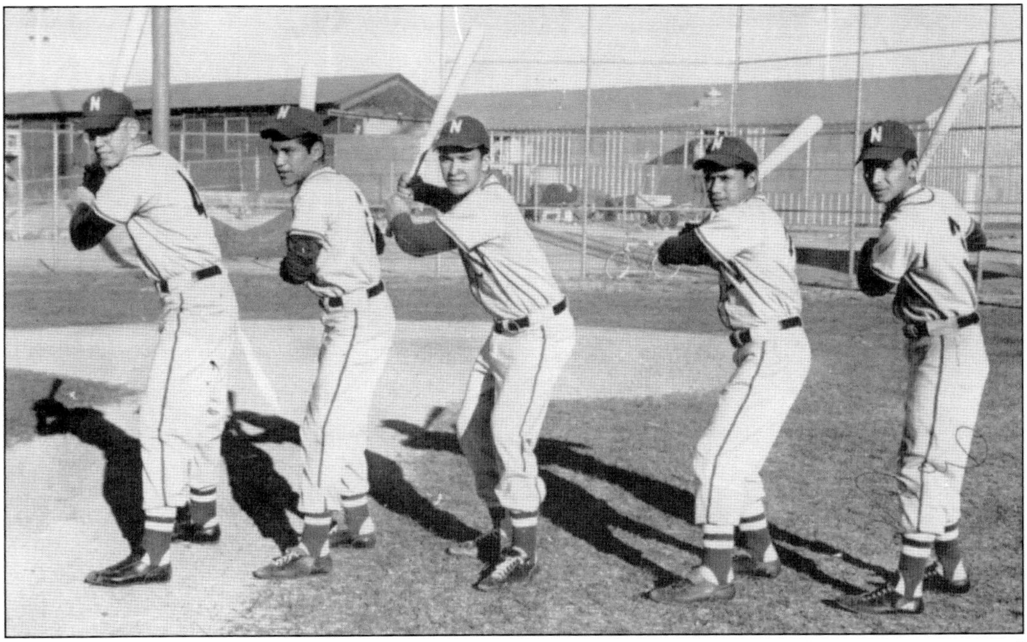

Batter Up. This picture was taken at the start of the 1958 baseball season. The Mustangs enjoyed wins in their first two games and went on to have an impressive finish. Each of the batters pictured sported an average of .300 or better. From left to right are Junior Willis, Joe Sanchez, Pete Mejia, Art Hernandez, and Raul Luna. (Courtesy of Needles High School.)

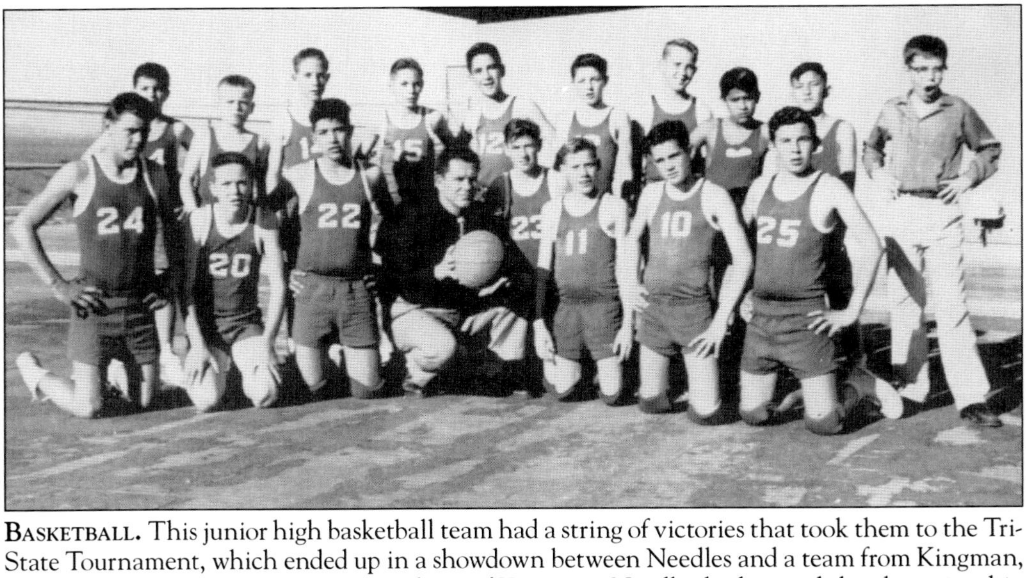

Basketball. This junior high basketball team had a string of victories that took them to the Tri-State Tournament, which ended up in a showdown between Needles and a team from Kingman, Arizona. The final score was 14-13 in favor of Kingman; Needles had missed the championship by one point. (Courtesy of Needles High School.)

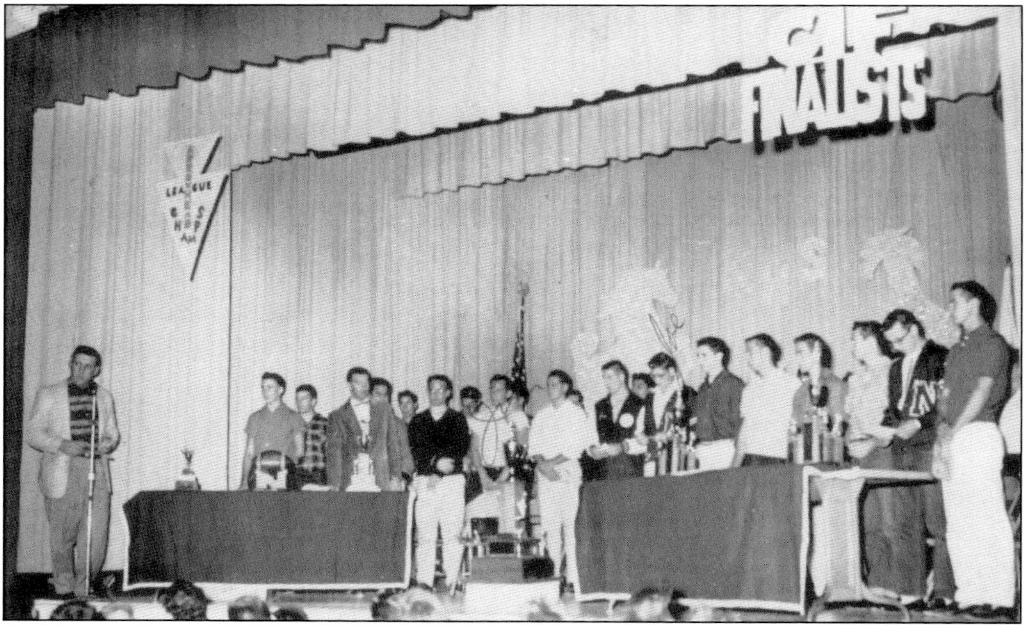

Football Team. In 1958, the Mustangs, under coach Jim Aitken, went all the way to win the Arrowhead championship. This put them in contention for the California Interscholastic Federation (CIF) championship for the second consecutive year. A win over Santa Clara took them into the CIF finals where they played Ramona. The win went to Ramona, 25-20. In this photograph, coach Aitken is conducting an awards ceremony for his CIF finalists. (Courtesy of Needles High School.)

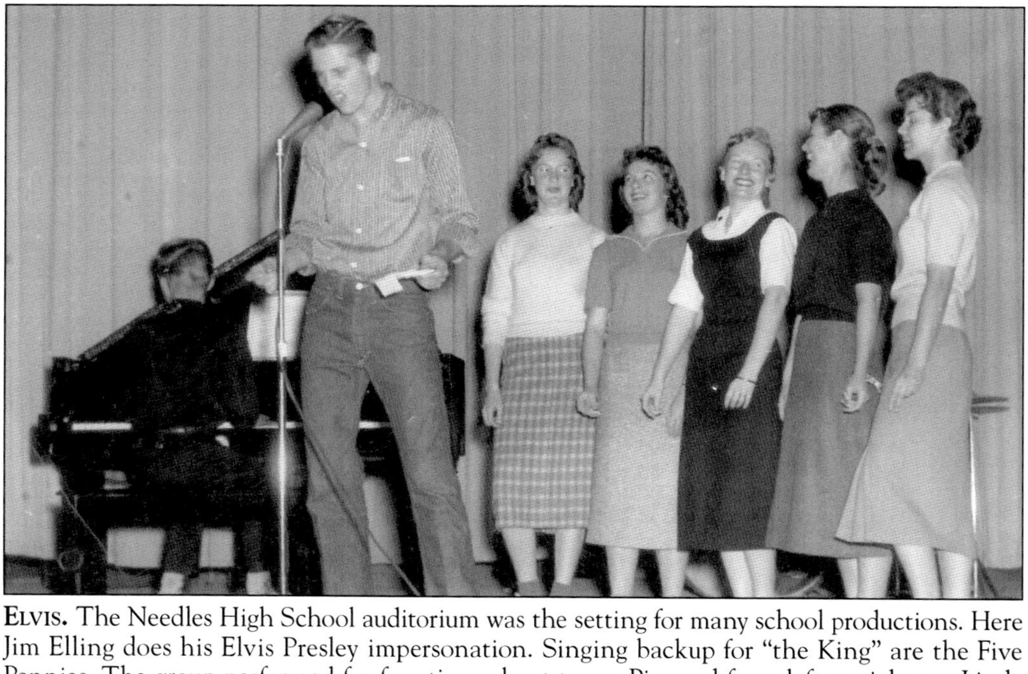

Elvis. The Needles High School auditorium was the setting for many school productions. Here Jim Elling does his Elvis Presley impersonation. Singing backup for "the King" are the Five Pennies. The group performed for functions about town. Pictured from left to right are Linda Kernaghan, Linda Fitzpatrick, Karen Moore, Nancy Morris, and Wanda Driscol. (Courtesy of Linda Kernaghan Wade.)

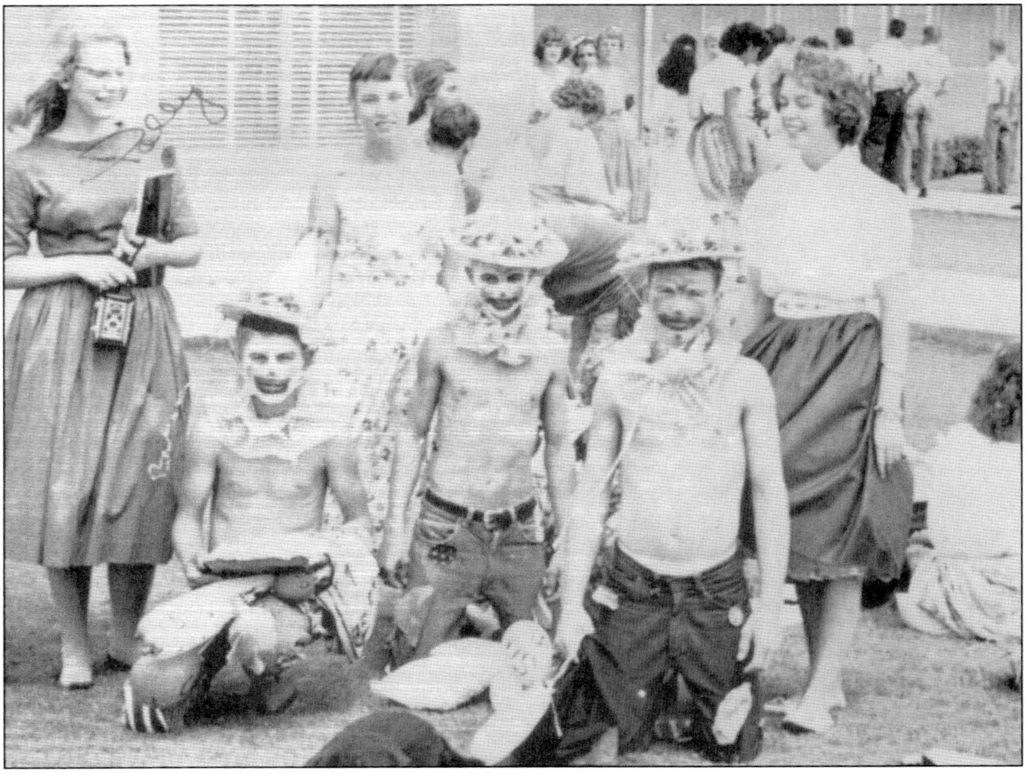

Slave Days. One of the activities at the start of high school each year was Slave Days. Seniors bid for freshmen, who were required to dress in strange attire. The "slaves" then carried the seniors' books and performed tasks for their "masters" throughout the rest of the school day. The money raised helped the seniors with expenses for their trip out of town on the Senior Sneak. (Courtesy of Linda Kernaghan Wade.)

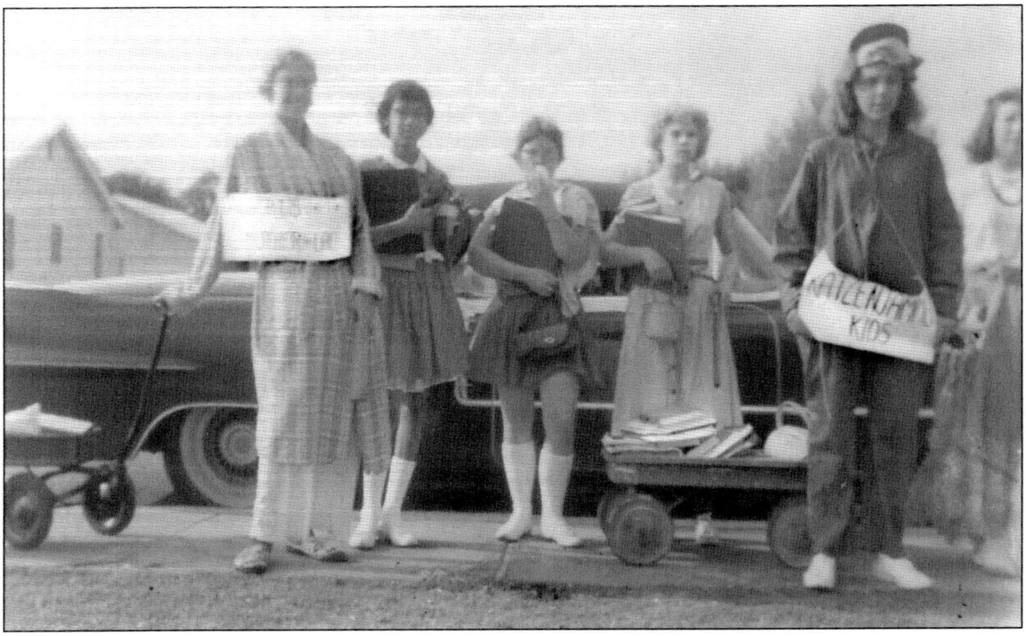

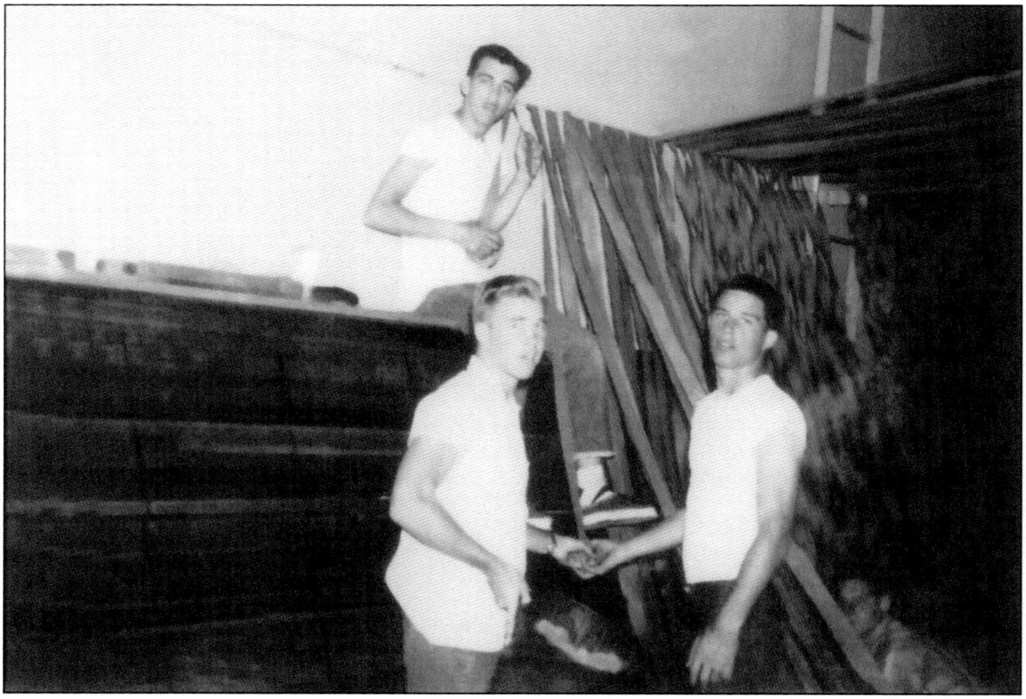

Junior-Senior Prom. Decorating for the 1959 Junior-Senior Prom are members of the Prom Committee, from left to right, Larry Pratt, Jim Shepherd, and in the rear, Danny King. The theme of the prom was "Dream." Below, teachers serving as sponsors for the prom and overseeing the preparation activities are, from left to right, Ernest Hadsell, Harold Rasplika, and coach Jim Aitken. (Courtesy of Carolyn Brown Holman.)

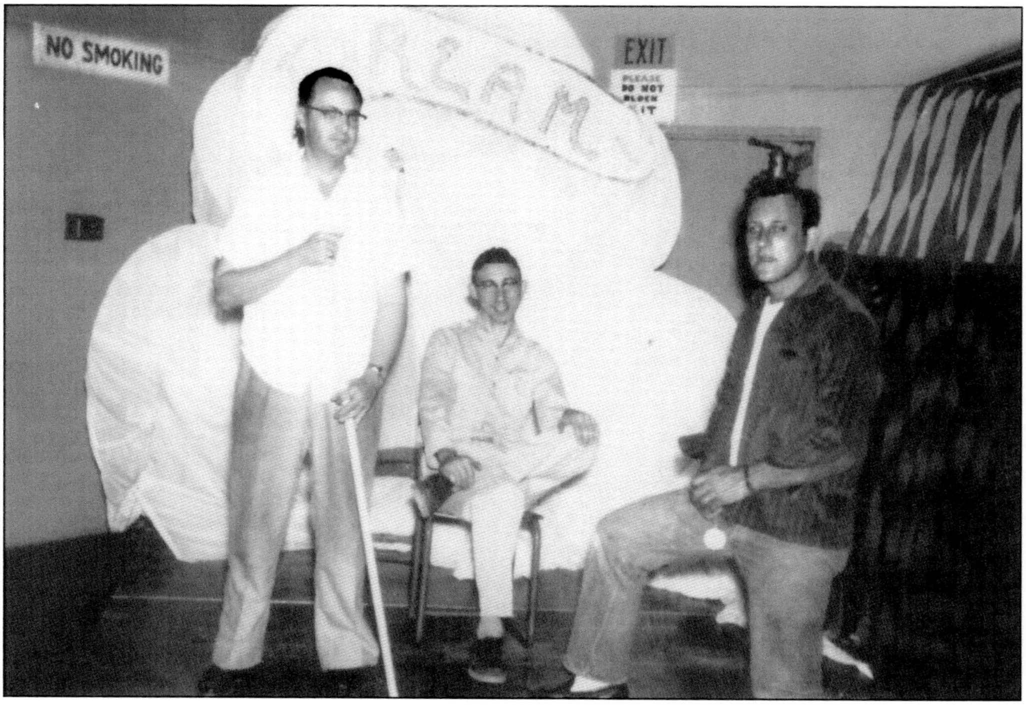

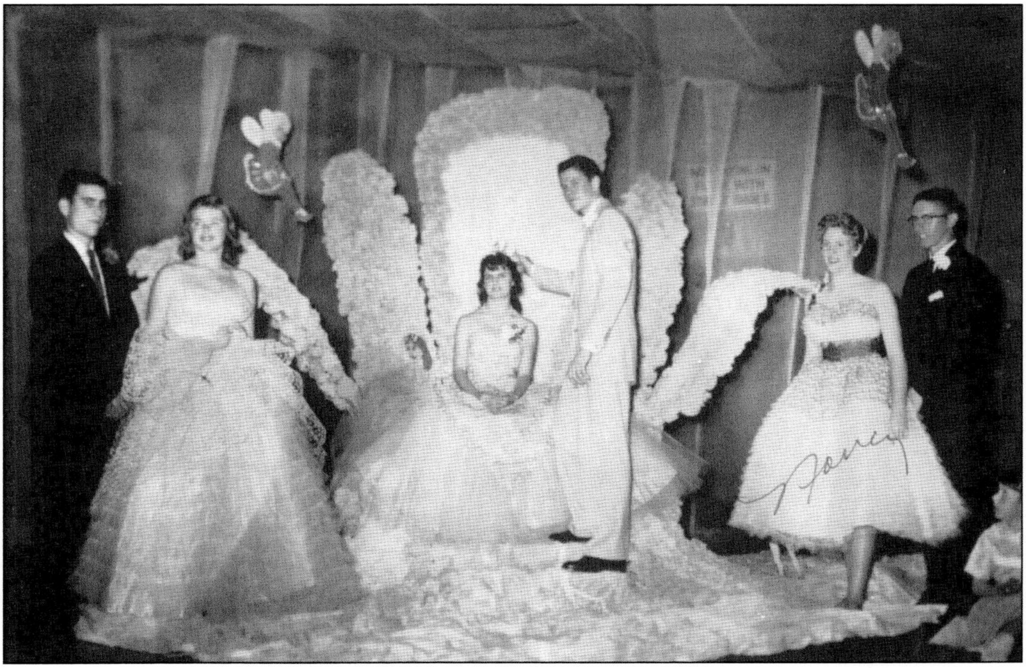

CORONATION. The traditional prom march takes place as the queen and her court are escorted by their dates for the evening. She is seated in a throne with fairies overhead, in keeping with the prom theme "Fairyland." In 1959, Janet Schwindt was crowned as the prom queen. Katy Reed and Nancy Poulson were crowned as princesses. (Courtesy of Needles High School.)

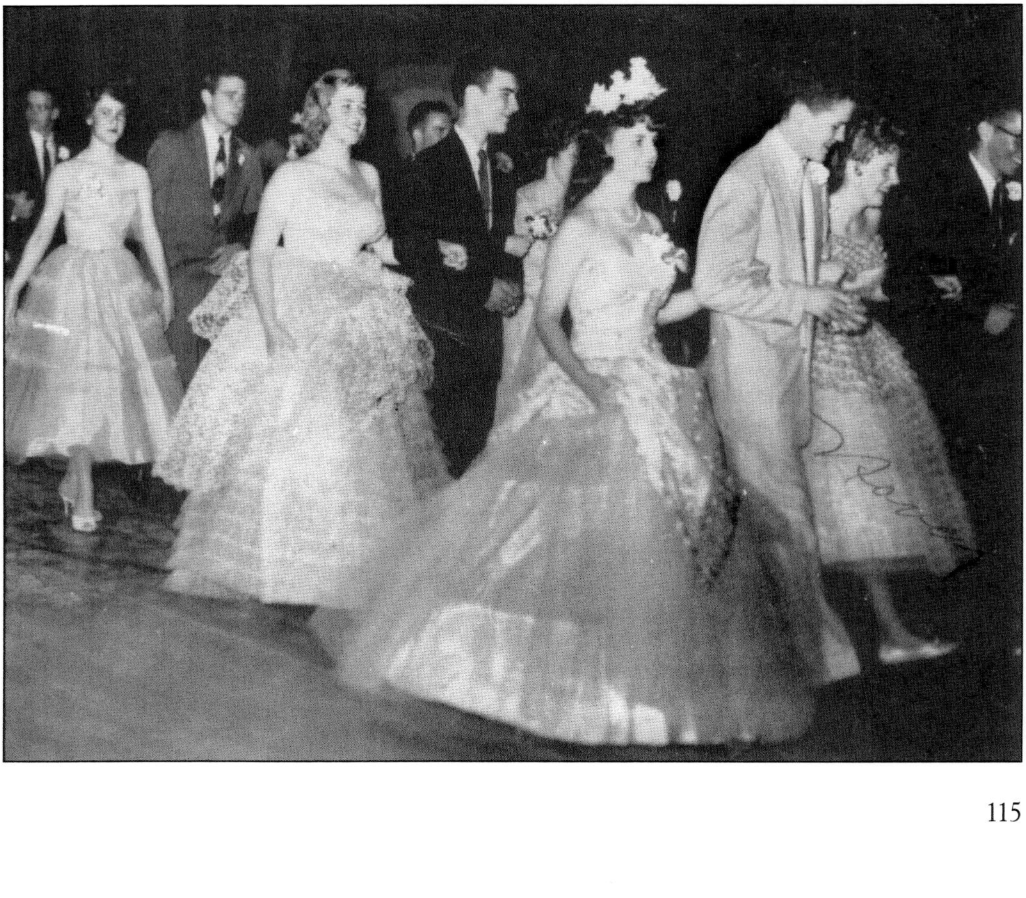

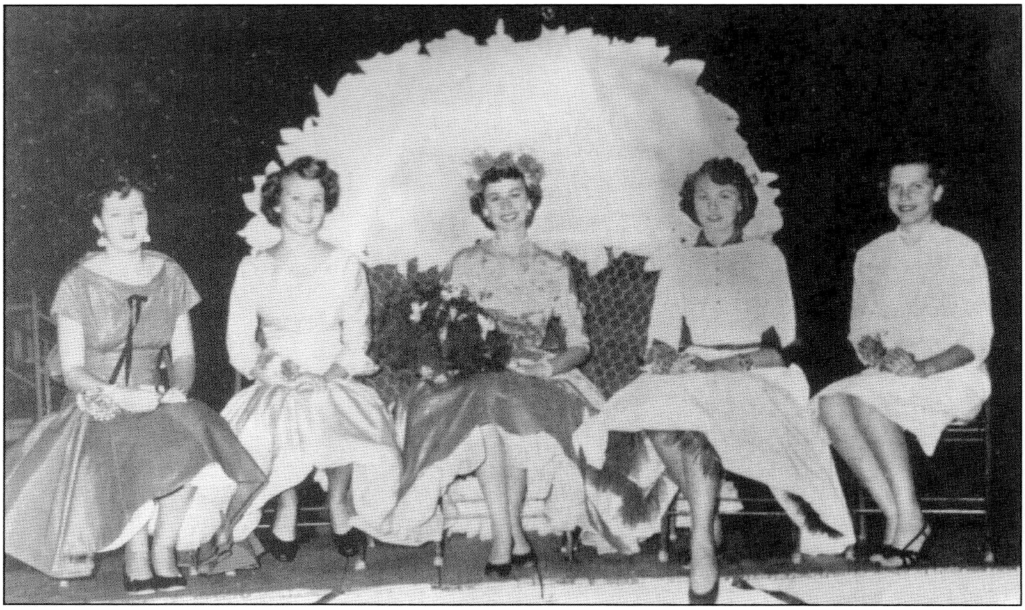

LOVELY WOMEN. The class of 1955 crowned the Homecoming Queen during the halftime celebration. Surrounded by her court are, from left to right, sophomore attendant, Linda Herring; freshman attendant, Ann Castle; homecoming queen, Colleen O'Conner; senior attendant, Gwen Advocate; and junior attendant, Linda Norris. (Courtesy of Needles High School.)

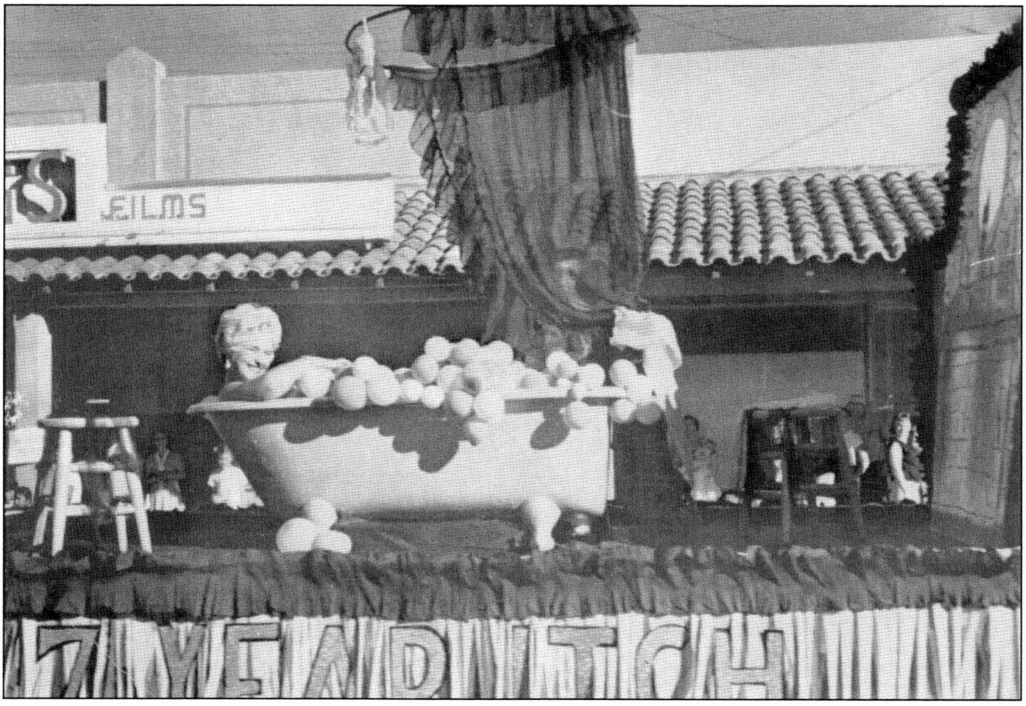

THE SEVEN YEAR ITCH. The theme for the 1955 Marathon Parade was "At the Movies." A favorite float in the parade was the Needles High School float. Blonde beauty Eileen Bailey lounges in a tub full of pink and white balloons as she portrays Marilyn Monroe in a scene from the movie *The Seven Year Itch.* (Courtesy of Eileen Bailey Driscol.)

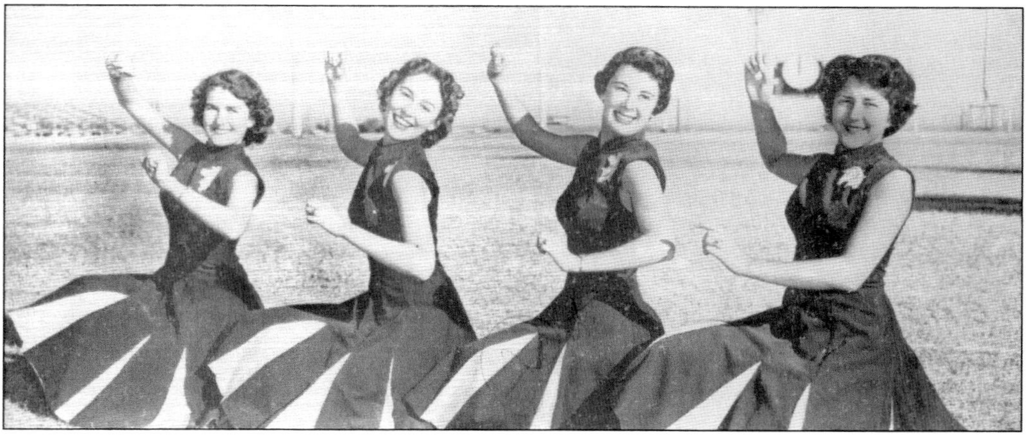

High School Spirit. Cheerleaders and twirlers were an important part of the school spirit through the years as the Needles Mustangs worked hard to get into the CIF playoffs in the 1954–1955 and 1958–1959 football season. Cheerleaders from left to right are Janet McMorris, head cheerleader Colleen O'Connor, Pat Lukin, and Gail Weaverling The 1959 twirlers in the picture below are head twirler Trisha Roark (left) and Barbara "Bobbie" Brooks (right). (Courtesy of Needles High School.)

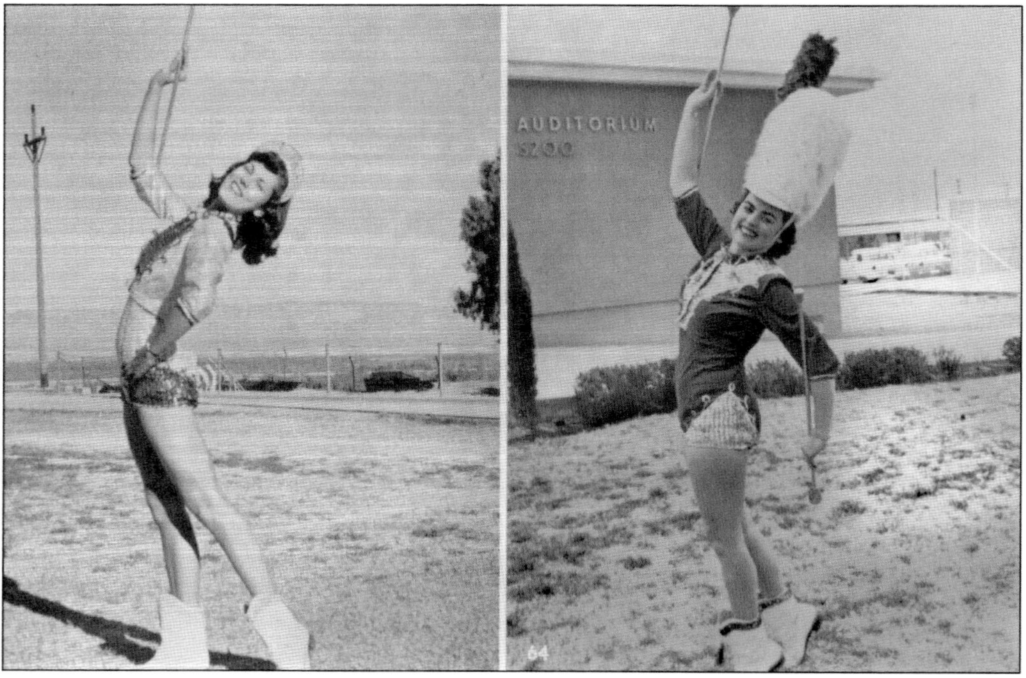

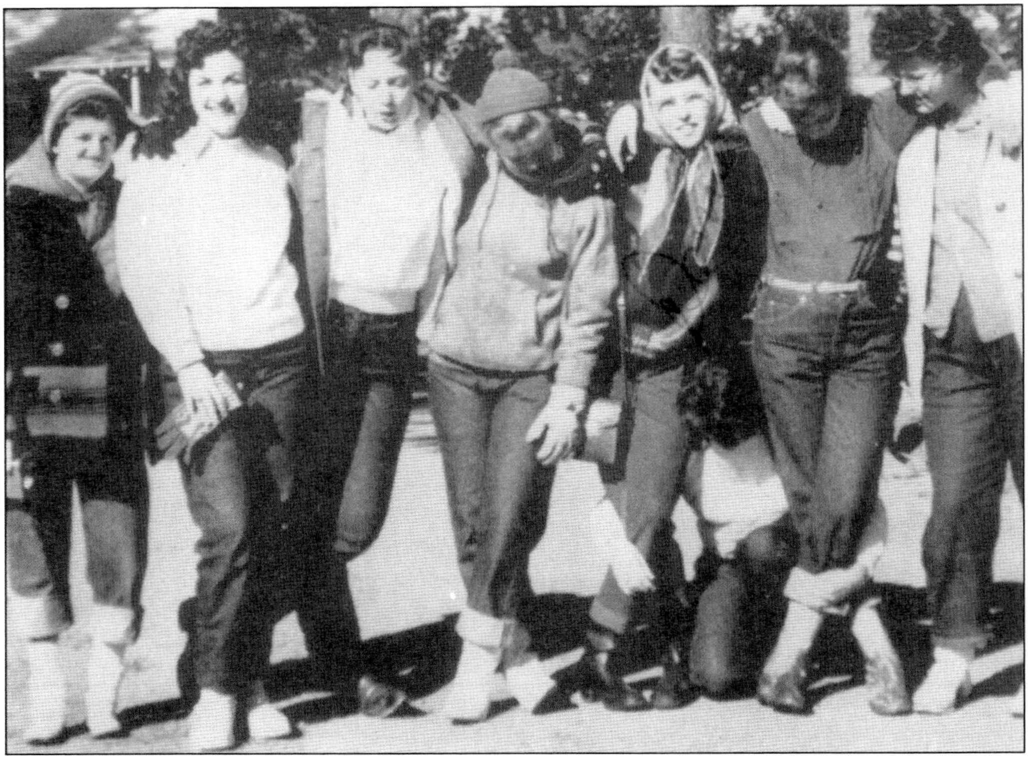

Senior Sneak. The senior class enjoyed a yearly tradition for all graduating seniors—Senior Sneak. The site for the 1959 Senior Sneak was Big Bear, California, where the class spent a weekend ice skating, skiing, and sledding. The group posed for pictures before boarding the bus home. Pictured above from left to right are Elaine Dunn, Patricia Barnes, Linda Stafford, unidentified, Donna Pearson, unidentified, and Myrna McKee. Pictured below from left to right are Rufino Hernandez, Jose Sanches, Sally Hernandez, Raul Luna, Rita Rameriz, Maria Proa, Pete Mejia, and Anna Marie Guerrero. (Courtesy of Needles High School.)

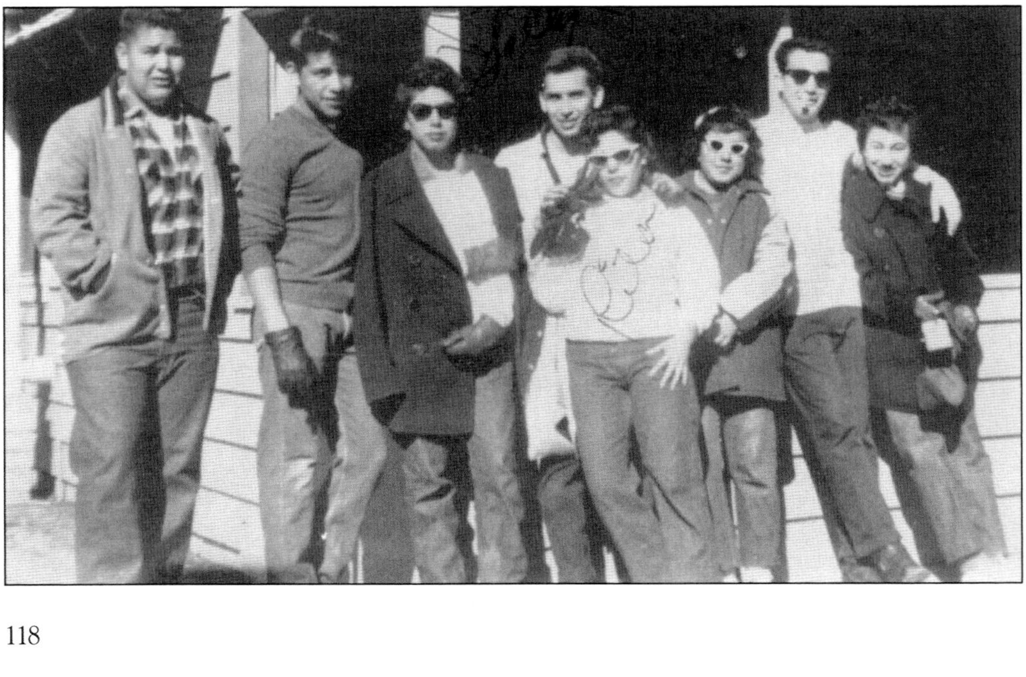

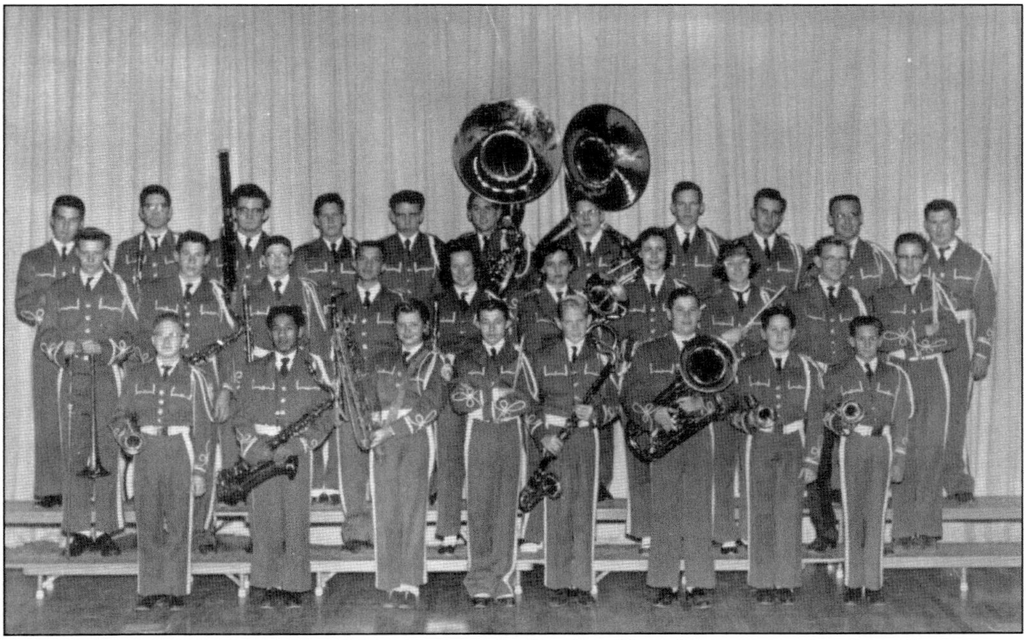

Senior High School Band. The 1958 senior high school band entertained with enthusiasm at all of the football games and traveled to the out of town games, driving the Mustangs on with their school spirit. They also participated in the yearly Marathon Parade and performed in other community functions. (Courtesy of Needles High School.)

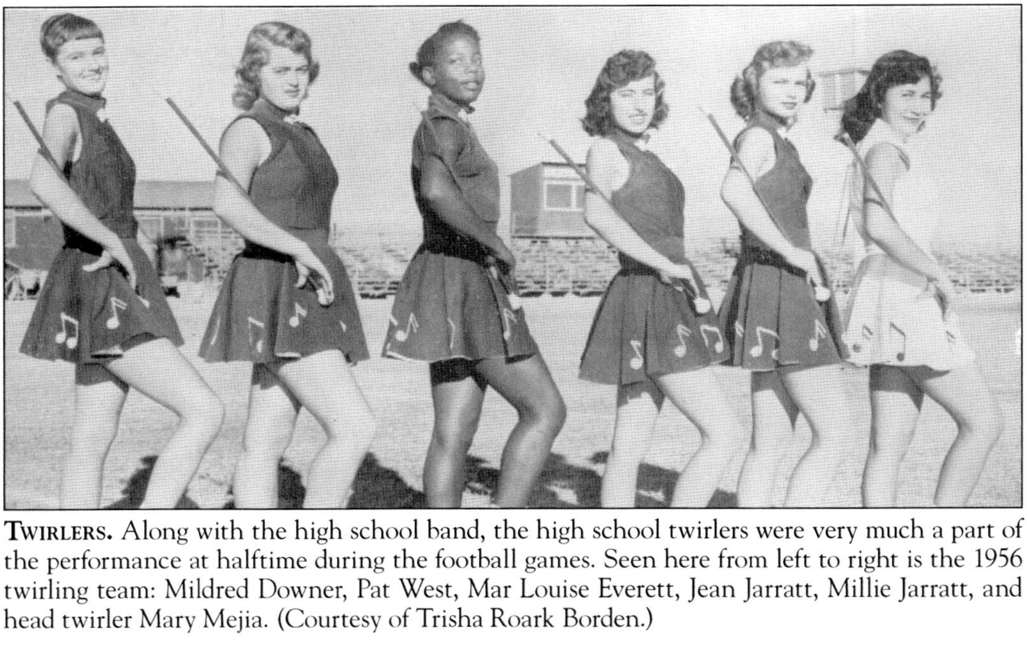

Twirlers. Along with the high school band, the high school twirlers were very much a part of the performance at halftime during the football games. Seen here from left to right is the 1956 twirling team: Mildred Downer, Pat West, Mar Louise Everett, Jean Jarratt, Millie Jarratt, and head twirler Mary Mejia. (Courtesy of Trisha Roark Borden.)

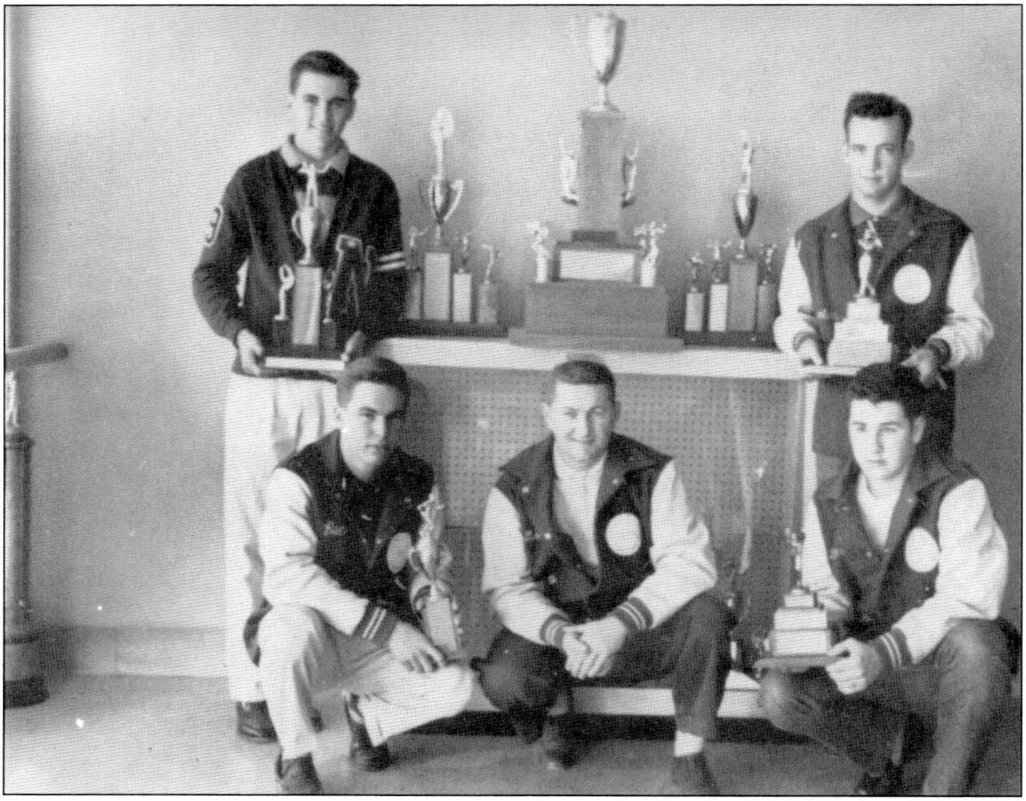

Lettermen. Pictured are new Needles High School varsity lettermen with coach Carothers (center). From left to right are Richard Parks, Carothers, Dennis Bender, Danny King, and Jerry Lyons. Each year the new members of the Lettermen's Club planned a spring trip for initiation. Several of the locations in years past were Big Bear and along the coast. (Courtesy of Needles High School.)

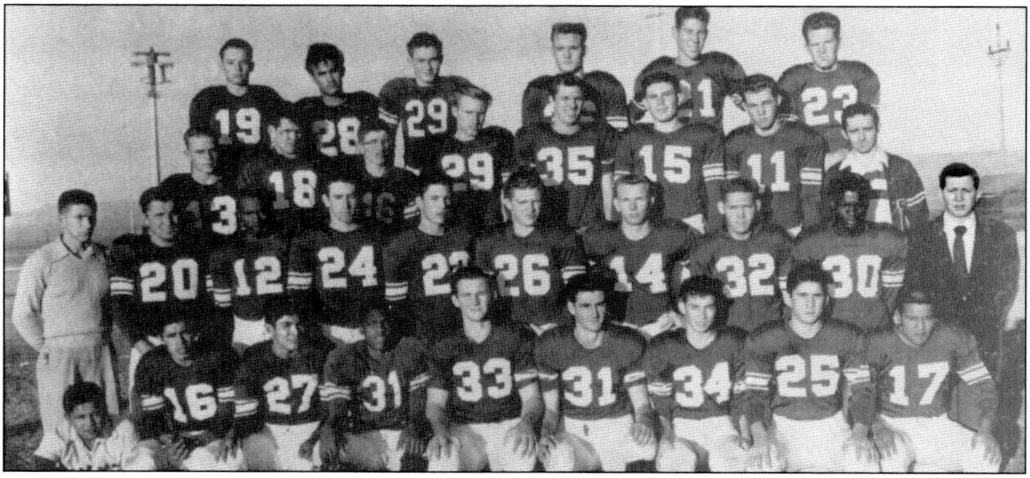

Varsity Football. The 1955 football team had six wins and three losses; in three games, their opponents did not even score. They beat Las Vegas 58-0, Blythe 13-0, and Desert 47-0. A fan favorite was Art Large, who carried the ball to the end zone time and again. (Courtesy of Needles High School.)

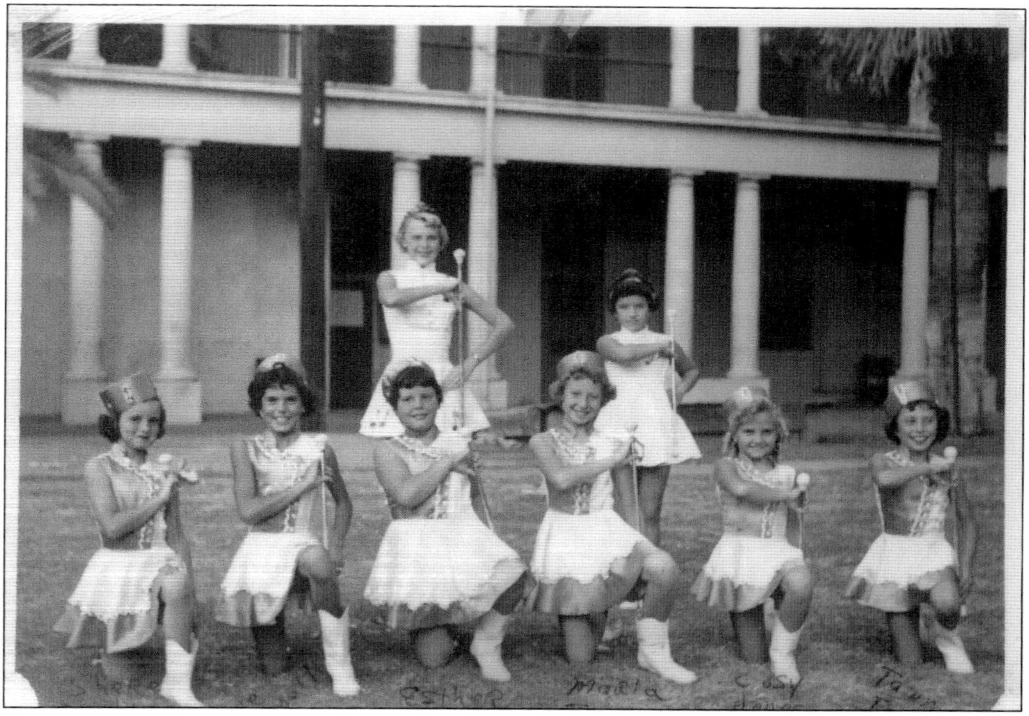

Twirlers and Cheerleaders. Pictured in front of the El Garces Harvey House as they practice for halftime at the football game are, from left to right, (kneeling) Sheri Dudley, Trisha Burt, Esther McConnell, Marie Tasker, Cosette Jones, and Jaye Burt; (standing) head baton twirler Bonnie McConnell and Tawn Temple. Below, 1958 cheerleaders pose in front of Needles High School for a picture for the high school annual. Pictured from left to right are Linda Daniel, Linda Fitzpatrick, Wilma Davis, and Linda Kernaghan. They were often referred to in private as the "Cheering Irish." (Courtesy of Trisha Roark Bowden and Linda Daniel Andrews.)

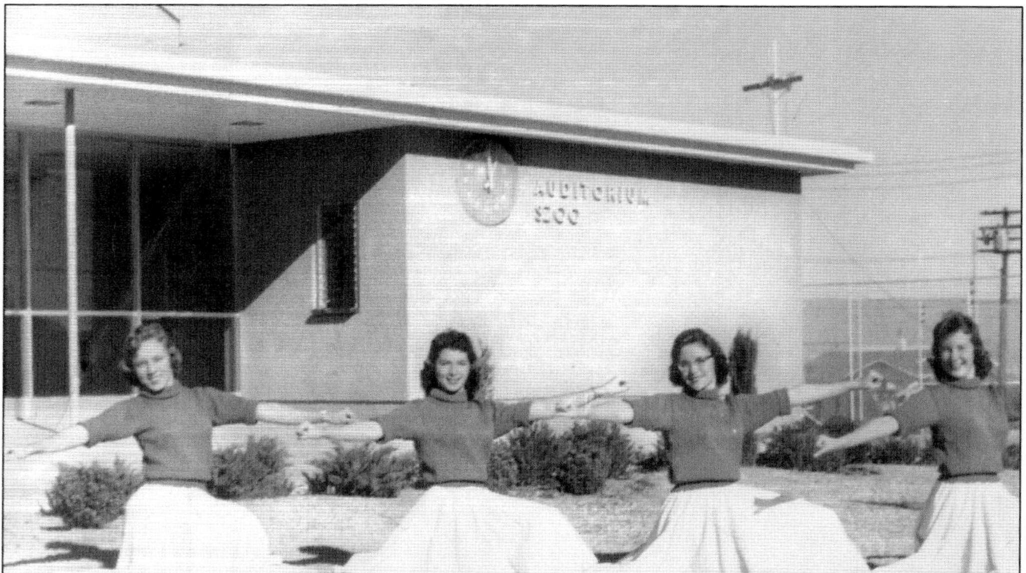

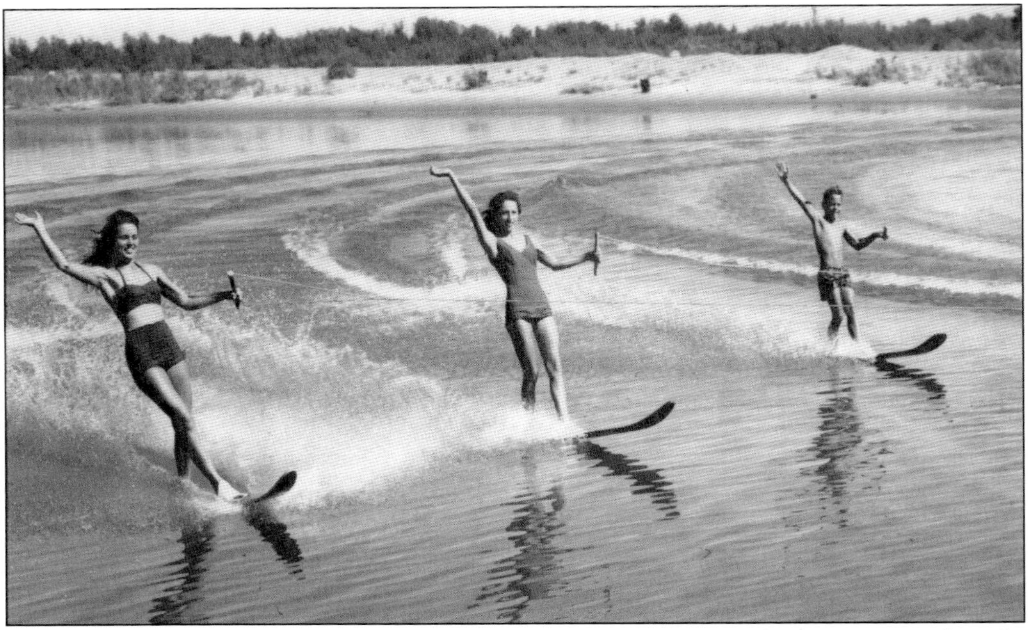

Water Skiing. Needles sits on the banks of the Colorado River, and it was a great place for summer activities. The beaches along the river were full of families and teenagers enjoying a relaxing weekend. Water skiing was an activity that was part of growing up in Needles. Skiing on one ski are, from left to right, Trisha Roark, Jaye Roark, and Chuck Roark. Below is Trisha Roark. (Courtesy of Trisha Roark Broden.)

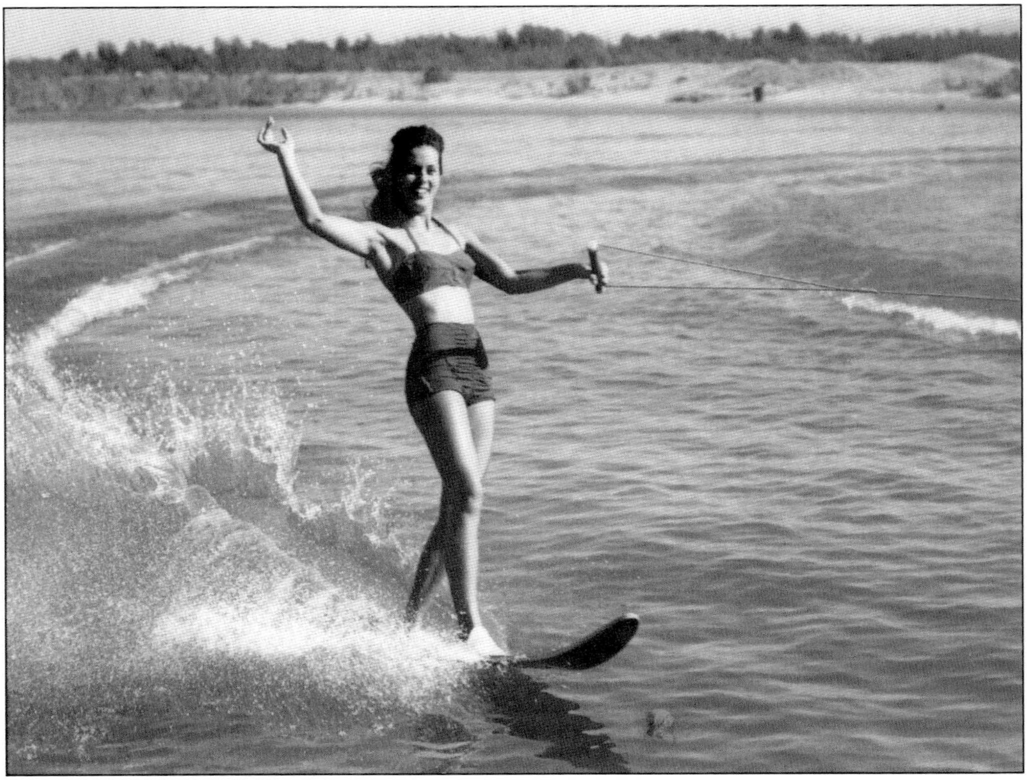

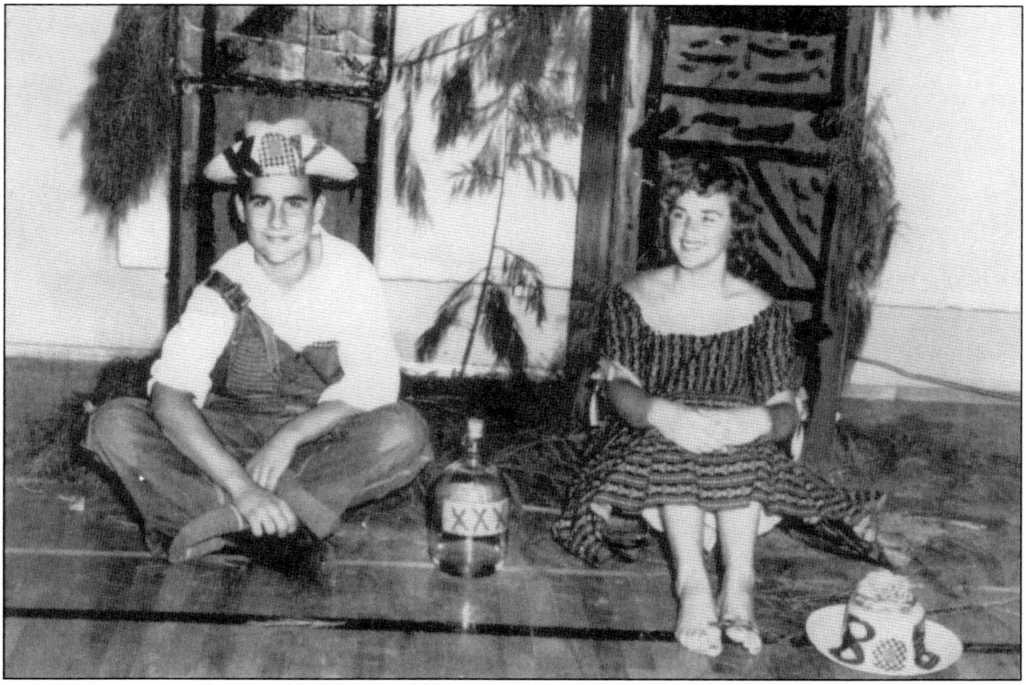

SADIE HAWKINS. The was one time in the year when it was permissible for a girl to ask a boy for a date. The attire for the evening was overalls for the guys and full skirts for the gals. Straw hats, bare feet, and painted on freckles finished off the Sadie Hawkins look. Here are Katie Reed and Bobby Robinson as king and queen of the evening. (Courtesy of Judy Orzel Browder.)

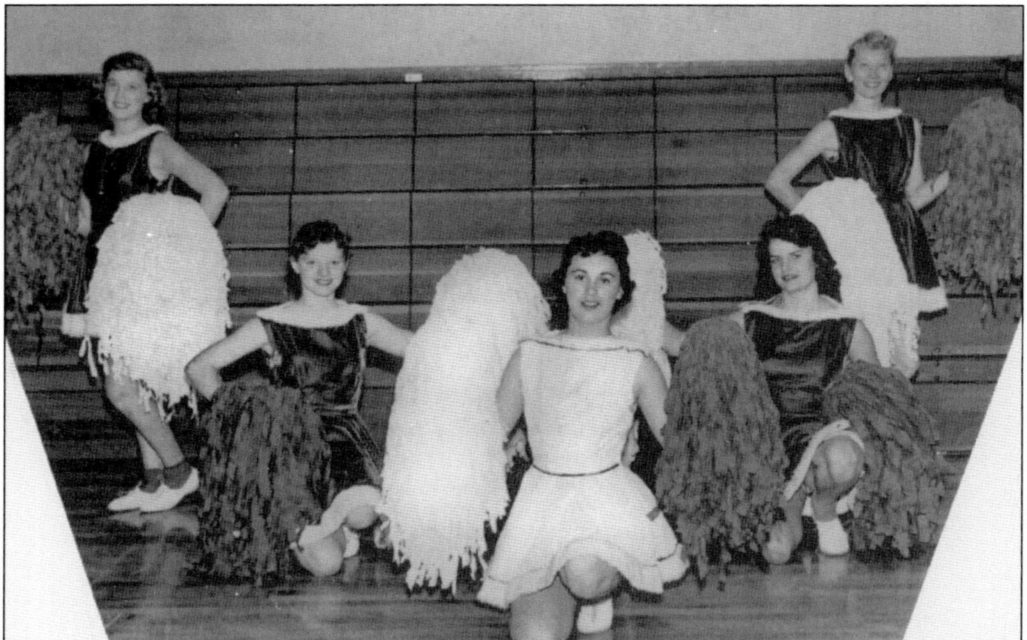

SONG LEADERS. The song leaders practice their routine for a pre-game rally in the high school auditorium. From left to right are Carolyn Brown, Twyla Wilburn, Dona Schulz, Janet Schwindt, and Carolyn Austin. (Courtesy of Needles High School.)

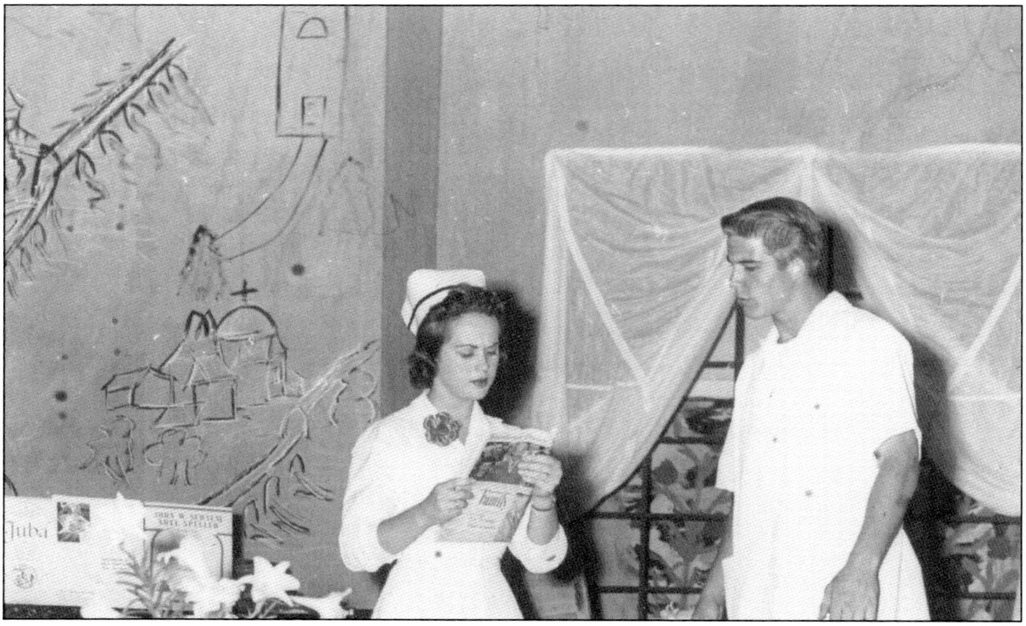

Thespians. The Needles High School junior class tested their acting skills in the yearly high school play. The class performed in the comedy *Curious Savage* by John Patrick about the humorously eccentric residents of the fictional Cloisters, a home for the mentally ill. Seen above are members of the Cloisters staff, Nurse Willie (Dona Schulz) and Doctor Emmett (Jim Shephard). Seen below from left to right are the actors playing the Cloisters's patients: Larry Pratt, John Lucas, Sandra Greable, Linda Daniel, and Linda Fitzpatrick. (Both photographs courtesy of Linda Daniel Andrews.)

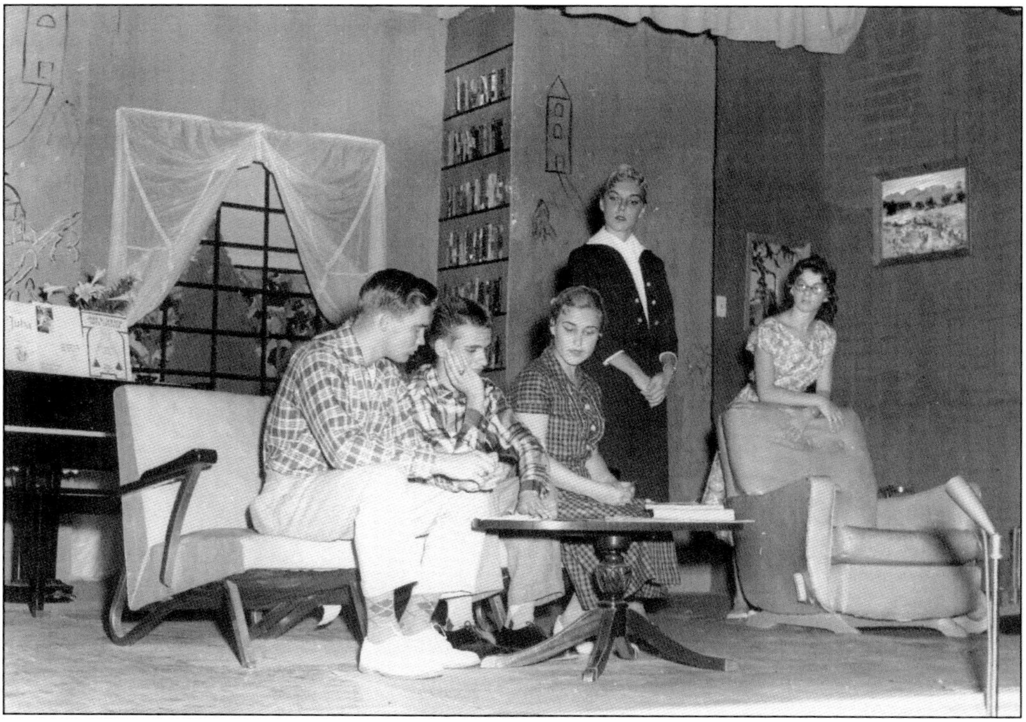

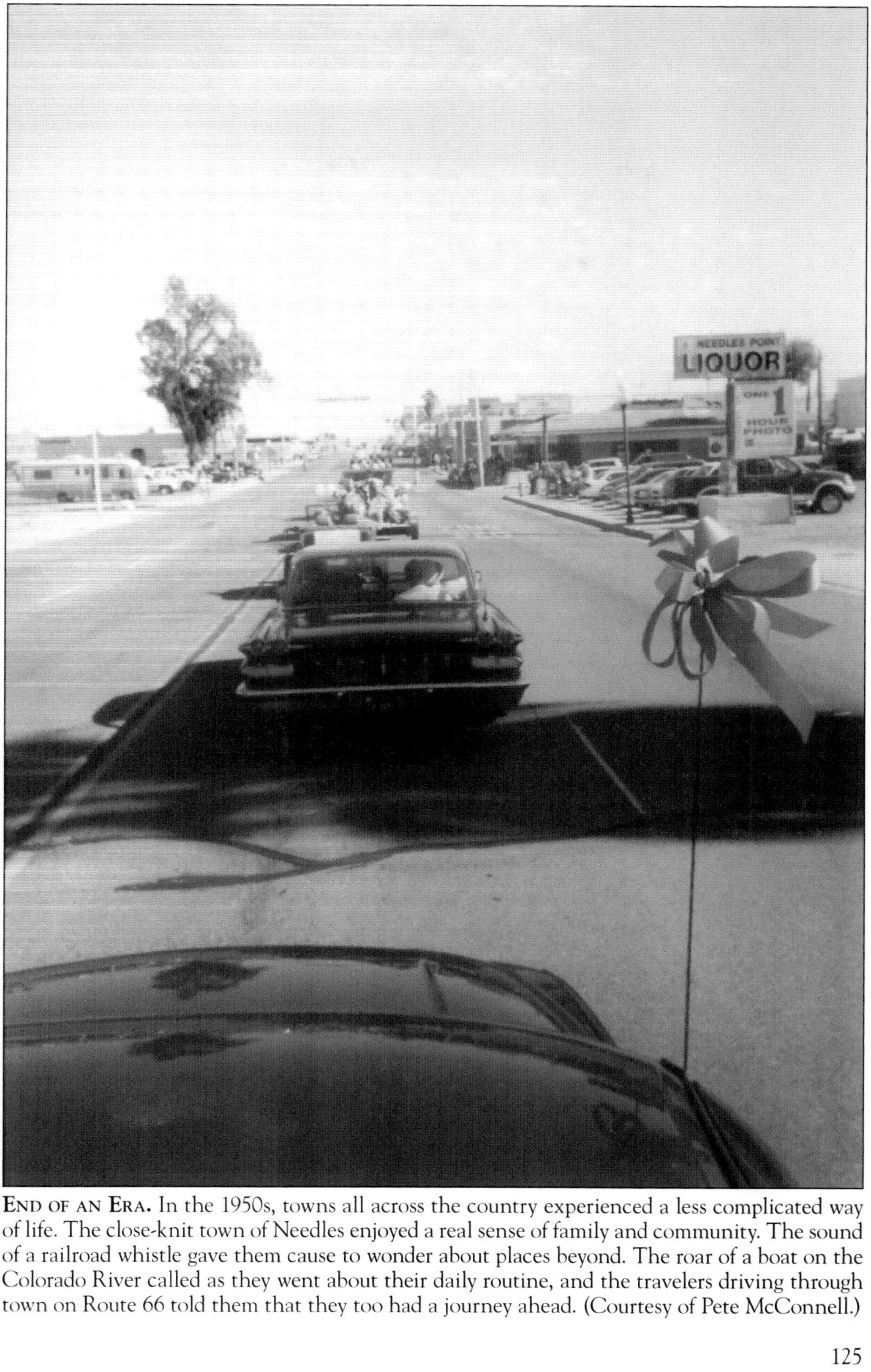

END OF AN ERA. In the 1950s, towns all across the country experienced a less complicated way of life. The close-knit town of Needles enjoyed a real sense of family and community. The sound of a railroad whistle gave them cause to wonder about places beyond. The roar of a boat on the Colorado River called as they went about their daily routine, and the travelers driving through town on Route 66 told them that they too had a journey ahead. (Courtesy of Pete McConnell.)

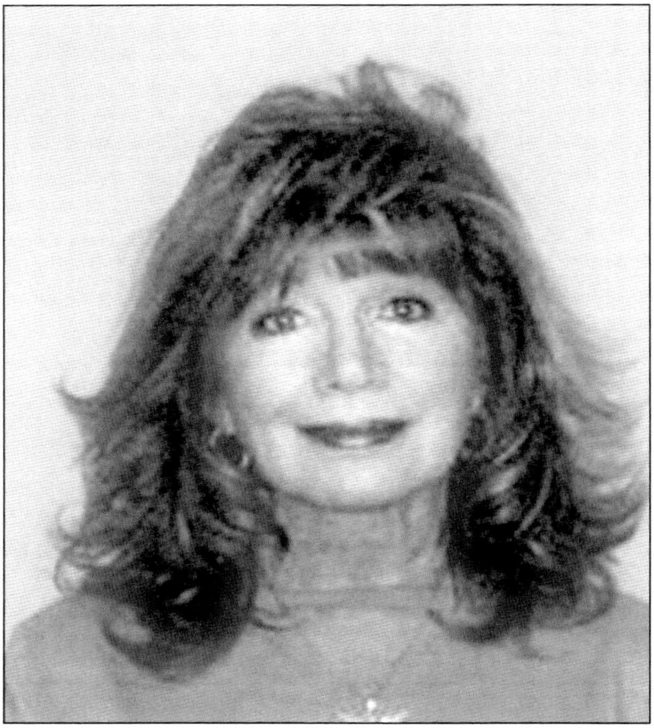

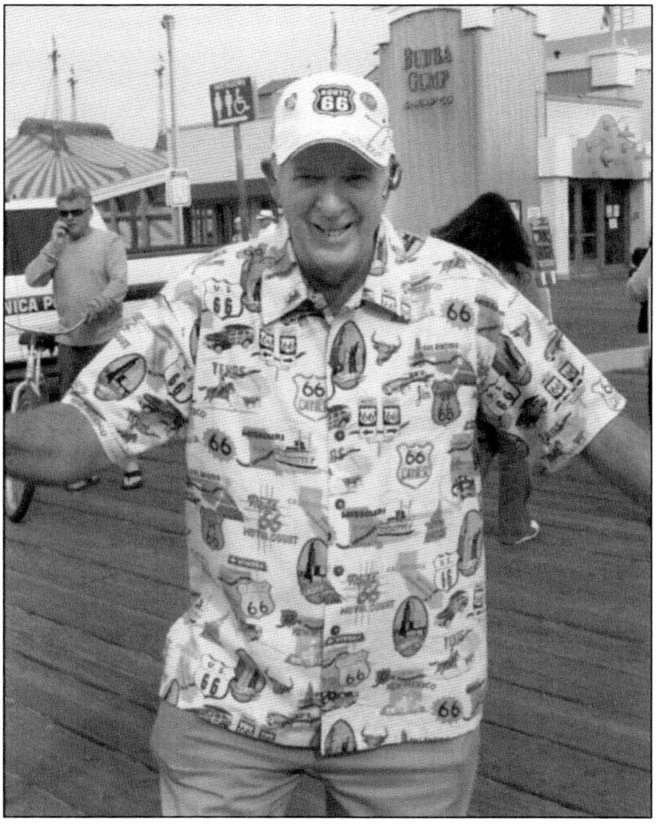

Meet the Authors. Linda Fitzpatrick is the mother of three grown children and the grandmother of 10. After graduating from Needles High School, she attended the Pasadena Playhouse, College of Theatre Arts, performing in stage productions in Los Angeles. She served as director of relocation for Walker and Lee Real Estate, department manager for Merrill Lynch Realty and later as vice president for Coldwell Banker, Southern California. Now semiretired, Fitzpatrick moved back to the Needles area and works to promote Needles. She was the recipient of the 2007 Humanitarian Award from the chamber of commerce. Jim M. Conkle has adopted Needles and spends much of his time promoting Route 66 and Needles.He is the publisher/editor of Route 66 Pulse Newspaper, cochair and host of the annual Will Rogers Awards event, cochair and founder of Route 66 Alliance, and a speaker, tour guide, media consultant, and event planner.

Bibliography

"El Garces Hotel and Train Station," Needles Chamber of Commerce.

"Historic California Post, Camp Ibis," The California State Military Museum World War II Desert Training Center, Bureau of Land Management.

Lingenfelter, Richard E. *Steamboats on the Colorado, 1852–1916*. Tucson: University of Arizona Press. 1978.

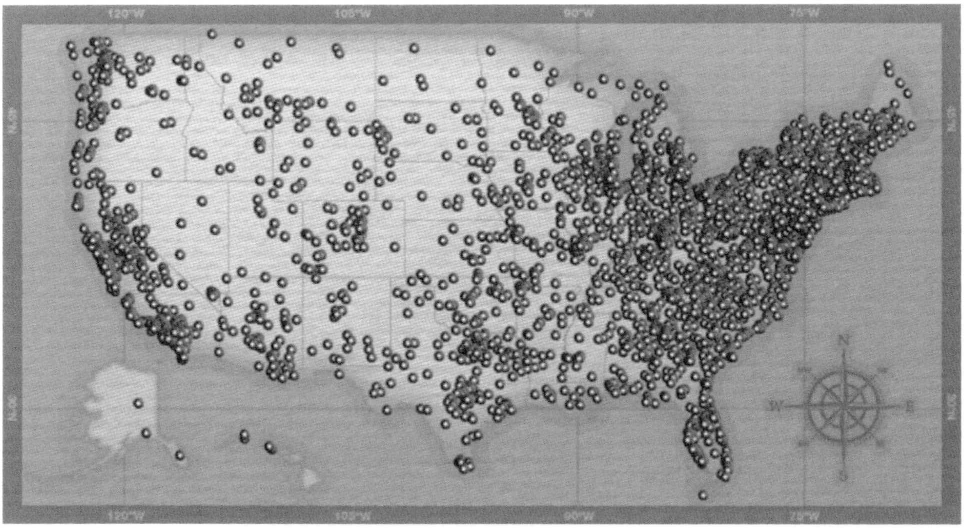